AGAINST THE GRAIN

AGAINST THE GRAIN

AN IRREVERENT VIEW OF ALBERTA

CATHERINE FORD

M&S

Library and Archives Canada Cataloguing in Publication

Ford, Catherine
Against the grain : an irreverent view of Alberta / Catherine Ford.

ISBN 0-7710-4775-4

1. Alberta. I. Title.

FC3675.F67 2005   971.23   C2005-903696-6

We acknowledge the financial support of the Government of Canada through the Book Publishing Industry Development Program and that of the Government of Ontario through the Ontario Media Development Corporation's Ontario Book Initiative. We further acknowledge the support of the Canada Council for the Arts and the Ontario Arts Council for our publishing program.

The excerpt on p. 128 is taken from *Dark Age Ahead* by Jane Jacobs. Copyright © 2004 by Jane Jacobs. Reprinted by permission of Vintage Canada, a division of Random House of Canada Ltd.

Typeset in Janson by M&S, Toronto
Printed and bound in Canada

This book is printed on acid-free paper that is 100% recycled, ancient-forest friendly (100% post-consumer recycled).

McClelland & Stewart Ltd.
The Canadian Publishers
481 University Avenue
Toronto, Ontario
M5G 2E9
www.mcclelland.com

1 2 3 4 5   09 08 07 06 05

In memory of my grandfather,
Clinton James Ford (1882–1964),
who was born in Ontario, adopted Alberta and never left.

And in memory of my father,
Robert Evans Ford (1917–1974),
who was born in Alberta and always returned.

Say, you chose him
More after our commandment than as guided
By your own true affections, and that your minds,
Preoccupied with what you rather must do
Than what you should, made you against the grain
To voice him consul: lay the fault on us.

– Coriolanus, Act II, Scene 3

Contents

Acknowledgements

I am indebted to the *Calgary Herald*, the newspaper that gave me my first job in 1964 and on whose Editorial and Comment pages many of these opinions have first appeared. Others, albeit altered by time and rewriting, have been published in the *National Post*, Montreal *Gazette*, and *Opinion Canada*.

I cannot imagine what my working life would have been, had I not had the great good fortune to work with and for the late J. Patrick O'Callaghan and the late William F. Gold. Both of them were, first and foremost, writers before being administrators. They brought with them a passion for words and ideas that inspired their staff. The former, as publisher of the *Herald*, made everything matter, from Irish ballads to politics. I miss both of them, still.

I am immeasurably grateful to E. Joan Abels O'Callaghan for permission to quote from her late husband's unpublished memoirs.

And I want to acknowledge Kevin Peterson, another former publisher of the *Herald*. He believed when one leaves work each day, the community should be a bit better place to live. His staff tried to come up to his expectations.

I would be remiss not to acknowledge my debt to Larry O'Hara, who, as the *Herald*'s city editor, gave his friend's inexperienced daughter her first job as a reporter . . . and then hired me back – twice.

I acknowledge with thanks the contribution of former Canadian senator and Alberta MLA Ron Ghitter, for his inspiration as a friend and for his permission to quote him extensively.

And thank you to friend and colleague David Bly, heritage writer for the *Calgary Herald*, who has not only shared the living history of Alberta with me, allowing me to steal – with permission – his research and hard work, but reminds all of us what the word "gentleman" really means.

I am also in debt to Leona Becker for her research work, including her patience in answering bizarre and occasionally stupid questions. She was indefatigable.

Most of all, I am indebted to my husband, Ted Busheikin, who actually chuckled in parts.

AGAINST THE GRAIN

Introduction

All I've ever wanted to do was write. That I would write was always clear, but how became obvious only when I realized, about age ten, there were real people behind the stories in the newspaper. I can do that, I thought. And so, for the past forty years, I have. And in all that time, mostly I have written about Alberta. I've spent nearly all of my working life here, and at the *Calgary Herald* in particular. I have been more than a bystander, but still an arm's-length observer to the changes that have turned Alberta into the economic powerhouse it is today. This past fall I retired, so this seems a good time to look back over those long years and set in writing my thoughts and observations about this province.

It is Alberta that has captured and held my heart and at times has broken it. With vast tracts of arable land, huge reserves of natural resources, and an ethos that arises from the difficulty in making a living from either, it could have been Utopia. It is not, but it remains a province where people value hard work and independence even for those incapable of doing or being either. This is not a province that takes kindly to freeloaders, welfare bums, unions, or whiners. We are not generous to the needy, the weak, the powerless, or anyone else dependent upon the state for a livelihood. It is a hard place with an amazingly large heart. We are open-handed and open-hearted to what could be called "good causes."

Volunteerism is our second job.

It is that sometimes infuriating spirit that keeps me in Alberta. There are years I despair for the arrogance of the place; years when the anger and mistrust of "the East" or "the government" or whatever burr has lodged under the saddle of the malcontents makes me wish my grandparents had stayed put in Ontario, instead of moving west early in the last century, or at least when given the opportunity, that I had reversed the westward flow and had remained in Toronto. But the call of one's heart is stronger than opportunity, and so I have always returned to the place I belong.

And therein lies my tale – how can an aging, liberal feminist find happiness in a right-wing, fend-for-yourself province? There is only one answer: It's home. I could not be more attached emotionally and physically to this strange and wonderful province. That is my only qualification for embarking on an adventure such as this.

Unlike other non-fiction books, this one has no voice of expertise, save those of the people I choose to quote, some extensively because I believe they have words worth repeating and remembering. In reality, there is no rhyme or reason in whom and what I've included. It is merely what struck my fancy – a problem I encounter each time I open a dictionary or an encyclopedia. I get distracted. I believe many people also do. That's why we find textbooks so numbingly boring – not because the lessons are uninteresting, but because there are so few tangents to distract the reader and take her down unfamiliar and unexpected paths.

This book is part memoir, part experience, part the voice of others, all gathered under fairly broad subjects. It has no political agenda. There is also (and blame my former day job as an opinion columnist for this) liberal use of the first person pronoun. Like the columns I wrote, regardless of their subject, I wanted this adventure not to be solitary, but to be a conversation between friends. And like friends – oh, hell, like my own mother – you don't have to agree with me. But if you have read this far, we are taking this trip together. Along the way, I hope to touch on the strata and nuances that are the people who live here and the province itself.

As those of us of a certain age learned in high-school Latin class, Gaul was divided into three parts – *tres partes divisa est* – and so, too, is Alberta, named for a daughter of Queen Victoria. The simplest division is geographical, lines drawn east-west, trisecting the province into almost equal parts – the northern wilderness, central farmland, and southern desert. Each district has its own agriculture, ecology, and culture, and while generalizations are possible, they go only so far. Unlike Upper and Lower Canada – Ontario and Quebec – settled by the privileged and adventurous of the Old World, ruled respectively by the elite Family Compact and Château Clique, Alberta arose out of a more basic imperative – need. The vast expanse of what was then the North-West Territories offered what the descendants of serfs, the second sons, and the poor but proud could not even wish for in the British Isles and across Europe – free land. Alberta was blessed by nature with riches in the land and above the land. There were sweeping acres of grassland, without enough water to grow wheat, but perfect for grazing cattle. There were lush valleys in central Alberta and rich loam in the north.

The CPR brought settlers to an outpost established to regulate the fur trade and control the whisky traders and natives from the south. People meant civilization; civilization meant order. Lured here by the railway and its offers of a quarter section (160 acres) for the price of only back-breaking work, Europeans seeking their own land flocked to Alberta. All the prospective homesteader needed was to get here, claim the land, and build a structure upon it. That those first homes were cut from the prairie sod mattered little, even in the middle of winter. For the immigrants it was a chance to be their own persons, to tip their caps to no one, and hopefully to prosper without the class structure and weight of history that limited their aspirations in the settled world.

Those first years taught newcomers that the weather would regulate much of their lives – hail destroyed fields tended throughout the summer; dry winds blew topsoil away in drought years; early frosts could kill a bumper crop. They would be at the mercy of luck and chance. The first settlers set the standard for hard work. The Americans who followed, bringing their cattle northward to lush pasture, set the attitude. Those early Albertans became the perfect people to welcome the industry that sustains us today: oil and gas. The oil business is like the weather – wait five minutes, it will change. There is always a break in the weather; there is always another boom-and-bust cycle. The children of the pioneers became the gamblers of the resources business, and they treated each bust with the kind of fortitude their forebears showed in the face of an angry God and His wind-driven blizzards: They hunkered down and waited for a break in the weather. Alberta's first producing oil field was located south of Calgary at Turner Valley, where vast deposits of natural gas are still pumped. The story is that a Calgary businessman, W.S. Herron, had noticed gas seeping near Sheep Creek. After buying seven hundred acres of land surrounding his discovery, he set out to raise money for exploration. He was spectacularly unsuccessful until he persuaded a couple of friends to come with him out to the country. Herron brought with him a frying pan and eggs, and when he reached the site of the seepage, he held a match to the rock fissure and cooked breakfast for his company.

That was all the encouragement needed and in the months between Herron's stunt and the outbreak of the First World War, the first real Alberta boom was on. Like so many other times, it fizzled. But the flame had been lit. It's still burning brightly, all these years later.

If I wax philosophical about the mainstay of Alberta's economy – Edmonton the blue-collar-and-workboots centre of the oil business; Calgary its white-collar head office – it's because, without oil and gas, we're just another hick province lacking the population to challenge the domination of Ontario and Quebec. Under our feet is 77 per cent of Canada's conventional oil and 91 per cent of its natural gas and bitumen and synthetic oil resources. They lie under 32 million acres of cultivated land and 21 million acres of wilderness.

It is the energy business and its wealth that makes the bullies back down.

The business is huge. Its companies inject $30 billion into the economy, generate a trade surplus of $14 billion or more, depending upon prices, employ directly and indirectly more than 240,000 Canadians, and hand over some $6 billion every year in taxes. A National Energy Board's assessment to the year 2025 indicates Canada has combined reserves and undiscovered resources of some 600 trillion cubic feet of natural gas, most of it in Alberta. Total production in 1999 was 6 trillion cubic feet. Alberta's oil-sands projects have produced more than 400 million cubic metres of oil since production started in the 1980s.

We are aided in our oil and gas ventures by the country's largest invisible minority – Americans. What many other Canadians fail to understand, and what far too many Albertans refuse to admit, is that the influx of Americans at the beginning of the twentieth century, and their continuing immigration as a result of the energy business, has had a profound effect on the ethos of Alberta.

The combination of Eastern European peasants lured by promises of free land, second sons of old British families and remittance men sent off to the colonies to ranch, American whisky traders and ranchers lured northward, made for a potent brew a few generations down the line.

One of the results was a continuing undercurrent of separation talk, invoked by the provincial government as a threat and by neo-conservatives as a promise. It will come to nothing, but it's a convenient facade. The proximity of the United States, emotionally rather than geographically – the closest major American city to Alberta is Great Falls, Montana, not exactly a hotbed of urban life – lends a credibility to the "threat" of moving south. Logic says it would make more sense for British Columbia to join Washington; for the Atlantic provinces to align themselves with Maine and eastern New York; and even for Ontario to annex Buffalo and take over both halves of Niagara Falls, than for Alberta to join the States. Except for the broad expanses of the plains and the north-south orientation of the Rockies, there is little to link Alberta and Montana. But it's a powerful threat, nonetheless, fuelled by the overwhelming presence of Americans in Calgary and their overarching influence in the oil and gas industry.

The business of alienation has its roots in history. As Alberta senator Tommy Banks said in the Senate:

Western alienation is not new. . . . While it is a problem for politicians, it is not a political problem. It is a sociological one. It is a problem of pride. A problem of being the object of disdain, or worse, of being ignored; not just in politics, but in everything. Politics is where it rears its tired old head most often and most visibly. It is also present though in commerce, in culture, in education, and in fact, in most aspects of everyday life in which there is any truck or trade of talk involving "westerners" on the one hand and "easterners" . . . on the other.

It is the same kind of quasi-paranoia (in the delusional sense of both grandeur and persecution) that Quebecers used to have vis-à-vis English-speaking Canada. The same that the whole of English-speaking Canada still has when it comes to the entire spectrum of our dealings with the United States.

By the way, when they really are out to get you, really do ignore you, or treat you with palpable disdain, it isn't paranoia.

Western alienation isn't simply a philosophy, it is a gut-level, at-the-coffee-shop, in-the-beer-parlour kind of reaction. It exists; it is enjoying a metaphorical fifteen minutes of fame and sunlight, but it is a chimera. It is also the kind of talk that occupies the far-right caucus of the Conservative Party while the Alberta government hews to a less-fractious reality.

At its root is not the desire to have a new country, as Quebec has worked toward for two generations, or the desire to join the

United States, as is said in frustration, but the desire to have the old country pay attention.

And yes, talk of Western alienation is getting tiresome, because those of us who live here know it is never, ever going to happen. As the population of Alberta increases, as more and more people throng to our cities, looking for jobs and new lives, the threat becomes even more of a joke. Immigrants aren't moving to Alberta to become Americans, and other Canadians aren't rooted in resentment. Everyone's too busy making a living to bother much about the old historical grievances.

Most of our citizens live in the north-south corridor that takes in Edmonton and Calgary. While our economy is based mostly on the rich natural resources that lie beneath our feet, we are quick to remind others of the prairie roots, the ranching and farming that is our heritage, regardless of the size of our cities. I've watched as the province has become more urban and liberal, but its politics more rural and right-wing. It is a curious dichotomy.

Alberta isn't a province of rednecks, although it is a compelling and handy stereotype to promote. Like all stereotypes, it contains at least a grain of truth. The red neck of the prairie farmer who worked the land from sun-up to sundown, plowing, harrowing, seeding, harvesting, all the time with the back of his neck exposed to the high, hot Western sun was a sign of hard work, not a hard head. These men and woman deserved our respect; instead, they gained our disdain and became a joke.

Their badge of hard work became a symbol of intransigence and ugly attitudes – indeed, a symbol of the kind of rock-ribbed fundamentalist Christianity that does not hold to the "love thy neighbour" commandment of the New Testament, but rather to the "eye for an eye" of the Old. I've always found it passing strange that the very people who proclaim their Christianity the loudest have clung the longest to the bloody-mindedness of the Old Testament's fearsome God of Revenge.

Their attitudes are, unfortunately, played out in public policy – the fight for equal rights for homosexuals in Alberta was seen as "those people" getting special rights; it took a court to rule in favour of the rights of same-sex couples to adopt, and the question of marriage for gays and lesbians was even more rancorous an argument here than anywhere else in Canada.

But just because we gave the rest of Canada Social Credit, Bible Bill Aberhart, and Ernest Manning; Reform and Canadian Alliance, Preston Manning, and Stockwell Day; Stephen Harper and the Conservative Party, does not make right-wing politics and thinking the only heart of the province.

There has always been a healthy left-of-centre wing in Alberta, one that mixes freely and well with its right-of-centre friends. At the level where intelligence is more important than the colour of your tractor cap, whatever differences exist politically are irrelevant. But the politics of anger and divisiveness suits many here, particularly those who do not separate their religious beliefs from their political actions. In promoting the singularity of the West, the handmaidens of the right-wing parties Alberta has birthed were the corporations and businesses who believe less in their social responsibility and more in their profits and personal gain.

A socially liberal country, after all, taxes its citizens to provide for the less advantaged, even those termed undeserving, a category that seems to include single mothers, homeless drunks, and anybody so lazy as to actually stay on welfare. But in Alberta, the poor are scapegoats, painted as a drain on "the system" by right-wingers who conveniently ignore the tax breaks and special perks that accrue to the wealthy, enabling them to become even more wealthy.

The all-too-willing accomplices of corporate greed are, surprisingly, the very men who should really be screaming at the injustice of "the system," the undereducated, economically deprived working-class men who, more than any other sector of the Canadian public, have seen their jobs stripped away through globalization. As a group, men of this disadvantaged class in Alberta, who are layoff roadkill or farmhands and labourers watching crops fail and their skills become irrelevant, are willing to march in protest over Ottawa's gun control and registration legislation, but believe they have nothing in common with the G8 summit protesters or any of thousands of radicals with privilege and education, young men and women just like them, who march for what they believe.

The redneck image does has an upside. It has been used to great effect by some of the brightest businesspeople of the province, content to make the ever-so-sophisticated Easterner believe they know nothing, all the while cutting deals that prove the sharp mind under that cowboy hat. More than a few of the downtown suits have gone to meetings in Toronto wearing cowboy boots instead of their usual Guccis, the better to promote the hayseed image and lull the men on the other side of the negotiating table into believing they were dealing with hicks. It has always worked to our advantage. And until Eastern Canada changes its own attitudes and reliance on stereotypes, it always will.

In Alberta, your membership is money, and special disdain is reserved not only for those whom we term different, but for those who can't, amid all this prosperity, share in it. For instance, every public library in Alberta, except Banff's, charges for membership, justifying an average twenty-dollar annual fee as the cost of issuing a library card and keeping track of who's got what and for how long.

The same kind of fancy talk justifies increasing user fees for all but the most basic of public services. Just as the lucrative gambling industry is a tax on the stupid, user fees are a tax on the poor. If you buy books rather than borrow them, who cares what the annual fee at the local library is? If you don't use the bus, what difference do increased transit fares make? If you don't visit public parks or go camping in provincial parks because you have a place in the Rockies or in the interior of B.C., what difference do the charges make?

This is the province that has, during the tenure of the Progressive Conservative government, charged health-care premiums to the oldest and sickest. It permits them to be booted out of hospitals (sometimes in the middle of the night) to fend for themselves, regardless of whether or not home care is available, while it boasts about not having a sales tax.

This is the province that justifies private hospitals as the panacea for waiting lists, even as its government created much of the log-jam in the public ones.

This is the province that used public money to oppose gun-control legislation and the dignity of universal human rights while it outsourced the care of the neediest and most at-risk children.

This is a province that philosophically opposes universal daycare and more publicly paid services for vulnerable and needy children, even as it rails against juvenile delinquency and out-of-control teens, and wants ever-harsher penalties for those in trouble.

This is a province with its heart in its wallet and its soul in utter darkness, so that it can't see the linkages between cuts in services and increases in poverty and life on the edge of disaster.

Albertans should be mad at all this, but most of us are not, because a canny government has promised us a better life through tax cuts. Even the Albertans who are getting shafted do not complain. It seems the only people who fume about taxes are those earning the most, those for whom a sweet deal has already been put into law.

If I have so much to complain about, why do I stay in Alberta? Because, all things being equal, it is easier to work to reform the things about a rich province that are bad, than it is to find enough money to reform a poor province. One of the privileges of citizenship and free speech is the right, if not the obligation, to tell the government when it has its head up its own ass; when it is so busy congratulating itself for helping its friends, it has forgotten about meeting its responsibilities.

This book doesn't purport to be a history of Alberta, an investigation of its people, or the last word in scholarship. I am neither historian nor social scientist; archivist nor political insider nor flunky. Nor is it a travel guide, although I will embark on a tour of sorts. I do not pretend to cover the length and breadth of this vast province in these pages. It is merely one woman's perceptions, opinions, ideas, and thoughts about her home over the years.

I am just one of more than 3 million people who choose to live here and who are tired of being described as rednecks, American wannabes, or whatever other description those who do not live in this province choose to throw at us.

I have taken the liberty of quoting from friends and strangers, letting their words, on occasion, fill in the gaps of my own experience. But essentially, this is a personal story, filled with the love and hope and anger of any intimate relationship. If there is a virtue to this approach, it is in its very lack of expertise. Why? Because most of us are not experts. And if we are, we are experts in limited fields. Most of us are merely citizens, getting through the challenges posed to us as citizens and communities as best we can.

We face the malcontents and the discontented with patience, if not understanding. There is a natural – and unfortunate – reticence to call our neighbours' opinions into question. After all, this is the prairies, where hail can batter a season's hope into the ground and one never knows when a neighbour's help will make the difference between surviving or going under.

Alberta is a complex province, still young and growing, still not sure what it wants to be when it grows up. I'm sticking around to see that. Living here is, if nothing else, always interesting.

1

The Land and the People

Alberta is a land of geological contrasts. So, too, are its people. It's trite to talk about flatland and mountains, boom and bust, black and white, right and left, native and newcomer, but that's what one has to talk about in order to understand this place.

Albertans deal with the contrasts and the uncertainties they bring every day. It makes us tough. Inside each of us is an uncertainty that has nothing to do with dreams, plans, or goals – it has to do with the land and its bounty. Farmer, rancher, oilman, skier – regardless of the business we're in, we are born into uncertainty and it keeps us wary of sure things in the same way our ancestors were wary of snake-oil salesmen. That wariness is nothing more complicated than the realization that all of this – a bumper crop, a gushing oil well, a boom in the stock market – can vanish in a moment. The land has taught us that through cycles of prosperity and poverty, through drought and deluge, through all the vicissitudes of weather. It's our legacy.

We Albertans are anchored to the land, even as we sit in offices forty and more storeys above it. Agriculture is one of the legs on the tripod of our economy. Scratch an Albertan – any Albertan – and you'll find a connection to the land in more than mere spirit. It is the land that roots us. It is also what makes us eternally hopeful. No one who has seen what the prairie can deliver in a bumper year ever loses the optimism that another harvest, another spring, another season awaits us. We just can't be certain when.

Like Scarlett O'Hara, Albertans know that all that really matters is land. That's what stays. It's what brought immigrants to Western Canada.

The Alberta most of us know is one part myth, two parts hope, and 100 per cent new. Not in the sense of just being uncrated, but because we have yet to become complacent about who we are, what we own, and the sheer scope of both.

There first was, of course, another Alberta and other owners. Europeans came here as interlopers and took over, settling the status of some of the First Nations through treaties, most notably Treaty 7, signed in 1877, in which the Blackfoot, Peigan, Blood, Sarcee, and Stoney ceded ownership of their territory in exchange for one square mile of land reserved for each native, some cattle, including a bull to be given to each chief, farm implements, and an annual treaty payment: twenty-five dollars to each chief; twenty-five dollars to each councillor, and five dollars to each tribe member. Chiefs also received, when the treaty was signed, a "suitable" suit of clothing, a medal, a flag, a Winchester rifle, and money to buy ammunition.

The treaty was between the Indians and the government of Canada, in the name of Queen Victoria, but the real organizer and beneficiary of the deal was the railroad. When British Columbia was admitted to Confederation in 1871, the government of Canada promised a railway to link the country within ten years. Until the First Nations conceded the land, the so-called National Dream was going nowhere. Treaty 7 took care of that. The natives still get their treaty money, but few of them have seen a cent of the billions of dollars in profit the railway made for developers and businesses. As for oil revenues, which have lined the pockets of so many Albertans and put Persian carpets on their hardwood floors, few of the original owners of the land and its resources benefit. The most notable exception would be the Hobbema-area Cree, whose reserves are about eighty kilometres south of Edmonton. The four bands, notably the Sampson Cree and the Ermineskin Cree, occupy land that is rich in resources. The Sampson Cree have accumulated more than $400 million in oil and gas royalties and each child has a trust account established at birth.

The Hobbema Cree are an anomaly, though. Most reserves in Alberta, indeed most reserves in Canada, struggle daily with poverty and hopelessness, caught between the well-meaning bureaucracy that comes with grants from the federal government and the certain knowledge they live in a kind of benign apartheid, battling the racism that makes an expression like "drunken Indian" tautology in Western Canada. They are, in a sense, legal wards of Canada and can thus be ignored by the provinces.

In light of that, and the treaty money still paid to the chiefs – which only serves to remind them of what they gave up – it's little wonder that negotiations with native tribes for any land concessions have been fractious since 1871. There is, though, a sort of ironic revenge being extracted: When the urban sprawl of Calgary butted up against the reserve of the Tsuu T'ina First Nation to the west and the city kept expanding ever-southward, the clamour of suburbanites for another north-south freeway – which, ironically, we call "trails" – became deafening. The easiest solution to the traffic woes of Calgarians living in the "deep south" was a road parallel to the Deerfoot Trail on the west side of the city. That would take it directly across Tsuu T'ina land.

This time, the natives weren't going to be bought off with a few dollars, a rifle, and a medal. For more than forty years, they were patient, they waited, and they drove the city administration crazy. Few people were betting against the natives getting the best of the deal, especially as the only other route for the road is right across an environmentally sensitive area called the Weaslehead.

For four decades, various city councillors, mayors, and lobbyists were flummoxed. Perhaps it was merely a long-delayed retaliation from the prairie gods. Then, in 2003, an agreement was signed between band and city for a land transfer after the Tsuu T'ina negotiated a provision for the city to build a roadway into their just-approved casino. There is, ahem, no correlation between

Calgary's need for a road and the Tsuu T'ina's desire for a money-making casino. For, it has come to this: The vast roaming tribes of Plains Indians, who supported their communities on the land and the buffalo, now see gambling as the future mainstay of their economy.

After Treaty 7 was signed, settlers arrived with their fences and notion that land could be owned by individuals and not communities (with the exception of the Hutterite colonies that dot the province and the communal Doukhobors and Mennonites). The buffalo gave way to huge herds of cattle roaming across rich pastureland on the dry southern plains and wheat, barley, rye, and flax in areas where the rainfall would sustain such crops. Irrigation boosted the yield of the dry southern areas, and for all the complaining about harsh winters and heavy snows, it was precisely that winter cover that nourished the soil. Years of light snows and too many chinooks meant lower yields at the next harvest.

Both the land and the weather serve to anneal the people into proud and independent men and women. It is no surprise, nor should it be, that most political protest movements have begun and flourished in Western Canada, particularly Alberta.

Anyone who likens the nationalist sentiments of Quebec and the emergence of the Parti Québécois and its federalist counterpart, the Bloc Québécois, to the rise of the Reform Party or any of a long history of pro-Western movements is conveniently ignoring the major difference: from the FLQ to René Lévesque to Lucien Bouchard to Jacques Parizeau, the aim has been to remove Quebec from Confederation. Only rarely has any Westerner suggested separation or its alternative – allegiance to the United States. That would probably be easier than their actual aim, which is to reform Confederation itself, to loosen the vice-like grip of Ontario and Quebec upon the Canadian body politic.

The statement about being a proud and independent people here in the West is not merely metaphorical. This is still not a tamed land – as any winter blizzard can prove. The veneer of civilization can be stripped away in the few hours it takes to blanket the country with white. Sometimes it is history that is eradicated as easily as the lush summer grass and time is its accomplice. We forget and destroy our past like small children careless with their toys. Sometimes it's necessary destruction, sometimes merely wilful, but there is always a cost. Some part of ourselves is always destroyed in the process.

Because Alberta is still "new," because its people always seem to be in a hurry, little attention has been paid to the past.

"No archaeologist will ever dig up Calgary layer by layer, as ancient Troy was brought to light," wrote *Calgary Herald* columnist – and native Calgarian – Allan Connery in 1978. "Here we scrape the site flat and start over."

We have, for example, nearly destroyed the sandstone buildings that are the West's unique architecture. Luckily, the few buildings left, including in Calgary, the city hall, McDougall School, which now serves as the southern site for the Edmonton-based Alberta legislature, the Central Library, and the old courthouse, have been designated heritage sites. Sadly, sandstone doesn't have the permanence of sturdier rock and brick and in order to repair the ravages of time and weather when the neglect started to show, it was necessary to import skilled tradesmen from Britain.

At the beginning, everyone was "imported," some more welcome than others. With the arrogance born of presumed privilege, the "white" settlers from across the British Isles and the European continent imported their prejudices. They tolerated the Chinese as long as they were building the railway, or, later, opening the ubiquitous restaurants that were a feature of every Western town. They could do the laundry, they could be servants, but they were never considered proper immigrants. Provincial and federal governments did everything in their power – including imposing the odious head tax on them – to drive the Chinese out of Canada, and if they persisted in staying, to ensure they could not bring their wives and children to join them. Anti-Chinese sentiment eventually resulted in a riot in Calgary's downtown Chinese district in 1892.

Other Asians fared no better, although the few Japanese immigrants were tolerated. As for black immigrants, who came largely from the U.S., the men had little choice but to serve as porters on the railway and the women as domestics: few other jobs were open to them. The most notable exception was John Ware, the cowboy and rancher freed from slavery by the American Civil War. Originally from South Carolina, Ware was hired to drive a herd of cattle north from Montana to southern Alberta. He liked the area so much he stayed, raised a family, and operated his own ranch east of Brooks.

It is curious that the blacks who settled in the northern rural communities of Alberta encountered little prejudice while those who chose an urban life met the same discrimination their brothers south of the border endured.

Albertans are barely two generations away from the immigrants who settled this province and who arrived with similar hopes, regardless of their circumstances: Alberta was a place where hard work meant more than family background.

Clinton James Ford – born in Corinth, Ontario, 1882; Bachelor of Arts, University of Toronto; gold medallist Victoria College; law degree Osgoode Hall – didn't set out in life to be either an Albertan or a lawyer. He wanted to be a minister, to serve God. How he ended up serving Mammon remains a mystery. At university, he switched from a course designed to equip him for a life of Bible study to one that would set him in a courtroom. His faded diaries from then are rife with references to church activities and youth groups but contain no mention of the decision not to make the church his life's work.

Still, all his life, his home and his wallet were open to the clergy, and his life was ruled by a strict Christian morality.

Abraham Busheikin of Gomel, Belarus, didn't set out in life to be an Albertan, either. Nor did he leave any written record why, as a young man of twenty-three, born outside the Russian Pale in 1887, literate, but not formally educated, he decided not only to immigrate to Canada, but to purposefully come to the wilds of Western Canada. Like millions of the disadvantaged and dispossessed, millions of the land-poor, Abe left his homeland to seek a better life.

While both men lived in the same city for the rest of their lives their paths were never designed to cross. Their lives were arranged around community and church, and neither man had a reason to know the other. But coincidence and, years later, marriage would link the two men.

They met once in a courtroom in Calgary in 1919, in a minor case involving a violation of the early-closing bylaw. Like most other upstanding Protestant cities in Canada in the early decades of the twentieth century, Calgary businesses closed all day Sunday and retail outlets closed at noon on Wednesday. Abe and his brother-in-law Harry Smith (the family name of Schumiatcher was arbitrarily changed by Canada Immigration) kept the family store, Harry's News, open in violation of Calgary bylaws. Clinton Ford was, that August, the city solicitor, responsible for ensuring such violations were prosecuted.

Both had arrived in the bustling prairie city in the shadow of the purple Rocky Mountains, to take up permanent residence, in 1912. And both eventually lived, unknown to each other, barely blocks apart, in Calgary's even-then tony Mount Royal district.

Clinton and the wife he had returned to Corinth, Ontario, to marry – Katherine Anne Evans, known for all of her life as Kate or Kitty – built their three-bedroom-plus-den house on two adjacent lots on Joliet Avenue for the munificent sum of six thousand dollars. In the 1930s, Abe and his wife, Eva Schumiatcher, the eldest daughter of a family of eleven, also from Gomel, built their four-bedroom, two-storey classic-style house on 7th Street, for about fifteen thousand dollars. (Both houses have now been renovated, but still retain their original style and exteriors.)

The two families, the Busheikins with their three sons, Joe, Judah, and Ted, and the Fords, with one daughter and three sons, Helen, Bill, Bob, and Tom, never met socially. There would have been a barrier between the two families, based on religious observances.

Clinton was a deeply religious man. His Bible, read nightly, was never far from hand. He was a regular churchgoer, one of the pillars of the Central United Church in Calgary and he eventually became the life president of the YMCA. His conversations were studded with Biblical references and his adherence to its principles, unwavering. His was not a surface belief, practised for the sake of appearances in a city where the majority of people still went to church each Sunday.

Abe was more sanguine about religion. Being Jewish for him was a cultural, rather than religious designation. His eldest son, Joe, and his youngest son, Ted, were bar mitzvah, but Judah, the middle son, refused the ritual admittance to adulthood. Abe himself would rarely attend synagogue. It was his mother-in-law who kept the religion active, as she did the Yiddish language she spoke all of her life. It was her only language, and while her children and grandchildren learned English, Chassia Schumiatcher never bothered. Like so many immigrants, and anxious to retain their cultural and linguistic heritage, the Calgary Jewish community set up and maintained a Yiddish-language school. Hebrew was used only on formal occasions, if then. To this day, the family can converse in Yiddish.

Calgary was no more, no less restrictive than other Canadian cities when it came to anti-Semitism. The virulent anti-Semitism of the Eastern European countries, that of the Poles and Ukrainians and the Germans, was not filtered out at the border and in enclaves of immigrants it flourished, quietly abetted by the less overt, but no less hurtful benign discrimination of the founding peoples of Canada. The prejudice was rarely acknowledged or argued until the Holocaust forced even the blindest citizen to recognize the discrimination that was all around them.

Both families also shared the pain of losing a child. Bill Ford died at nineteen, electrocuted by a high-tension power line at the top of the 14th Street South hill, when he climbed the pole to retrieve a friend's entangled kite. Judah Busheikin died at twenty-seven from hypertension, a disease now controlled easily by medication. Both families struggled to deal with their loss.

The two families' stories as immigrants – one from Russia, the other from Ontario, and just one generation from Ireland – eventually came together years later, when Clint and Kate's granddaughter

Catherine, married Abe and Eva's son Ted. They now live equidistant from the homes in which they were children.

This is but one minor story in the narrative of the West. There are thousands of similar stories, of families who, in whatever old country they came from – and yes, Ontario and Quebec can be included in that description – would never have countenanced intermarriage. But the old rules didn't long survive the move. Those men and women who decided to take a chance on Western Canada soon found their sons and daughters mingling, marrying, and making the West a new kind of society, one based on merit, money, and motivation.

Marriages – the dynastic variety – have never attained the importance they were accorded in older societies. (By the same token, the stereotypical trophy wife – the young thing superglued by money and attention to the middle-aged business executive, and all-too-willing to provide an aging Lothario with a second, or third, family so that he can finally play Dad and be proud of himself – is more readily accepted.) Intermarriage, intermingling, interbreeding – call it what you will, we Albertans are mostly mongrels. We are a Heinz 57 people, a mixture of cultures and ethnicities that defy the *pure laine* attitudes in provinces such as Quebec.

Senator Tommy Banks, from Edmonton, pointed this out in the Red Chamber in a March 2001 debate, when he said "We mongrel Canadians – who have always been the dominant demographic of the West – are largely outsiders." The paper presented by the senator, written by Satya Brata Das and Ken J. Chapman of Cambridge Strategies, was an attempt to understand the disaffection of the West. We have become, says the paper, the Third Solitude:

> There are two streams of Western disaffection. One is born of confidence, the other of fear. The first is rooted in cosmopolitan urban cities, the latter in its smaller centres and rural communities. Yet both share the view that the country east of the Manitoba border is an older Canadian model, one

with little relevance or resonance for people west of it. If the older Canada represents Two Solitudes, then the nine million people of the West are Canada's Third Solitude.

The majority population of the West is of neither French nor British descent – indeed in Winnipeg, Vancouver, Calgary and Edmonton, fewer than one in six citizens are of pure "founding nations" heritage. Canada's largest urban centres are havens of cultural diversity; and the West is, in fact, the most diverse part of the country, especially in its metro cities.

Statistics from the 1996 Canadian census tell a tale: in Calgary, only 13 per cent of the population were of British or French descent; in Edmonton, 11 per cent. (Winnipeg and Vancouver, the two other cities surveyed, were not much different, at just less than 13 and just over 13 per cent, respectively. By contrast Toronto's population is about half foreign-born, although the numbers are not directly comparable because Canada's biggest city was not surveyed independently, in the same manner as the four cities already mentioned. In the census data, about 24 per cent of Ontario's population identifies itself as ethnically of either British or French descent.)

What Senator Banks was attempting to do in the debate was what frustrated Albertans have been trying to do for generations – tell Ontario and Quebec that while we are Canadians, we are of different stock, have different needs and desires, and deserve to have our interests taken into account, regardless of the overwhelming number of Ontario voters and the constant threat of Quebec separation. What we lack in population, we make up for in our contribution to the economy of the country. The very Canadian Charter of Rights and Freedoms entrenches the idea that minorities must never be held hostage by the whim of the majority. Yet for all of our history, the West has been in just that position. Little wonder there is talk about Western alienation and separation.

As the senator's presentation stated:

When the West mentions "founding nations," we think first of Siksika, Cree, Haida, Dene, Peigan, Inuvialuit, Nisga'a. To the enlightened and cosmopolitan Westerner, everyone outside the First Nations is an immigrant. We are proudly Canadians, but we know we are newcomers, nonetheless.

The disaffected of the urban West are the flag-bearers of a new era of lean government and low taxes, driving the fast train to the frontiers of the global economy. The new face of alienation is born of confidence not fear. It is not the face of the victim, but of the presumptive master, railing at an old order that will not fade or at least get out of the way. There is more than a touch of American influence here, because this "get out of the way or we'll move south" shout is loudest in Calgary, the most American-influenced city in Canada.

Curiously, any comment – no matter how mild – about the American flavour of the southern half of Alberta evokes the complaint that one is "anti-American," as if comparisons are, in and of themselves, odious. Yet we are not Americans (and we have no bananas), we are Canadians. And yes, there is a difference, one that some of the loudest voices in this province refuse to accept.

If there is a basic, easily stated difference between Canadians and Americans, it is in the philosophy of personal privilege: Americans believe unless they are specifically prohibited against doing something, it's their right to proceed; Canadians believe exactly the opposite. It is the supremacy of the individual over the collective in the United States and the opposite in Canada.

Such an attitude, while not shared by everyone in Canada, is such a cultural phenomenon that it is manifested in such treasured social programs as universal health care and the natural reticence to apply a means test to everything done for the common good. It was, after all, in Canada that the baby bonus was a staple of life from 1945 to 1992. It meant every child received a monthly benefit from the federal government, a cheque made out, deliberately, to the mother.

(Perhaps the thinking, based in a sort of Scots Presbyterian suspicion of drink and carousing, was that the mother would be more likely to buy diapers for the baby and shoes for the children, and the father would waste it on booze and smokes.)

The explorers came for the adventure, the settlers came for the land, but it took a natural wonder to bring the tourists.

2

Yahoo, It's Calgary

When Joni Mitchell, a native Albertan, wrote and sang about paving paradise and putting up a parking lot, I wonder if she had Calgary in mind. Thirty-five years after she wrote "Big Yellow Taxi," there's not much paradise in Calgary's footprint. We used to boast that our city would never have the problems of pre-amalgamation Toronto – an inner-core city surrounded by burgeoning, self-governing boroughs perpetually whining about inadequate freeways into Toronto – because Calgary had annexed enough land for all eventualities. But we've gobbled up all the land set aside all those years ago, and then some. There's not much of a joke left in the prediction that Calgary will grow until it reaches the Banff National Park gates. We've already turned a long stretch of the Trans-Canada Highway between Calgary and Banff into little more than an access road to new developments.

The real way to appreciate the monster that is Calgary is not by car, but by air. And at night. It's not much of an exaggeration to say that you can see Calgary, an ocean of orange glimmering in the night sky, from hundreds of kilometres away. To approach Calgary airport from the south means flying directly over the city's expanse, which stretches across almost 722 square kilometres and fills the horizon. The only "dark" spot left is Nose Hill Park, a wide expanse of tall-grass prairie, rising nearly two hundred metres above the Bow Valley. For centuries this land provided rich pasture for the buffalo and it still feeds smaller animals such as coyotes, rabbits, porcupines, and the ubiquitous prairie gophers. It is now completely surrounded by urban sprawl. Somehow, in a city rapacious for development – 16,500 building permits worth $2.4 billion were issued in 2003 alone – the city has managed to preserve this chunk of nature, smack in the middle of Calgary. Maybe somebody was listening to Joni Mitchell.

Calgary, although sprawling, is not without beauty. The late Richard J. Needham, for long years the resident curmudgeon at the *Globe and Mail*, went to Toronto from Calgary. In his final column in the *Calgary Herald* in February 1951, he wrote about arriving in Calgary in 1936: "Seeing Calgary for the first time on one of those blue-and-gold mornings, we were enchanted by the clear, tangy air; by the sense of freedom and adventure; by the feeling that we were spiritually, as well as physically, on the top of the world."

His words presaged those of Joni Mitchell. "The old town was kind of beaten up in those days," wrote Needham. "But we think . . . that people had more fun then, that it was a friendlier place, that it had a spaciousness and graciousness which have since contracted. Calgary is half again as big as it was when we came and the merchants love it, but a lot of Calgarians don't love it and we can understand why. Something has been lost."

Exactly thirty years later another journalist wrote about Calgary in the midst of an economic boom as having "winter in its heart."

"It's a city long on money and short on heart," I wrote after returning from Toronto in 1981 to yet another stint at the *Herald*. "In a few years, we've managed to destroy – almost – its environmentally fragile beauty, and the famous Western friendliness is disappearing."

A month later, Calgary mayor Ralph Klein, in his first political job, made his famous "creeps and bums" speech to, of all groups, the Calgary Newcomers' Club. His actual comment was that Calgary didn't want and had no need for "a lot of creeps" coming to town, that the city didn't need unskilled workers without the money to take care of themselves. If there was any doubt in other Canadians' minds that Calgary was hick cowtown, this cinched it. Klein made headlines across the country. What he didn't make was any apology for saying that the fast-growing city needed skilled people with education and technical expertise.

The bottom fell out of the boom soon after Klein's outburst, but our attentions were diverted by the excitement of having been awarded the 1988 Winter Olympics.

How many Calgarians does it take to screw in a light bulb? A million: one to screw in the bulb and 999,999 to tell everyone what a great party the Olympics were.

They were. Because the Calgary organizing committee negotiated a more-than-$300-million contract with ABC for the television rights in the U.S., the Games were a financial success, unlike Canada's other Olympic foray, in Montreal in 1967.

The blowhards brag about the surplus resulting from the lucrative television contract and its use as an endowment for future Olympians and training, but the real legacy of the Olympics was the pride in the city the Games brought to all of us and the spotlight Calgary shone on the two-class system of privilege and power that existed in the International Olympic Committee.

The Calgary media were the first to highlight the arrogance and sense of entitlement that abounded throughout the IOC. That was the chink in the door that later gave way to the scandal of bribery and vote "payments" that cleaned out the ranks of the committee. The insight into the rarified world in which IOC members lived came because this was the first time the Winter Games had been held in a city with major media outlets. Never before had they been open to examination by reporters other than sportswriters.

What the world saw was sparkling snow and ice, the majestic Rocky Mountains, the up-close-and-personal attention paid to such stars as the East German figure-skating phenomenon Katarina Witt; the men's figure-skating showdown between "the Brians" – Canadian Brian Orser and American Brian Boitano, the eventual winner; the hapless Jamaican bobsleigh team, which we took to our hearts; and the clueless British ski jumper Eddie Edwards, known as Eddie the Eagle. What writers and reporters in Calgary saw was the lavish lifestyle of IOC members, the privileges they demanded, and, worst of all, the empty reserved seats front and centre at prized events. The picture of those empty seats, surrounded by a sea of excited – and paying – ticket holders was enough to embarrass the IOC into releasing their unused spaces for general admission.

More than a year earlier, the enterprising – and crooked – ticket manager was discovered selling seats to Olympic events, priced in Canadian dollars, for the same figures in U.S. dollars. He was pocketing the difference in the exchange rate. It was a crafty scheme and only uncovered because Calgary had a lot of reporters looking at all aspects of the Games, not just the competitions. Sleepy Alpine towns that usually host the Olympics are picturesque, but they lack big-city media.

The takedown of Olympic "royalty" was a case of the Calgary media pointing out that the emperor was wearing no clothes. Calgary doesn't take kindly to aristocratic attitudes. This is a city where the cat can look at the queen, where your worth is measured by your achievements (if not your outright wealth) rather than the colour of your blood. Perhaps it was the subtlest of peasant revolts, but on the street IOC members were just people, and we treated them as such. They were shocked.

One of my favourite stories comes from Joseph D'Angelis, owner of La Chaumière, at the time (and still) Calgary's premier classic French restaurant. If you were somebody, you dined at La Chaumière, with its impeccable service and cuisine. But nobodies ate there too, as our money was the same colour. One company tried to book the restaurant for the entire sixteen-day run of the Olympics, but D'Angelis refused. He passed up a guaranteed profit for a single reason: his local customers. The visitors would leave after two weeks, but his regular customers would still be here, and there was no way D'Angelis was closing his doors to them for this important civic celebration.

There may have been a lot of overblown comments about how the Games were world-class and the best ever, but there was one genuine world-class experience: the enthusiasm of the more than ten thousand volunteers who gave up their own lives and business for those two weeks.

Since 1988 there has been much talk about the legacy of the Olympics, even though Canada Olympic Park is really only used for parties atop the abandoned ninety-metre ski jump and tourist runs down the bobsleigh and luge tracks. Easy ski slopes, ideal for learning before one ventures out to the mountains, snowboarding pipes, and Nordic cross-country trails are the most-used facilities by residents. The real legacies are the speed-skating oval at the University of Calgary and the Pengrowth Saddledome, the home of the Calgary Flames and visiting rock stars and evangelists. Legacy is one thing, aesthetics are another. Only the most optimistic of local boosters would call the Saddledome a thing of beauty, even as its contoured roof dominates the eastern skyline.

Maybe the true beauty of the city can be seen only in a narrow focus: dawn reflected in the golden glass of downtown office buildings; the hoar frost clinging to trees and bushes, sparkling in the sunlight; the horizon-to-horizon arch of a winter chinook keeping the cold at bay, if only briefly. There are glimpses of manufactured beauty – the Family of Man statues outside the Calgary school-board offices, their elongated bronze forms seeming to dance on the grass; sandstone buildings like the old courthouse, which now overlooks the downtown light-rail transit tracks, but is still majestic; the Devonian Park at the corner of 8th Avenue and 8th Street S.W., a symphony of concrete and water, an oasis in the midst of high-rises.

Perhaps the most welcome beauty in Calgary are the one-hectare Devonian Gardens on the third floor of the downtown Toronto-Dominion Square. Opened in 1977, it is one of the largest indoor gardens in the world – more than twenty thousand plants in 135 varieties – and while some Canadians may be blasé about flowers and greenery, they must live in Vancouver or Victoria. There is nothing to compare with visiting these gardens when it's minus 30°C outside.

It's warm, it's humid, it's quiet. And it's almost possible to believe the real world is far away. If you plan well, you can get there from any downtown office building without ever venturing outside, thanks to the "Plus-15" system that links downtown buildings fifteen feet above street level. It's a bland and featureless journey – a maze that's occasionally difficult to figure out – but what it lacks in beauty and style it makes up for in practicality.

Practical is a good way to describe both Calgary and its citizens. Stubborn might fit, too. As would independent and determined.

Then there's our silly side, which we show to the world for ten days every summer when we all pretend we're cowboys. It is, of course, the Calgary Stampede, the name of which is always followed by: The Greatest Outdoor Show on Earth.

No matter how hokey, the Stampede has a grip on the city. And no Calgarian escapes the allure of the Stampede if the love affair begins in childhood, as mine did. Whenever I get too cynical or too angry, I remember what it was like to be four years old and wide-eyed at Kids' Day. That hot July day is sunburned into my memory and may well be responsible for my sometimes inexplicable optimism. Out of all the thousands of children at the Stampede that morning in 1949, I held the winning ticket for the two-wheeled bicycle. Well, truth be told, my father held the ticket and read out the number before swooping me up and carrying me down what seemed like interminable sets of stairs onto the stage set, front and centre of the rodeo infield. Brand-new mayor Don Mackay put the CCM bicycle in my hands. I can still feel the hot tarpaper burning through the soles of my red sandals, the bumps of the rubber grips in my four-year-old hands, and the joy in my small heart. A two-wheeled bicycle! Mine!

This was even better than winning the pony or the rabbit, the other prizes on offer, both of which would have been instantly banished from my grandparents' city house, where my parents and I lived at the time, to friends in the country. But a bicycle I could keep. First, though, it had to be changed from a boy's bike to a girl's. That meant prying my fists from the handlebars.

Fifty years later, the organizers allowed me back up on the stage for Kids' Day 1999 to make the presentation of the bikes to the two lucky children holding winning numbers. Giving away a couple of bikes has been a staple of Kids' Day at the Stampede for as long as anyone can remember. Nobody gets a pony any more, and I didn't see any rabbits as prizes, either. But, sadly, the bicycles – now donated by the Calgary Police Officers' Union – don't come in all their brand-new splendour: they come as gift certificates. But just about everything else was the same as I had remembered – the good-natured crowds despite the cold rain, the pancakes and sausages (free breakfasts all over the city are a hallmark of the Stampede), and, most of all, the children. Thousands of kids and thousands of parents. Millions of smiles. Just as I remembered.

Most of my blond hair now comes from a bottle, and it has been more than half a century since it was tortured into ringlets. And while I own a two-piece bathing suit, the chances of my wearing it in public are remote. But inside my heart still lives the tomboy, who stood on the stage in the two-piece green gingham playsuit, complete with ruches and ruffles. It is she who is responsible for most of my good feelings about the Calgary Stampede. It is her I remember when the "modernization" of the Stampede threatens to overwhelm the historical reality of life in the Canadian West.

The Stampede has changed in those fifty years, and it now features a Wild West shootout, just like in the movies. The Stampede has always been an amalgam of the real and the fanciful: the true nature of pioneer life in Calgary shoulder to shoulder with romantic dime-novel scenarios.

Even the very first Stampede in 1912 had that curious mixture of reality and revisionism, a celebration of a way of life already dying by the turn of the last century. It was a combination of a Wild West show – vaudeville on horseback – working cowboys competing for prizes, and an agricultural fair. At the time of that first Stampede my grandfather was building his first and only house on Joliet Avenue atop the south hill of the city. He and his wife would raise four children there as the city – and the Stampede – grew around them. Like most Calgarians, my grandparents' heritage owed more to farming than ranching or cowboys, yet Guy Weadick's dream of an enduring "Western" show found room for them, too. The first agricultural fair, out of which grew Weadick's vision of working cowboys competing in a rodeo, was held in Calgary in 1886. Some of the same competitions still exist.

Years before he would become an august judge, my grandfather – the son of an Ontario farmer – was an organizer and president of the Alberta Poultry Association. The poultry exhibit was a mandatory stop on the Stampede grounds for me as a child. And I was expected to appreciate the subtle beauty of Rhode Island Reds. I didn't.

Most of my Stampede memories, though, centre on my father, who was born and raised in Calgary. It was Dad who took me on all the scary rides and didn't seem to mind the one time the combination of being shaken around and too much cotton candy got the better of me, and I threw up all over him. It was Dad who arrived home one Stampede parade afternoon followed by an entire Highland regimental pipe band, which paraded after him from 14th Street to our driveway. To this day I have a soft spot for pipers, drummers, and men in kilts. And, not surprisingly, for Scotch.

On parade day, we always headed down to the courthouse, which fronted 7th Avenue, to watch from the upstairs offices, and I'd dream about being a majorette at the head of a marching band. Years later, I would sneak into the publisher's office at the old *Calgary Herald* building and watch the parade from a window over the intersection of 7th and 1st streets. And even more years later I finally realized my childhood dream of riding in the parade, when the newspaper sponsored a chuckwagon and driver Ray Croteau let me tag along – still the excited kid.

To an outsider, the ten days of the Stampede look like mayhem, but it is actually controlled chaos. And there is a difference between the two. Visitors just need to know the following Seven Highly Effective Rules for Stampede Enjoyment:

1. The cowboy: Everyone is a cowboy during Stampede. "Cowpoke" is the gender-neutral term. You will be able to tell the difference between the two. But you might not be able to tell the file clerk and the CEO apart. The man in the ratty hat and jeans could be the owner of the biggest oil company in the city. So remember cowboy manners and be polite to everyone. Take no chances. Dance with everyone.

2. The food: Stampede meals consist of five important food groups: beef, beans, beer, and before noon, pancakes with sausages or bacon. You need only remember the colour brown. If it isn't brown, it doesn't qualify as Stampede food. Black – as in grilled to the consistency and colour of charcoal – is passably acceptable. Greens are what you feed your horse. If you're eating fusion or other sissy food, get out of town. The only "exotic" food that is authentic is Chinese, the historic staple of Western towns. Beer is optional in the morning, although liquor is indeed served at 8 a.m. The official meal of the Stampede is breakfast. Don't miss it, because breakfast is the base for day that might include a substantial number of liquid refreshments and other meals of such fleeting sustenance as donut holes and corn dogs.

3. The dress: Western, of course. Open to wide interpretation. Jeans and shirt as a minimum. Boots, hats, string ties, and all the other paraphernalia of cowboy culture is at your discretion. Newcomers may think they can avoid dressing Western, because they see no use for this stuff the other fifty-and-a-half weeks of the year. But this is Calgary, pardner. Cowboy shirts and vests, hats and boots, will appear like magic in your closet. You might as well give in as soon as you move here. The good news is that the longer you wear cowboy boots, the better they feel.

4. The hat: Not mandatory (this is a July event, after all) but should you want to complete your ensemble with a genuine hat, in Calgary it isn't a Stetson, it's a Smithbilt, made right here by a company started by my husband's uncle, Morris Schumiatcher/ Smith. (After Morris started Smithbilt Hats he switched its

name from Smith to Schumiatcher and back again, until settling on the family's real name.)

Once you've purchased a fancy felt number and put it on,
don't take it off. (It is the only type of headgear acceptable
indoors.) A real cowboy doesn't take his hat off for a variety of
reasons, but we drugstore cowboys don't take our hats off for a
very specific reason: hat head. If your hat flaunts feathers,
beading, sequins, or comes in any colour other than brown or
black – white if you are the Stampede Queen or one of her two
princesses – you are a tenderfoot. You will be considered fair
game by the barkers on the midway.

5. The language: The official Stampede cry is "yahoo" or "ee-
   haw." Feel free to burst into either version anytime the mood
   strikes, regardless of venue. (Except, maybe, church.) "Howdy"
   is also acceptable.

6. The real stampede: This comprises the infield rodeo, nightly
   chuckwagon races, crafts and art shows and competitions, the
   wonderful animals and the evocative rich smells of the horse
   barns, the Indian village, and anything that celebrates this city's
   agricultural and ranching heritage.

7. The not-real stampede: Here's where you'll find cacti, Texas long-
   horns, Navaho blankets, and turquoise jewellery, Weadickville
   and Nashville North, although both offer the kind of West people
   not steeped in Canadian history actually believe. Why would
   something as blatantly fake as shootouts be featured at the
   Stampede? That's simple: more than $125 million from 1 million
   visitors by the end of these ten days.

The whole idea is to have fun, as long as you remember it isn't
real. The "real" West in Canada was settled by Easterners,
Europeans, French and English, brought here by the railroad. This
wasn't Dodge City, it was civilization. In the real Canadian West the
North-West Mounted Police and the Canadian Pacific Railroad
came before the settlers. Early Calgary did have a wild side, but six-
shooters weren't much a part of it.

Even so, the attitude of the Wild West, of a land of independence and entrepreneurs, lingers to this day. Calgary is a city whose overarching civic culture – one that newcomers seem to imbibe as readily as though it were a founding myth – carries an inbred aversion to governance. This is in contrast to the "government as partner" ethos of Vancouver, Edmonton, and Winnipeg.

Senator Tommy Banks said of Calgary:

It would be wrong to evoke from the singularity of Calgary any sort of general conclusion about the disaffection of the West as a whole, or indeed about the other metropolitan centres. Yet many influential people in the four Western metro cities contrast their civic polity (that process of organized and civil society) to what is perceived to be a sclerotic Centre-East rooted in French-English squabbles. . . .

In some Western circles there is a nastier anti-government sentiment that is fundamentally opposed to the compassionate state, because it still finds its antecedence in the peculiarly American mythology of triumphant individualism. Like the Calgarian leaders, they are unable to reconcile their new-found wealth and power with the culture of grievance that informed their upbringing.

Culture of grievance be damned. The culture that really matters owes much of its existence to that new-found wealth and power and the oil business. For little in the way of public festivals, art, or organized activity takes place without the involvement of the oil business. Calgary (with Banff) has an international writers' festival because Enbridge underwrites it, just as it underwrites both Word on the Street and Alberta Theatre Projects' annual playRites festival of new Canadian plays.

Every facet of city life is touched by corporate sponsorship. Both Petro-Canada and Renaissance Energy help fund the Calgary Philharmonic; BP Amoco, Petro-Canada, and Nova Chemicals are involved with the Calgary Opera; Imperial Oil, Petro-Canada, and

Amoco assist the Alberta Ballet Company. Name it in Calgary, and an oil company has helped.

In reality, the business of oil and gas anywhere in the world is a dirty, filthy enterprise for gamblers. The kind of person who drills for oil on the basis of geological guesswork is one who must be ready to take the chance that the hole will be dry, or as in the case of the tar sands, the cost of recovery too high. Men and women with that entrepreneurial spirit are rare, yet there are thousands of them in this city, their accents belying their origins in Dallas or Houston, London or Oman. Calgary's largest invisible minority is Americans. Indeed, the ritziest inner-city neighbourhood, now called Mount Royal, its mostly French-inspired street names completely mispronounced by Calgarians, was originally known as American Hill. (I once lived, as an adult, around the corner from my childhood home on Vercheres Street. The dispatcher for Checker Cabs called it Vercherry.)

The cattle business brought the first Americans north, but oil and natural gas started the boom in immigration.

Say Calgary and think oil.

Starting about 560 million years ago, layers of rich organic material were buried by the earth's restlessness until, after at least 1 million years of intense pressure and heat, the Rocky Mountains emerged and the transformation of muck into coal, oil, and natural gas was completed. All that remained was the wait, until the hydro-carbons worked their way upward through layers of rock. That wait was over in 1883 when a railway crew near Medicine Hat found natural gas instead of the water they were drilling for.

In 1912, an entrepreneur named Eugene Coste set out to supply all of southern Alberta with natural gas. The house he built that year still stands. Its owner today is another oil-company entrepreneur who endured with ineffable good humour the distinction of holding title to the property ranked number one on the city market-value tax assessment roll, until an $11-million-plus mansion was built in Pumphill.

Just a few blocks over from the Coste House is the two-storey house built by my grandfather the same year. It, too, still stands.

Now, though, it is surrounded by the city. What had been, in my grandfather's time, farmland and prairie to the horizon, is all development. There's a small black-and-white photograph in my album, sent to me a number of years ago by a total stranger, looking north and showing my grandfather's house on Joliet Avenue on the horizon. In the foreground is a contented cow. She's surrounded by lush grass pasture. Now, less than one hundred years later, there are nothing but houses, businesses, roadways.

All that growth owes its existence to natural resources. And it is Alberta's rich deposits of natural gas, oil, and coal that make this province a bank vault filled with riches.

Canada isn't the biggest producer of energy in the world (we're fifth), but we have – particularly if the tar sands are taken into account – the greatest sustainable supply. Even better, we are economically and politically the most stable source of energy. No war will threaten our oil fields; no civil or sectarian strife will shut down the wells.

Why are Albertans so smug about our riches? Because constitutionally, we own what's under our feet. (Some of us, older Albertan families, still own original oil leases, not sold or surrendered to the government. They remain the only mineral rights owned entirely by citizens, not by the province, and are leased on the same basis for exploration as all others.) Our hearts, particularly the hearts of Calgarians, pump oil – a rich, viscous liquid that courses through our arteries, until it is impossible to remember how it wasn't always so. The energy business is a part of our body and our politic as no other endeavour is. We don't have to like it all the time, but we must admit to it.

Until oil and gas took over, it was coal – one of the steps between rotting vegetation and diamonds – that bolstered the Western Canadian economy, coal for the railroad as it snaked its way across the country. Like most houses, Grandfather's was originally heated by coal, which was delivered by the ton and shovelled into the basement to be fed into the furnace.

Abundant coal deposits were discovered here in the late 1880s by James McMillan, a government land surveyor, and in 1889, Ad McPherson and J.J. Cooper opened a mine just west of the town of Black Diamond. Each year, they delivered 650 tons of high-grade coal by wagon cart to meet the CPR line in Okotoks, about forty kilometres south of Calgary.

Most of the coal in Alberta is bituminous, ranked second highest in quality, used to make coke for the steel industry or to generate electricity. In 1997, bituminous coal accounted for 41.2 million tonnes or 52 per cent of Canada's total coal production. The softer, lower-ranked sub-bituminous coal is mined here too. It contains more moisture, making it less economical to transport long distances. But in 1997, 25.7 million tonnes were produced to generate almost 90 per cent of the province's electricity.

Coal fell out of favour with the development of cleaner fuels, but it has never been replaced. And every time the price of gas and oil increases, coal becomes more attractive. Coal never quite vanishes over the horizon for the simple reason that Canada has enormous reserves of the stuff – over 8 billion tonnes. Those reserves contain more energy than all of the country's oil, natural gas, and oil sands combined.

We live above vast deposits of coal, oil, and natural gas, all laid down when the dinosaurs roamed Alberta. It's little wonder that the mascot for the Calgary Zoo is Dinny the Dinosaur, upon whose huge painted green concrete tail I used to climb as a child. I'm sure modern managers of the zoo would prefer a less archaic mascot, but it would cost more to dismantle the tons of concrete that are Dinny than to preserve him. And it is a constant reminder that the resources under our feet started to form about the time the real Dinny roamed the land northeast of the inland sea that is now downtown Calgary.

When outsiders talk about the need to diversify the Albertan economy, we point them to the universities of Calgary, Alberta, and Lethbridge, and welcome them to the reality of life in Alberta. We can research and study any worthy subject. We have competent scholars and brilliant minds. But nothing works when the oil business doesn't.

I am just as dependent upon its fortunes as if I were employed by Petro-Canada.

I could have been rich had my grandfather, Clinton James Ford, thought more about money than public service; had he taken his law degree, and as his partner, Eric Harvie, did, amassed oil and gas leases. Instead, the firm of Ford, Miller and Harvie broke up. Ford became city solicitor, judge, and eventually, Chief Justice of Alberta and the Northwest Territories. Harvie became a legend of business acumen and accumulated wealth.

Family gossip says the partnership disbanded because Grandfather believed that taking the mineral and resources rights of the farmers and ranchers in payment for legal work was denying their birthright.

Harvie's legacy puts Olympic boasting to shame: Calgary has public parks and institutions, such as the Glenbow Museum and the Devonian Foundation, because of the largesse of my grandfather's law partner and Eric Harvie's family.

Us? The Fords have memories instead of money. But the family still owns some of those original oil and gas leases. Every year, they bring in royalties. Not enough to make any of the now fourth generation of Fords wealthy, but enough to remind us our roots are deep in this resource-rich soil.

3

Welcome to Paradise

Banff is the destination of choice for tourists. It is not the destination of choice for locals. This isn't to say Albertans ignore Banff, but that they seek out specific attractions in the park – the backcountry trails for skiing in the winter and hiking in the summer – that the tourist who stays in the town misses.

Banff is in danger of being loved to death. This love affair has been carried on since 1885, when two railroad workers "discovered" what the local natives had always known: natural hot springs high in the Rocky Mountains, which the local tribes considered to be healing waters. Anyone who has skied the Rockies on a bitterly cold afternoon and then immersed herself in the spring – nature's original hot tub – believes the natives were right, the sulphurous smell notwithstanding. The federal government moved quickly to set aside ten square miles of the Northwest Territories to protect this natural phenomenon from being exploited by commercial interests. That ten square miles became Banff National Park, the oldest, best-known, and most beloved park in the country.

That fight goes on to this day – conservationists and environmentalists who want to protect this beautiful patch of the planet from development versus business and commercial interests who see the wilderness as one giant theme park to be exploited. Businesses argue that restrictions placed on the expansion of the town of Banff hinder their right to a reasonable return on their investment; environmentalists argue that any further encroachment into the wilderness will mean the death of wildlife whose migratory patterns have already been disrupted by development. So far, it's a tie: the federal government has further restricted expansion, there is a "need to reside" rule, but businesses still flourish and prosper.

For more than a hundred years tourists have been flocking to this small mountain town first named by Europeans on the railroad maps as Siding 29. By 1886, Siding 29 had been moved three kilometres, renamed Banff for the Scottish hometown of the railroad president, Donald Smith – Lord Strathcona – and the tourist boom was on.

The hot mineral waters – steaming even during winter's icy grip – soothed sore muscles and spirits. It didn't take any genius to figure out that rail travellers would be attracted to "take the waters," as centuries of Europeans had been doing in spas such as Baden Baden and Bath. The knowledge that the wilderness contained mineral baths to rival any in Europe would lure travellers to the mountains, the new railroad would bring them, and all they needed was accommodation.

In 1888, the majestic Banff Springs Hotel, built of massive grey and purple rock from Mount Rundle, opened its doors. It has dominated the town of Banff, the valley, and the fortunes of the region ever since. Not surprisingly, it resembles a great grey Scottish castle and its spires echo the peaks of the surrounding mountains. It was an instant hit. It captured the hearts – and the money – of wealthy travellers. Nothing has changed in all these years.

The thousands of staff needed to operate an exclusive hostelry came from across Canada, beginning with Calgary and included, before the Second World War, my father, Bob Ford, whose experience as a bellhop taught him, he said, too much, too soon. (Being asked to find "companionship" for a male guest took him by surprise, but even more stunning was the offer of a twenty-dollar tip to do so, smack in the middle of the Depression. Dad assured me, when he told me this story, that he hadn't the faintest idea what the American guest was talking about. He also learned about the artifice of movies and makeup, when he met the likes of Ginger Rogers in the flesh, and realized the tall, beautiful woman dancing with Fred Astaire was rather homely, freckled, and short. What she lacked in real beauty though, she made up for in golf, according to my father.)

Banff took hold of my father's heart and held on, as it does with most native Albertans. His own father, from the farming flatlands of Southwestern Ontario, first came West for a summer job at the cement plant in Exshaw – a carbuncle on the park's landscape that still exists, having been grandfathered, so to speak, when it became obvious (thankfully early in the history of the national park) that to permit further mining of the limestone mountains would seriously affect the tourist business. Wealthy American and European tourists did not want their vistas marred by belching smokestacks and grit in the air. The Exshaw plant is still there and, I believe, acts as the greatest advertisement for government and legislative control over development since the 1885 government of Canada recognized the need to protect some of the park's pristine beauty.

As the traveller to or from Banff rounds the great sweep of Lac des Arcs, about ten kilometres east of Canmore, they can see across the narrow "lake" (it's actually just a broadening of the river) a mountain that is slowly but inexorably disappearing as its mineral resources are stripped away. It is, aside from commercial and residential development beyond the national park's borders, the single most stunning difference in the landscape over the years. Mountain time is usually measured in hundreds of centuries, not years.

After working in the heart of the Rockies, and recognizing that a farm boy didn't stand much chance of breaking into the staid Toronto establishment with its family law firms and old-boy connections, Grandfather returned the following year and made Alberta his home, completing his final year of law here, instead of at Osgoode Hall in Toronto. Either the mountains or the Western freedom to succeed or both had captured my grandfather's imagination. He returned East only long enough to marry his childhood schoolmate, Kitty Evans, and to honeymoon in Niagara Falls – where else? – before coming back to Calgary.

My husband's family has reel after reel of home movies of their convoys to Banff every summer, along the two-lane blacktop that was the connecting highway. A trip to Banff was the highlight of my childhood, too. Seen in sequence, the home movies eventually change from scratchy, black-and-white eight-millimetre to colour film. What hasn't changed, though, is what brought all of us over the generations to Banff and its surroundings – the mountains and the blue and green lakes; the smell of pine and spruce, the larch and the trembling aspen; buffalo beans and western wood lilies; wild roses and Indian paintbrush; the heavy saskatoon berry bushes – all the nature that explodes around the visitor if he has enough sense to stop and look. A photograph taken today from the outlook on Sulphur Mountain would not be substantially different than the first photograph taken from the same vantage point a hundred years ago. We haven't quite paved over paradise, although we're trying.

On one side of the sometimes rancorous discussion over the future of Banff are the very commercial interests an earlier government worried about, but not quite enough to keep out of the park. Today, the Cave and Basin hot spring, which started it all, is closed to the public, a safety hazard with no available wherewithal (read millions of government dollars) to renovate.

Unlike Yellowstone National Park in Wyoming, which has been scrupulously protected by, ironically enough, the most pro-free-market government in the world, Banff was up for grabs. And grab it we did.

There has always been something mystical and magical about the Rocky Mountains. In Canada they form a 1,200-kilometre wall of snow-covered purple and grey jagged rock extending northward from the U.S. border to the Laird River basin. They were a formidable barrier. While European explorers are credited with finding the mountain passes through them, it was the native peoples who knew the routes first. In one memorable example, in their historical exploration of the lands west of the Mississippi River, Meriwether Lewis and William Clark used a map first drawn by Old Snow – Ak ko makki – an Alberta Blackfoot chief and subsequently copied by a British cartographer. David Thompson, whose name graces the highway west from Red Deer to Saskatchewan Crossing (literally the place where the North Saskatchewan River can be forded) is credited with finding the northern route to the Pacific Ocean. His name is the one in the history books. Yet he followed a route already set out by Jocko Findlay, the mixed-blood son of one of the founders of the North-West Company.

It's no secret why the names credited for exploration of the West are white, male, and British or Scottish – as a British dominion, Canada was naturally considered part of the White Man's Burden. Without native guides, some of whom were women – Sacajawea is the most famous example – many of the explorers would have failed. But the arrogance of the white explorer did not permit him – and the society paying for his travels – to consider the First Nations spread across the entire face of North America as anything other than ignorant savages.

After two hundred and more years, we're finally learning that Europeans encountered cultured and thinking peoples. Today, anthropologists and cultural scientists are slowly but irrevocably unravelling the racist history we still study, but it's an uphill battle against prejudice and generations of teaching and training.

Regardless of who first crested them, the Rockies have lost none of their enchantment. Yet as civilization crawls up their face, they have lost a considerable amount of their appeal for many Albertans, who find it necessary to go farther and farther afield to escape civilization. It isn't ennui that keeps us away from the well-travelled and trammelled destinations, but exasperation. There is no better example of paving paradise than Banff.

I know of few people who see Banff as a destination any longer. Far more attractive is its neighbour, Canmore, outside the national park gates, where there is still a feeling of community on the main street, and the prices of goods are given in Canadian dollars, not Japanese yen or American greenbacks.

Banff is, of course, an international destination. It is probably churlish of people like me to complain that this small town, never intended as a metropolis, has been inundated with day trippers and rich tourists.

But the town is the sad victim of its own success – overrun with people who love it too much, overwhelmed with its own publicity, the Niagara Falls of Western Canada with high-end shopping in place of the wax museum and the tacky attractions of Niagara. Like Niagara, the natural beauty is still there, but you won't find it in the town of Banff, unless you keep your chin raised and your eyes focused on the top of Mount Norquay or Sulphur Mountain and away from the crowd of people wandering aimlessly up and down Banff Avenue or spilling drunkenly out onto the streets when the bars close. This is the "mountain experience" for the tourists. The real experience is in the backcountry, on the hikes and the trails, at least on those that haven't been ripped to shreds by mountain bikes and off-road vehicles. While it is foolish to hope a national park with the Trans-Canada Highway bisecting it could be saved from the fate of being too popular, there are still environmentalists and ecologists desperate to stop the park from becoming a national theme park with the only item missing being fuzzy mascots.

There have been small victories, although the word *victory* depends on which side of the development argument you stand. The operative word is *small*. For example, Banff has a shopping mall, but it doesn't have a Ripley's Believe It or Not! museum of oddities. More than a decade ago, Banff turned down a surefire money-maker in favour of, dare it be said, taste. Anyone who has visited the town of Niagara Falls knows that Ripley's is to museums what Tang is to orange juice. Yet nothing is so gross that tourists won't pay good money to see it, and such exhibits are a boon in tourist destinations. The secret is children. Ventures such as Ripley's make money because they offer family entertainment in places where such entertainment

is limited. But Banff decided the price was too high in terms of tack-
iness: lime-green, polyester-doubleknit tacky; plastic forks and paper
plates tacky; varnished redwood bars with pulsing neon lights – that
kind of tacky.

Both the Horseshoe Falls and the Canadian Rockies are two of
the most enduring wonders of the world, renowned around the globe,
symbols of Canada that stand alongside the Royal Canadian Mounted
Police. And both Niagara Falls and Banff are towns whose lasting
appeal owes more to God than the good sense of their developers
and businesses. Only the geography is different. Banff townsite,
hemmed in as it is by the Rockies, is proscribed in its development and
squished into its natural setting. Every new street, every storey of
every new building, every bit of new development encroaches further
on the once-pristine beauty of the surroundings. Every pop can tossed
in a ditch, every heavy foot in the surrounding alpine meadows, and
every camera-toting hiker and trail-destroying mountain biker diminishes the park's natural beauty and value. The trick is to balance the
needs of visitors, the rights of the townsfolk, and the inherent right
of the environment to be protected.

Banff has nowhere to go; Niagara Falls can keep right on growing
until it meets St. Catharines or falls into Lake Ontario. It is impossible for the town to place the falls from which it takes its name in
jeopardy, because the Niagara Parks Commission controls both
Horseshoe Falls and the surrounding shoreline. The commission has
permitted few encroachments, meaning the natural physical beauty of
the area is preserved. Huge shade trees, grassy parks, and walkways
mark the area near the gorge and the whirlpool and the foaming
Niagara River. It is a sight to rival the Rockies – as long as you don't
look over your shoulder.

But Banff's bad luck is to be Canada's first national park wholly
in Alberta, where the voices of environmentalists are routinely
drowned out by the complaints of developers and businesspeople who
see the easy access to such natural beauty as an excuse to expand and
to bring more and more people into the area. It's an exponential
erosion of the natural setting – the more rooms and entertainment

and attractions are designed for tourists, the more service personnel are needed, the more infrastructure must be built to support the resorts and hotels, the restaurants and the shops.

Those who complain that Banff was never meant to be the Aspen of the North, the Whistler of Alberta, but to be an example of preservation of wilderness are routinely dismissed. Even as we welcomed a new millennium, the then-sitting federal minister responsible for Banff – the hapless and unloved Sheila Copps – was being demonized for her attempt to preserve the wilderness around Banff. She blotted her environmental copybook, though, with the ludicrous exercise of "celebrating" Canadian history by putting up cut-out "statues" of Canadian heroes outside the park's administration offices.

I'm still not sure what she was trying to achieve, other than the Disneyfication of Banff – where regional interests and reality are secondary to the fantasy that all parts of the country and culture are the same. Under that kind of thinking, why don't we just celebrate Canadian history with a series of theme parks, in various convenient locations? But the Disneyfication of Banff is not the real issue. The real issue is the globalization of culture that makes all places look the same and diminishes and destroys the unique history and culture that once existed.

Nobody goes to Paris to eat at the Burger King on the Champs Élysées. The McDonald's in Moscow became a tourist attraction when it opened – because it was about the only place in the city where one could be served food with a smile and without the attitude – but nobody visits the Russian capital for that express purpose. A downside of globalization is the ubiquity of the T-shirt culture, fast-food restaurants, and tacky souvenir sales all around the globe. Yet compelling arguments are made that global corporations are merely supplying what countries want – a Western, particularly an American, cultural experience.

Meanwhile, we Calgarians don't go to Banff any more.

We live, though, in a diminishing world, the wilderness being given over to golf courses and destination resorts and where the sounds of helicopters over the Rockies now joins with the lonely whistle of the locomotive heading through to the Pacific. The federal government can dictate development in the national park, but it has no control outside the gates of Banff. Housing developments now crawl up the slopes of the Bow corridor between Calgary and Banff, condos and townhouses and retirement homes for the baby boomers – often garish and ill-built pimples on nature's face.

Solitude is precious and vanishing. But Silvertip and Kananaskis are still golf courses to die for – Silvertip with its spectacular fairways and greens built into the side of a mountain overlooking the Bow Valley and Kananaskis with the Kananaskis River meandering through the course. The hazards on both courses are just as likely to be resident bears as sand traps. (The bears have the privilege.)

In the backcountry, the problem always has been the effect of humans on the ecological balance. It doesn't take much ignorance to destroy fragile alpine meadows or present a danger to wildlife, it just takes a few ignoramuses. But "a few" can be thousands. Several million tourists a year visit the Banff, Jasper, Yoho, and Kootenay parks, which straddle the Alberta–B.C. provincial border, and the southern Waterton Lakes Park, attracted by the wilderness and spectacular scenery and the hiking, biking, and camping opportunities. Even though the parks comprise hundreds of thousands of square kilometres of wilderness, the trails and campgrounds are crowded all summer.

City people whose garbage is picked up weekly, whose toilets flush into municipal sewer systems, who rarely have to worry about what they throw away, all too often take those attitudes into the wilderness, and the more they've paid for the privilege, the more sense of entitlement they seem to bring. While resorts such as the Banff Springs Hotel or Château Lake Louise – and all such established businesses – have expensive and extensive disposal systems for everything from garbage to sewage, the wilderness itself can't do anything when hikers and bikers attack it.

This isn't a new problem. Ken Jones, the first warden of Mount Assiniboine Provincial Park, said in his memoirs that the worst wildlife he dealt with was the two-legged variety.

Jones says that when he took the job in 1967, "The main problem was the mess that was being created. The worst stuff was the tins and foil wrap. A lot of the campers were very careless about their garbage, leaving it scattered about. A lot of them packed in booze, wine, whiskey and even beer . . . it seems that they could carry in the full bottles, but couldn't carry out the empties. . . . It took me two summers to clean up the trash that had accumulated over the years."

Now, all these years of consciousness-raising later, the garbage still litters the trails and the backcountry.

Almost as bad are the whims of government, for whom the optics are often more important than the facts. Mount Assiniboine Lodge is a case in point. It is the single development – except for a few camping spots and day cabins – at the base of one of the most photographed mountains in the Rockies.

The problem was one of borders: Mount Assiniboine Lodge is in British Columbia, the family who still runs it lives in Alberta. This posed a problem only for the deep thinkers in Victoria.

The national and provincial parks are contiguous through the mountains and most of the time the visitor would be hard-pressed to decide which side of a scree is in Alberta and which is in B.C. Mountain people are, in the main, less concerned with political geography than they are with protecting the mountains they love. So when the province of British Columbia decided it didn't like or approve of the optics of having a family that lived half the year in Canmore, Alberta, run the lodge at Mount Assiniboine in B.C., everyone who had ever had the wonderful experience of staying with Sepp and Barb Renner was surprised. No, they were astounded at the insult.

The Lodge is a heritage site at the base of the mountain, snuggled into the alpine meadow at the edge of Lake Magog. It was built by the CPR in 1928 as part of an original concept of wilderness tourism, and as a destination for the trail rides that would bring tourists over the mountains. The horses were eventually banned, but people are still permitted – thirty a night, for a two- or three-night minimum (depending on the day of arrival) – because there are only two ways of getting to the lodge: the eight-hour hike over the pass or the short, thrice-weekly helicopter ride.

Next to the Lodge and its six log guest cabins are more rustic cabins for overnight hikers, overlooked by a B.C. Parks ranger's office and public campgrounds – the same campgrounds that Jones bemoaned took him two years to clean up. Even with that development, 85 per cent of the land is left in its natural state.

The Renners have held the concession for the Lodge since 1983 and have spent years fixing the crumbling structures and chasing down the authentic furniture of the period. What they couldn't find, Sepp built. The family – Sepp, Barb, and their three children, including Canadian Olympic cross-country skier, Sara – poured their love and energies into the facility, only to be told in 1996 to get out.

The official words from the B.C. government were more politic than "get lost," but the effect was the same: the family was deemed politically incorrect. The "why" will forever be buried in the archives of the provincial government and the hearts of the bureaucrats who decided a couple who lived in Alberta couldn't be in charge of the B.C. site. The provincial government awarded the contract for the Lodge to a subsidized B.C. business. The public outcry was loud, long, and national.

The tendering process that took the Lodge from the Renners was tossed out. For once, public input and outrage meant more than political connections, development interests, and back-patting. By late summer of 1997, the Renners were again awarded a ten-year contract to operate the Lodge.

The reason so many Canadians are so loyal to the Renners is simple: They get it. They get what it's all about. Unlike other destinations – Banff comes immediately to mind – that's why Mount Assiniboine can claim more than three-quarters of their visitors are from Alberta and British Columbia – including an out-of-shape newspaper columnist who, after a couple of years, still can't believe she walked huffing, puffing, and complaining all the way, to the top of a ridge just to see if Cerulean Lake really is the right colour blue. It is.

During all of the confusion over who should operate the Lodge, no words of criticism passed any of the Renners' lips. Their concern, they said, was not the politics but the business they call "a living museum," and the people who return year after year. (The Lodge has a 100-per-cent occupancy rate and a 70-per-cent return rate, even though there isn't much in the way of indoor plumbing or running hot water.) The attraction is the wilderness. Those who need television and noise don't come to the Renners – the closest cash machine, convenience store, and television are an eight-hour hike away. If you want wine with dinner, you hike in with the bottles. Those who want the beauty of the mountains, a chance to hike and climb, and the comfort of good food and company, come back year after year.

Mount Assiniboine commands everything below it, rising nearly four thousand metres straight into the clouds. Like other World Heritage sites, visitors are awed by the spectacle laid out by the hand of nature millions of years ago. It seems ludicrous to consider boundaries in this wild land where mountains and the men and women who love them share more with each other than with any political jurisdiction.

There is more to Alberta tourism than the mountains, although you'd be hard-pressed to find someone from Germany or Switzerland who's here for the waving fields of grain.

What Europe has is history, even in its mountains. What Canada has is sheer size and majesty, available nowhere else but the Andes and the Himalayas, and there's no equivalent of the Banff Springs Hotel in Machu Picchu or Nepal, short of the Royal Palace.

Yet the visitors can still surprise us. Germans come for the "Western" experience, to visit ranches and act out the life of a cowboy. The Swiss come to see if the mountains here are anything like the mountains there. They aren't, the Rockies being a few geological generations younger. The Japanese come on package tours, and when the bottom fell out of the Japanese economy, there was near panic in Banff, Lake Louise, and Jasper, all destinations for Asians. Mostly, though, the Europeans come to Alberta and our

mountains because of the solitude and the wilderness. A few kilometres off the Trans-Canada Highway, it's as if humans never set
foot in this beauty.

There is also more to Banff than the town of Banff, as any backcountry hiker will attest. The national park, a World Heritage site,
is more than 6,600 square kilometres in size, bordering Jasper
National Park and Yoho National Park in British Columbia. There
are more than 1,100 kilometres of trails through the park, ranging
from pleasant strolls your great-grandmother could manage to the
most difficult of terrains. And all through the park are campsites and
hostels for travellers whose budgets don't cover the expense of
staying at the Banff Springs. The Alpine Club of Canada also main-
tains a network of high-country huts and shelters.

Don't even think of venturing off the paved roads of Banff
without preparation. That booklet given to you as you enter the park
isn't just advertising, it's serious. There are wild animals here and they
have the right-of-way. Smart hikers go nowhere alone, go nowhere
without telling a responsible adult where they are going and when
they are returning. Cars may screech to a halt whenever a bear is
spotted at the side of the roadway, or a troop of alpine sheep calmly
licking the salt off the asphalt, but only a fool gets up-close-and-
personal with them. This isn't Disney, it's reality. Although most of
the wildlife – with the exception of the brazen elk walking around
Banff townsite – are shy and furtive, preferring to stay as far away
from you as you want to stay from them, to a bear, you may be a
threat to her cubs. To a cougar, you're lunch if you are small enough.

In any confrontation, remember the wildlife usually wins.

And in any confrontation with Nature, you will always lose unless
you are prepared. And that means even for a quick stroll in the woods,
bring water, clothing for sudden changes in the weather, extra food,
sunscreen, waterproof matches, and a survival blanket. (One of those
silver things that roll down into a cigarette package size.) All of this
may seem too much trouble for a day's hike, but pretend you're a Boy
Scout – be prepared for any eventuality, including getting stranded
overnight, caught in a sudden blizzard or a thunderstorm. The most

important equipment to bring to the mountains is a healthy respect for the vicissitudes of nature. Oh, and if you run into a grizzly bear, play dead. The first time I heard this advice, I burst into gales of laughter. Play dead? I'd be comatose with fear.

Along with this advice, guidebooks warn visitors that access to many of the trails is difficult if you're used to using public transportation. Public transportation, like so many other public services, is almost non-existent in Banff. Ironically, there is no longer any regular train service, either.

The only way of experiencing the breathtaking vistas available to train travellers is to pay the premium price for a seat with Rocky Mountain Railtours, a private company operating a two-day train service to rival the Orient Express – at least in terms of cost. There are still trains running through the Rockies, their whistles echoing off the mountainsides, but the passengers are coal and oil, containers and cars, all the freighted goods heading one way to the Port of Vancouver, and the other across the prairies. Train travel fell victim to the age of speed, and to put blame where it is deserved, to neglect, economics, inefficiency, awful service, and lack of passengers. All of this was compounded by the chronic inability of the railway to get the cross-Canada train to run on time. Hours-long waits for scheduled service were part of the "romance" in this part of the country.

It only took about one hundred years to drive the national dream into the track bed. It was, then, a national scandal. Now, not many of us care. The train doesn't stop here any more, and we barely notice.

What we do notice, at least those people paying attention, is the creeping privatization of public services.

Where humans live, they need services. Not just the obvious ones in a tourist town – the restaurants and bars, the hotels and motels, the gas stations and grocery stores – but the ordinary services city dwellers take for granted. Schools, medical clinics, and hospitals, a fire department, policing, and such amenities as a public library.

The Banff Public Library, an unprepossessing brown building at the corner of Bear and Buffalo streets, doesn't look much like the headquarters of a revolution, but it is. That the "revolution" never extended beyond the town boundaries is not as important as the principle being upheld.

The Banff library refused to get on the Alberta political bandwagon of user-pay. Banff town council, the library board, and the library staff decided to mark the millennium in 2000 and the fiftieth anniversary of the library by offering free memberships to local residents. Within a year, this small public institution in a town where prosperity is determined by tourists had recorded the highest usage and membership ever.

All the other libraries in Alberta, save one, charge a fee, negotiating their way around legislation by saying the "membership" fee is for special services, like issuing a library card. (The exception is the library in Lloydminster, the town straddling the Alberta-Saskatchewan border. The library there is governed by Saskatchewan's Public Libraries Act.)

Libraries are just a single example of the user-pay attitude of the province. Across Alberta, the people least able to afford luxuries are paying the most for them, if you consider access to library books, public recreational facilities, sports teams, schools, all of which come under the rubric of "user-pay."

Thoughtless people believe user fees are logical. They argue the truly needy are exempt. Right. Life is just one jolly means test around here. They refuse to see that a level of public and social service is expected of a province, of a government, and particularly of a people.

We don't live in isolation, we live in communities, and we look to our communities to care for us.

4

Highway 93 and the Road to Kyoto

As much as the Trans-Canada Highway discourages lingering and gawking, silently demanding motorists put pedal to metal and drive at least 120 kilometres per hour – even though the speed limit is 110 – Highway 93 from Lake Louise to Jasper positively begs for a slower pace. Turn off Highway 1 and you lose the steady stream of freight traffic, propelled by drivers who couldn't care less about the scenery, as long as they can get from Calgary to Vancouver in under twelve hours, give or take a few weigh scales or radar traps. They have no time for or interest in the scenery or the wildlife munching along the verge.

The dearth of heavy truck traffic may not be the main reason to meander along Highway 93 – colloquially referred to as the Icefields Parkway – but it's one reason. The better reason is this is the most spectacular highway short of two: the Sea to Sky Highway from Vancouver to Whistler and the Italian mountain road that links Naples and Positano. (Best done at twilight just as the lights flicker on up and down the mountainside, reflected in the calm waters of the Mediterranean.)

Such scenic routes make up in enjoyment what they lack in speed.

It's just under three hundred kilometres from Banff to Jasper, and the optimistic tourist might calculate the trip will take about three hours, then add another hour or so to get to Banff from Calgary. And, yes, it could. Given a clear day, dry roads, and no radar traps you could make the trip from Calgary to Jasper in four hours. But why would you want to?

Why hurry through the changing scenery offered along the roadside? Instead, take the time to see what we're doing to the landscape and then ponder whether the Alberta government is correct in dismissing fears of global warming. Remember when U.S. president Ronald Reagan announced that acid rain was caused by bee poop? That's about the level of intelligence brought to the discussion of global warming, greenhouse gases, and the threat to the environment, not only for us, but for the world.

Granted, to compare Canada or the United States to such monstrous polluters as China or Russia is ludicrous. But just because other countries are worse polluters than we are is no excuse to add to the problem. And we are adding to it – although when Canadian prairie farmers talk about the drought that has plagued their crops for the past few years, and the eastern half of Canada is deluged in the summer and ice-bound in the winter, while the western half doesn't get enough snow in the winter or enough rain in the summer, the connection is rarely made. If blame is laid, it is on Nature, as if the perfect balance Nature presented for this planet is somehow affected by outsiders. Aliens, perhaps. Satan, some would say.

The evidence of global warming is right there, on Highway 93. Here, one doesn't need to be an environmentalist to see with her own eyes the destruction of the glaciers. All one needs to do is stop on the way to Jasper and ponder the Columbia Icefield, the largest mass of its kind in the Rocky Mountains. While six glaciers contribute to the accumulation, it is the Athabasca Glacier that dominates and is visible to tourists. (The Dome and Stutfield glaciers form part of the scenery also.) But Athabasca is the dominant one, and just as the limestone mountain in Exshaw slowly disappears from constant mining, so too goes this particular glacier.

I can remember, as a child, that the glacier came almost to the edge of the highway. I imagined I could step from car door onto glacier ice – if my parents would let me. Now the distance between child's foot and ice mountain is merely a fanciful memory, and it is obvious to an adult's eye fifty years later that the ice has noticeably retreated from the highway. Tourists are still taken onto the icefields by special vehicles with huge puffy tires to grip the ice and snow, the better to supposedly leave no trail, but it is impossible to ignore the degradation of what is a World Heritage site. (The vehicles, called Snocoaches, are the most ecologically friendly ever used on the ice and are built in Calgary specifically for Brewster Company, which operates the icefields tour. All but one are stationed at the Columbia Icefield. The other is used by the American government in Antarctica.)

Experts say the glacier cover in the Rockies is at its lowest ebb in ten thousand years; meanwhile, as late as 2003, Alberta Environment was denying a proven connection between human activity and global warming. The government frames the debate not as a question of what, but who. It's sort of like: yes, greenhouse-gas emissions exist, but we aren't responsible.

Tourists can still see the icefalls, crevasses, and moraines (think of these deposits as glacier garbage, the debris that collects in a glacier's trail, much like teenagers and their bedrooms) and still enjoy this particular wilderness experience, but even the most blind Albertan can't help asking where will it end.

The icefields glaciers are remnants of the great ice age and the glaciers that once covered the mountains. Although only a small part is still visible from the Parkway, the icefields are calculated to be more than three hundred square kilometres of ice to a depth of 350 metres. Like the Great Wall of China, the Columbia Icefield is recognizable from space.

Why worry about one glacier in the midst of such a mass of ice? Because melting ice from the Athabasca Glacier forms the headwaters of the Athabasca, Columbia, and North Saskatchewan rivers. Those rivers are the lifeblood of the land. Endanger them and endanger all of us. UNESCO puts it this way: "The Columbia Icefield

in Jasper is regarded as the hydrographic apex of North America."
The only other one in the world is in Siberia.

In the 100 years from 1900 to 2000, the glacier receded 1.5 kilometres (a blistering pace when non-cataclysmic geographical changes
are measured in millimetres) and scientists estimate 16 million cubic
metres of water has been lost. Not just any water, but clean, fresh
water. Water frozen before air pollution existed.

There are few other places where you can casually drink the
water as it comes from its source. Scientists estimate the glacier melt
as more than 99 per cent pure, freezing as it did before there even
was such a thing as industrial pollution or technological advances,
maybe even before the vegetation turned to coal. Not all water in
the mountains is safe to drink from its source. Visitors to Banff are
cautioned not to think that because the water looks crystal clear it
is clean enough to drink. A particularly nasty water-borne parasite,
Giardiasis, otherwise known as beaver fever, lives in the waters
around Banff. I know it's risky to drink the groundwater near any
human settlement, but I have drunk water straight from Heart
Creek – as it flows down through the small community of Lac Des
Arcs to the Bow River – for years without any ill effects. Perhaps I
do so because I still can. I don't like my chances – or the creek's –
of thriving through another couple of generations. David Schindler,
a University of Alberta professor of ecology, told a Banff conference that southern Alberta, including the Rocky Mountains, will
be two degrees warmer in twenty years. Those of us warm-blooded
creatures who live through the indignities offered by winter – the
garage door freezing shut at minus 40°C – might like a few degrees
of warmth in January's darkness. But, of course, such thinking is a
case of be careful what you wish for, you might get it.

An average temperature rise of just two degrees would mean
the end of the glaciers and the reduction of such rivers as the Bow
and the Elbow, both of which flow through Calgary, to little more
than streams. The city would be hotter and drier, and the costs of
municipal water supplies would be "astronomical," said Schindler.

Warnings such as this have had little effect on the mindset of many Albertans whose thinking isn't focused on what we leave behind, but on how we can exploit it now. Much of the shortsighted reaction to environmental damage is led by the province itself, and when it comes to a choice between jobs and nature, between business and wilderness, the former wins out in almost every case, even if development is precluded by the province's own legislation. A case in point is the dam across the Oldman River in southern Alberta, built in 1992, which has altered forever what had been one of the last free-flowing rivers in this part of the world. To put up the dam as an aid to irrigation of the desert-like region, Alberta had to violate its own laws. Was anything done? Only protests by what the province would call the usual malcontents – environmentalists, natives, ecologists, and wildlife experts. But here was a conflict between farmers and the future. The farmers won.

One of the problems of getting the message of global warming through to ordinary people is simple: We don't like scare tactics and we don't believe exaggerations. And for many Canadians who live with clean air and clean water, the idea that the world is polluted is a joke. They've never been to Mexico City or Beijing; to Rome or Moscow, all monster cities where the air has the texture of Styrofoam and the taste of car exhaust.

The second reason is more philosophical. When Canadians are polled about environmental issues, we are overwhelmingly in favour of preservation, protection, clean-up, and all the motherhood issues. Indeed, if Canadians are asked whether they'd pay a little more for heating or gasoline if it means preserving the environment, we agree it would be worth it. The difficulty is nobody can tell us how and when and how much. As a friend in Ottawa's federal bureaucracy put it to me: "If you ask about clean air and water, everybody says yes." He paused for a moment and then added: "In the abstract."

Both sides of the debate have done an abysmal job of explaining the situation to the ordinary Canadian, who should not be expected to understand "carbon sinks" and "carbon sequestration."

We only barely comprehend the translation of "anthropogenic climate impacts" to mean the effects on climate caused by humans, not nature.

On one side are those who believe the world will end with a bang when we finally extinguish ourselves and on the other those who believe the world will end with a whimper when corporate profits dry up.

The much-maligned Kyoto Protocol is an example of good intentions screwed by politics and greed. Canada signed it, over the objections of provinces such as Alberta, but it's a paper tiger, toothless and irrelevant despite its high-toned rhetoric. Maybe if the framers and the protesters against Kyoto had stood at the foot of the Columbia Icefield and pondered where the ice went, there would at least have been a greater understanding. As it is, the United States did not sign the accord, so it's largely useless, except as a talking point.

There is a wealth of well-meaning protocols, agreements, and conventions to which Canada is a signatory – from the United Nations convention on the Rights of the Child, to the Code of Conduct for Responsible Fisheries. We are eager to affix our country's name to documents that promise better conditions for all, human and non. It is in the doing we fail, not in the promising. Even though eighty-four countries, including Canada, signed the agreement, which calls for meaningful reduction in emissions of greenhouse gases, there has been little agreement about the basic premise: that global warming is occurring. Politicos still argue about it while businesses stand behind whatever spurious "investigation" has decided there is no link between emissions and global warming. The Alberta government was four-square against the Kyoto accord, claiming no definite proof carbon dioxide and other hydrocarbon emissions affect climate.

On the way from Banff to Jasper take a side trip; stand in front of the icefields and ask yourself, Where did the ice go? Ponder the bizarre weather patterns we're now seeing in Canada: ice storms in the east and drought in the west to cite two recent environmental disasters.

No, I don't believe everyone has to bicycle to work or turn the thermostat down to sixteen Celsius. But I do believe it would be sheer stupidity to ignore the warnings of global warming and the dangers inherent in using fossil fuel just because a coalition of vested interests characterize such worrying as needless and pathetic.

Maybe the non-smoking lobby and its tireless and unceasing hectoring over the past thirty-some years is worth using as an analogy. The same tactics to deny global warming were used by tobacco companies in the early days of the campaign to eliminate smoking. First, deny there's a problem. Second, lie about the science or buy your own scientists to refute any claims of danger. Third, marginalize the opposition.

But the anti-smoking groups never gave up, even as they were excoriated and dismissed by a smoking public. Now, no doctor would stand up and defend smoking as a healthy activity. Governments have instituted stiff legislation on smoking and concomitant taxes, even as tobacco continues to be a legal product. Even the most fervent supporter of the right to smoke – and I count myself in pre-abstinence days as one of those – doesn't argue today that smoking is not harmful and that second-hand smoke can be just as bad.

A wise management expert once drummed into my head that any action or any change will usually be greeted with skepticism and reluctance. The instigator of change must learn, he said, to "appreciate the time delay." It took the non-smoking lobby decades to change habits and win acceptance, but it succeeded. Today it's the turn of those who warn of the danger of global warming to be met with anger and denial from the people who benefit from lax regulations and co-operative governments.

A few generations ago, the engine of Alberta's economy was coal. Any suggestion that the use of coal was polluting the air and presenting a health danger was greeted with hoots of derision from the coal companies, somewhat like the sounds coming out of governments dependent on oil and gas revenues and royalties.

Still, consideration must be given to what is seen as the unfairness of the Kyoto Protocol, that developing countries such as China, India, and Mexico are exempt from its provisions, even as they continue to befoul their own air with impunity. Canadians live in a clean country: our air is clean; our water safe for most communities, and our lives are blessed with all the riches of nature. Yet the Kyoto agreement calls for the people of Canada, by 2010, to reduce their consumption of those riches and cut back greenhouse-gas emissions to 6 per cent below 1990 levels, a figure now considered unreachable in practical terms. (By 2005, Canada's greenhouse-gas emissions were 30 per cent higher than in 1990.) Meanwhile the overpopulated, pollution-spewing developing countries are exempt because their per-capita emissions are not as high as those in the First World. Even an idiot can understand that global warming is global, not regional, and unless everyone's in the game, nobody can win.

The idea of setting an example doesn't sit well here in Alberta. We are more into fair play than altruism.

You probably won't consider all that while gazing in awe at one of the country's major glaciers, especially if you're there to soak up the majesty of Nature. You won't be alone there. Highway 93, the Icefields Parkway, delivers Nature big time to more than 2.5 million travellers each year. More than two thousand vehicles a day drive the highway in the summer, occasionally dodging grizzlies and bighorn sheep. The lucky ones take their time and discover what's waiting just off the beaten path, so to speak.

Just over thirty kilometres south of Jasper is Athabasca Falls, where the Athabasca River drops twenty-five metres into a gorge. The area is well-travelled and convenient for tourists, laced with trails and pathways, and rife with destinations – Sunwapta Falls and Stanley Falls (neither as spectacular as Athabasca) and picturesque lakes, such as Buck Lake and Osprey Lake.

After a lifetime of exploring the mountains and their attractions, even as a mere dilettante and not an adventurer, they delight me every time. Nothing, though, could possibly compare with the experience of biking or running that highway, and when the Banff to Jasper race was cancelled in 2000 after twenty years, it was mourned in runners' circles and clubs around the world. The original organizers, the University of Alberta–based Chasquis Running Club, gathered nine teams for the first heady, around-the-clock race. The last relay in the original twenty-four-hour format attracted 116 teams of seventeen runners each, from around the world. It was the most spectacular relay race ever organized and had as its high point, both literally and figuratively, Sunwapta Pass at 2,035 metres. On the first weekend in June, for a complete circle of the clock, through every possible weather, runners were strung along the highway between the mountain towns. Some teams couldn't complete the run in twenty-four hours and some couldn't finish at all, but according to my giddy stepdaughter, who ran one year with a team of women from Edmonton, just being in the race was a thrill.

But environmentalists, wildlife experts, and Parks Canada stepped in with concerns that the race was affecting nocturnal wildlife and damaging the environment. It took until 2005 to remount one of the world's favourite races as an Alberta centennial project. Some of the glamour was missing. No more the haunting beauty of a moonlit night. No more the effort to reach Banff from Jasper propelled only by human feet. The reconstructed race was held in two segments run at the same time: from Banff to Saskatchewan Crossing and from Saskatchewan Crossing to Jasper. Twelve hours instead of twenty-four. Daylight only.

Jasper, 287 kilometres northwest of Banff, is sort of the poor cousin to the more attractive tourist destination of Banff. Jasper has never enjoyed Banff's worldwide popularity. Part of the reason is the difficulty of getting there – at least a four- to five-hour drive from either Calgary or Edmonton, the time depending on the season and the weather. Leaving Calgary in the middle of an Indian summer only to meet winter halfway to Jasper is a common experience. Like Banff, the premier hotel just across the river outside town – Jasper Park Lodge – began life as a railway lodge, built in 1922 on the shore of Lac Beauvert amid one thousand acres of wilderness. Its championship golf course rivals that of the Banff Springs, including the errant elk and occasional flock of Canada geese. The reward for making the drive is a less-crowded park experience than Banff.

Part of the difference between Banff and Jasper is the geography. In Banff, the mountains are on top of you, looming overhead, seemingly guarding the town. Jasper, on the other hand, is set on a spacious, mountain tableland at the north end of Jasper National Park, where the Athabasca and Miette river valleys meet.

The town of Jasper still retains some of its small-town feel. The stores aren't quite as in your face as in Banff, and the restaurants are not so determinedly cool, although you know you're not in Kansas any more when the menu features the line, in impeccable English only: "For the convenience of our visitors from abroad, the management reserves the right to add the customary gratuity to the bill." Were there truth in customer relations, it should read: "All you Japanese who don't tip because it isn't customary in your country will find a 15-per-cent service charge added to your bill." After all, our delight at the friendship and goodwill brought into our province by travellers and tourists from around the world is tempered by the fact they represent money, and that we like almost better than anything.

Once each year, on a slow weekend in the shoulder season (not quite winter and not yet summer) the Jasper Park Lodge is invaded by hordes of women in pyjamas. Literally. The Ultimate Pyjama Party, now held at various upscale resorts in Canada and the U.S., originated at Jasper when two enterprising Calgary women – Helene Oseen and Nadia Piatka – acted on their belief that women would enjoy a weekend away with just "the girls."

Most of us remember the fun of pyjama parties when we were kids, and Helene and Nadia (who now lives in Buffalo) offered a grown-up version. Buses from Edmonton and Calgary deliver a couple of hundred women anxious for a good time to the doors of the Lodge on a Friday afternoon. Some of us, with the assistance of various libations and hors d'oeuvres (the kind we usually only make for company instead of for ourselves), have already started the "good time" on the bus. Past pranks include trying to horribly embarrass the male driver by hanging our brassieres from the rear-view mirror. One year the driver joked that the bus company held a lottery to see who would drive the bus from Calgary. He grinned widely: "I won," he said.

It is difficult to explain to someone who has never been to the isolation of Jasper why it is the perfect get-away place for a bunch of women. It's just far enough from home that only a dire emergency could bring a wife and mother back during those two days. It's far enough away that it feels like a genuine break from real life, and as guys say, it's a "road trip," with all of the attendant highjinks.

This isn't a self-improvement, make-over weekend, it isn't a trip to the spa (although one is available), and it certainly isn't serious. After the Friday night reception, it's a full Saturday of sometimes silly girl stuff, a Saturday night banquet complete with karaoke and a chance to let loose on the dance floor with your girlfriends, and a Sunday brunch buffet, which only seems to extend from one wall of the dining room to the other. The weekend has, for nearly a decade, given busy women an excuse to follow through on the song "Girls Just Wanna Have Fun."

Aside from the slower pace, one other difference to mention between Banff and Jasper is that travellers can take a regularly scheduled train – the Snow Train – to get there. (No word on what the Snow Train is called in the summer.) While it's possible to take the train all the way across Canada and pass through Jasper to Vancouver, it remains one of the most boring, bum-numbing experiences available – three days of endless nothing and a few hours of spectacular mountain scenery. Anyone who still considers the train a romantic mode of travel would be well advised to fly from, say, Toronto to Edmonton and then catch the train for the five-hour trip to Jasper. But be warned – the scenery from Edmonton to Jasper is nothing to write home about, either, except for the last run from Hinton to Jasper.

A better bet, although I may be considered an Alberta traitor for suggesting it, is to fly to Vancouver and take the eastbound VIA Rail train to Jasper. The overnight, eighteen-hour trip winds through the coastal mountain ranges, along the Fraser River, over the Yellowhead Pass, the border between B.C. and Alberta, and the Continental Divide. Train travellers exchange the jaw-dropping view of the Fraser Canyon in daylight for a daytime arrival in Jasper. This timing is probably a case of some VIA manager reckoning that what the customer doesn't know won't hurt him. Tourists who have never seen the Fraser Canyon by rail, especially on a brilliantly sunny winter's day with the light reflecting off the soft powder snow, are unaware of what they are missing. There's also a more commercial reason for the overnight train: VIA Rail and the Great Canadian Railtour Company, a private interest which took over VIA's Rocky Mountain daylight service, share the same track. The fancy-named, Oriental Express–inspired, luxury Rocky Mountaineer has first call on daylight service. And not to forget the reality of the rails these days: the over-burdened, pushed-to-capacity Canadian Pacific freight division trains take precedence over all.

Any trip between Alberta and British Columbia must cross the Continental Divide, the point from which all the water to the west flows to the Pacific and all the water to the east drains into Hudson Bay or the massive eastern Canadian river system and eventually the Atlantic Ocean.

The Columbia Icefield meltwater feeds the creeks and rivulets that eventually join the river system, but up close, the visitor can marvel at the trickle that splits itself in two, one stream heading to the Pacific, the other to the Atlantic.

5

The Promised Land

Moses never saw the Promised Land, having ticked off the Creator. In retaliation, God sentenced His servant, who carried the Ten Commandments down from the mountain, to forty years of wandering in the desert, never asking for directions. Northern Alberta isn't the Negev, but it too is a promised land and Albertans also spent forty years looking to cash in on the promise. Think two words: oil sands. Unlike Moses, we didn't need directions. We knew exactly where the promise lay, what it was embedded in, and how valuable it could prove to be to the Alberta economy.

The promise of wealth inherent in the rich but sticky deposits in the Athabasca tar sands still tantalizes us. As early as 1892, the Edmonton *Bulletin* reported findings of oily deposits at St. Albert, a French-speaking town that would, within 100 years, become a suburb of the provincial capital, Edmonton. The newspaper wrote: "Whether or not the tar is a sure indication of a profitable petroleum field, there is no doubt of the genuineness of the find and as little doubt that it is not confined to that single location."

No doubt at all. The tar sands stretch from Cold Lake and Lloydminster to the upper reaches of the Athabasca River. They are, in total, larger than the area of New Brunswick. Four different deposits stretch east to the Peace River, with the Athabasca deposit at Fort McMurray the largest of the four. It covers an area twice the size of Lake Ontario, according to *Canadian Geographic*, about 4.3 million hectares.

An estimated 400 trillion cubic metres and more of recoverable oil foiled all attempts to recover its riches profitably. Until now. As the price of energy climbs inexorably skyward, the cost of extraction, which depends on steam generation to recover heavy oil from sticky deposits buried too deep for surface mining, becomes more affordable. What was considered so expensive in the 1980s that it shut down all plans for the massive Syncrude project in Fort McMurray is now economically feasible. The tar-sands plants can now produce oil at eleven dollars a barrel, while the world price has reached forty dollars per barrel.

The peculiar properties of the oil sands were first discovered by the Cree who lived along the lower Athabasca River and used the oil-impregnated soil to waterproof their canoes. Alexander Mackenzie, who lent his name to the Mackenzie River, was the first European to describe the deposit in the late 1700s, but it would be more than 150 years before anyone thought of the tar sands as more than a curiosity. Until then, the fur trade was the prime business for the area.

Salt deposits were mined, in the middle 1920s, before the oil sands, although history tells us of one Thomas Draper experimenting in using the oil sands for paving roads. A few years later, and a couple of generations ahead of reality, Alcan formed the International Bitumen Company, and the notion of mining and extracting the oil was first proposed. The problem was how to separate the oil from the sand; to extract what was valuable from what was merely in the way.

In 1964, Suncor started building the first experimental plant to extract the oil north of Fort McMurray. The town's only prior experience with such interest and an influx of people (about three thousand) was during the Second World War, when American troops arrived to protect the supply lines for materials moving to the Northwest Territories.

What was, in 1964, the Great Canadian Oil Sands (known as Suncor after amalgamating with parts of the Sun Company in 1974) was determined to take the bitumen of the tar sands and turn it into something usable. Within ten years, a second plant, Syncrude Canada, was being built amid great hope that this oil reserve, estimated as larger than that of Saudi Arabia, would bring prosperity to the region and stability to the oil market.

It hasn't quite worked out that way, although in terms of continued prosperity, the oil-sands projects represent the hope of the future – as long as that future continues to keep oil prices above thirty dollars per barrel. While I know almost nothing about the oil business, I do know what it does for this province, and that magical thirty dollars per barrel has always been assumed to be the point where extracting the oil from the sand became worth the cost. In the spring of 2005, with gasoline prices in Alberta creeping toward one dollar a litre, a benchmark already passed in other parts of the country, thirty-dollar-per-barrel oil began to seem a floor, rather than a ceiling. With prices soaring past fifty dollars per barrel, the future looked prosperous for oil-sands production. But we are people accustomed to the vagaries of fate: in 2000, thirty-dollar-per-barrel oil seemed a bonanza, given that in 1999, the price bottomed out at ten dollars per barrel.

The thirty-dollar-per-barrel benchmark estimate for profitability in oil-sands production is rationalized because of the effort of extraction. It takes about two tonnes of oil-impregnated soil to produce one barrel of crude. In forty years, the extraction process has been modernized and made less costly, and now Suncor and Syncrude together account for about 18 per cent of Canada's crude-oil production. That might not seem much right now, but facing a future of limited oil supplies around the world, that amount can only increase.

Not everybody in the northern third of Alberta is involved in the oil business, but everybody benefits from it. Albertans call it the "Alberta Advantage," and yes, it's always capitalized. The Advantage makes up for isolation, lack of services, loneliness, and living in an area that charitably can only be called "interesting," regardless of the Fort McMurray and other northern tourist associations. Northern Alberta has its own beauty, but it isn't a tourist destination except for trappers and fishers, for hunters and explorers. The single exception in northern tourism may be Japanese travellers awed by the spectacle of the northern lights and a chance to go ice-fishing or experience a dogsled ride.

Fort McMurray is literally at the end of nowhere. The highway continues north for only another 100 kilometres. There is literally no place to go except back to Fort McMurray, and you have to drive three hundred kilometres farther south to Lac La Biche to meet another highway. The road into the Northwest Territories goes through the Peace River Valley, which is only about 385 kilometres southwest as the crow flies. But the crow doesn't need roads. Humans do.

Little wonder that places like Fort McMurray have a tough time attracting the professionals any city needs. The perennial shortage of doctors is a particular worry, despite best efforts to recruit physicians to practise in the north. The town is estimated to have half the number of physicians it needs to meet the provincial patient-physician average of 500 to 1. That's the bad news. There is good news: the population of Fort McMurray, as is the population of most northern cities, is overwhelmingly young and robust. There is therefore less need for doctors than in the south, where the numbers of aging seniors skew the medical/hospital statistics.

As a result of the boom-and-bust cycle of the oil business, Fort McMurray is (half-) jokingly referred to as Newfoundland's third largest city, after St. John's and Corner Brook. The north attracts young men eager to earn a higher-than-average wage and is a magnet (as is most of Alberta) for workers from the Maritimes. Why young people from the Atlantic provinces flock to Alberta is simple: according to Statistics Canada, the unemployment rate for fifteen- to twenty-nine-year-olds in the Atlantic provinces is a national high of 27 per cent. The rate for the same age group in Alberta is a national low of 11 per cent. They come here for "the Advantage."

First coined by Alberta premier Ralph Klein and the Tory government in 1996, the phrase "Alberta Advantage" has taken on a life of its own, unencumbered by reality, disparate economic situations, or diverse opinions. It is, for all intents and purposes, a mantra, replacing the licence-plate slogan, Wild Rose Country. We may live in "wild rose country" but our hearts are closer to our wallets than the outdoors.

Metaphors aside, the Alberta Advantage has captured the imagination of those who prosper from the good life that is Alberta. For the rest, for the Albertans who are poor or homeless, unemployed or living from paycheque to overdue bill to hampers from various food banks dotted throughout the province, and for the more than twenty-seven thousand Albertans receiving assistance through social services, the Alberta Advantage is a large and not-very-funny joke. This is the dark side of Alberta's prosperity, and under Ralph Klein that darkness has included deep cuts to medical care and to the health system; to education and to cultural programs.

In the Klein years homelessness and unemployment grew while both were explained away as products of prosperity. Homelessness was the dirt swept under the living-room carpet, and it was suggested the homeless on the street were bums who choose to be there rather than living in their own homes or apartments or rooms. This lie has rarely been examined for the foolishness it proposes. The boom in the province meant low-cost housing was scarce, if available at all, and what subsidized housing existed was filled to capacity. For the forgotten poor, for the working poor, there is no Alberta Advantage.

But for those who do prosper, it is magic.

In a study entitled "State of the West," the Calgary-based Canada West Foundation laid out in numbers the Alberta Advantage, its inheritors and its victims. The province most often compared to Alberta – its neighbour to the west, British Columbia – on the surface looks as prosperous as Alberta. But the numbers don't lie. The story is in the debt-to-gross domestic product ratio: Alberta's dropped from 30.1 per cent in 1994 to 8.3 per cent in 2000. B.C.'s rose from 23.1 per cent to 24.3.

The story also lies in the provincial gross domestic product per capita: in 1999, Alberta's was nearly 40 per cent higher than the Canadian average – at $34,200 – and just behind the American average, after adjusting for the difference in the dollar and buying power. Ontario's GDP was second at $32,200. After that, there's a nearly ten-thousand-dollar drop in provincial GDP with the four Atlantic provinces scoring a pathetic $21,000 per.

But tough negotiations with the federal government over off-shore oil revenues has made the future brighter for the Atlantic provinces, particularly Newfoundland and Labrador, and Nova Scotia. The premiers of those provinces, respectively Danny Williams and John Hamm, held Prime Minister Paul Martin to his election promise: 100 per cent of the offshore profits were to go to the provinces. The notion that the lands clinging to the east of Canada would ever be more than Confederation's poor cousins suddenly changed. Not that the West in general and Alberta in particular paid much attention: our gaze was locked into the stock ticker that showed almost daily increases in the per-barrel cost of oil. Even the most pessimistic of naysayers began to believe in the early months of 2005 that the boom really was back, and as the apocryphal bumper sticker promised: "This time we won't piss it away."

What was a $6-billion provincial debt in 2001 was paid off on the last day of March 2005, no doubt giving rise to speculation that waiting a single day, until April 1, would be seen as an April Fool's joke, rather than reality. The final payment of a debt that had peaked at almost $23 billion in 1993 happened without fanfare and without fireworks on an ordinary Thursday afternoon. It didn't even make the front pages of Alberta's major newspapers.

Now, Albertans are looking for payback. A proposal to eliminate provincial income taxes has already been made, a benefit that would put thousands of dollars into the pockets of each Albertan. Again, though, those who pay the most and have the most would benefit the most. Prosperity is ours, but at a price.

A United Nations Human Development Report puts prosperity in global terms: in 1999, the combined worth of the world's wealthiest two hundred people was equal to the income of almost half the population of the globe. That's a ratio of 1 to 30,000,000. In dollar terms, those two hundred people are worth US$1 trillion. For those of us more visually attuned, that is $1,000,000,000,000. And those are American dollars.

The disparity of wealth is nothing new, nor does the notion that so few should own so much cause much of a ripple in the corridors of power. The notion of too much going to too few is not popular, not in the Western world.

Closer to home, the Parkland Institute, associated with the University of Alberta and described by its detractors (usually with a curled lip) as a left-leaning, anti-government think-tank has reported just how disparate the Alberta Advantage is. Alberta has been booming, but mostly for the already well-to-do. Statistics Canada figures, used by the Parkland Institute, show how that disparity has grown since the last, disastrous downturn in the economy.

Late in 1981, the bottom seemed to fall out of every sector in Alberta, aided by a government that tried to ignore the recession. Good-time budgeting, in a bad-time economy, blinded far too many Albertans to the truth of the recession. Still, even in those terms, the richest 10 per cent of Alberta families had, in 1981, an income fourteen times higher than the poorest 10 per cent. Less than a generation later, in 1997, the richest group was earning twenty-two times more than the poorest.

Says the Parkland Institute report: "Economic benefits are not trickling down to Alberta families. In the final analysis, the most wealthy will continue to reap the benefits of the Alberta Advantage while middle- and low-income earners continue to work harder for less."

Since my return to Alberta from Ontario in 1981 – just as the bottom was about to fall out of everything – until now, my personal fortunes, as an Albertan, have gone from deficit through debt to real prosperity. Even more surprising, this has happened despite what so many Westerners see as a crippling tax burden imposed by

Ottawa, designed to prevent entrepreneurs from raking in their well-deserved fortunes.

It has happened despite the recent mad cow crisis, when a single animal in a northern Alberta farm was discovered to have bovine spongiform encephalopathy, which slammed shut the U.S. border and caused a general panic. In answer to the BSE furor, Premier Klein remarked casually that the farmer in question should have "shot, shovelled, and shut up." That sentiment, shared but unspoken by many Alberta ranchers, farmers, and others dependent on the lucrative American beef market, is an excellent example of how the premier can hone in on the unspoken attitudes of Alberta's rural constituency.

Prosperity has happened despite the drop in tourism, occasioned by the SARS battle in Toronto, which resulted in geographically ignorant Europeans and Asians cancelling trips to Banff and Jasper.

That so many Albertans have prospered so greatly in the past two decades and into a third, despite their opinions of the rapaciousness of the Ottawa tax regime, is seen as a testament to the Alberta spirit. Few in Alberta in general and Calgary in particular will ever be willing to forgive the federal government for the National Energy Program, which we believe stripped Alberta of $6 billion in royalties – yet to be repaid. That the NEP was seen, from the other side of Canada, as benefiting the energy-poor provinces by sharing the wealth through a common Canadian price, cuts no ice in Alberta. We are the little red hen with a new twist to the story: It's our oil. We own it, we extract it, we market it. If we want to share our energy, we get to decide with whom and under what conditions.

If the phrase "Alberta Advantage" is a mantra, it joins NEP for its powerful message. Mention the NEP anywhere in Alberta and stand back and wait for the predictable reaction. Most of it will be negative and much of it will hint that another such federal money grab is always just around the corner.

When then prime minister Jean Chrétien held a federal Liberal caucus meeting in Edmonton in the summer of 2001, he gave an innocuous speech about Canadian attitudes about sharing. He suggested the good fortunes of Alberta were in danger of fostering envy in its neighbours, and as Canadians, Albertans should be willing to share the wealth.

The reaction was instantaneous and negative. The temperature in the Edmonton meeting room seemed to drop ten degrees within seconds. By the following day, pundits and columnists were talking darkly of son-of-NEP. Within the week, it was conventional wisdom that the prime minister and his Liberal cronies would just as soon steal all of Alberta's wealth as look at us.

Was the former prime minister being provocative? Was he, in fact, making a disguised grab at Alberta's wealth?

Nothing so nefarious. He was merely repeating another kind of conventional wisdom, one that far too many Albertans refuse to admit: that there are genuine fears in other parts of Canada that Alberta's success will harm the consensual nature of the country. No less an august publication than *The Economist* looked at this very phenomenon more than a year before the prime minister opened his mouth in Edmonton.

"Alberta's politicians are promoting a robust, American-style agenda of less government, more individualism and more private profit. And they are being successful enough to make opponents fear that caring, consensual Canada might become a clone of its southern neighbour."

For many Canadians, particularly those living in the West, this is not a bad prospect. They believe the closer Canada gets to the United States, the better. They promote open borders and aren't scared of being overwhelmed by American businesses or practices. These are the very people who vigorously supported the North American Free Trade Agreement, and see any problems with NAFTA as being caused by Canadians unwilling to give up so-called socialist practices, such as universal medicare and government ownership, in order to level the playing field.

While such aggressive business attitudes are admired by many Albertans, they are nonetheless anathema to those Canadians who believe we should put the common good before private profit.

These disparate philosophies will never be reconciled. But, maybe, there is common ground somewhere, as the former prime minister's rather banal speech in Edmonton might suggest.

But Jean Chrétien's mild comments about "sharing the wealth" in Canada caused a rush to man the ramparts in Alberta, with dire predictions the federal government was planning to revive the hated 1980 National Energy Program. The overreaction on the part of business leaders and oil and gas interests vitiated against even discussing the prospect of sharing anything. (To a right-wing Albertan, "sharing" is defined as being gouged out of his hard-earned money, in the form of sending tax dollars to Ottawa.)

None – *none* – of the fears and predictions that Alberta was about to be robbed blind were real. The scare was made out of whole cloth by conservative commentators willing at all counts to believe the worst of any Liberal government. But few in Alberta ever stop to think whether there is any reality in these dark conspiracy theories.

But then 9/11 happened and one of its consequences was that it made both Americans and Canadians realize how valuable an assured supply of energy and natural resources is. And it fed right into the conspiracy theories of a nefarious federal government raising the spectre of public ownership of private resources.

It suits Alberta to promote such fears to keep the wolf at bay, but such an attitude is more American than Canadian. The primacy of private ownership over the good of the common weal is to be expected in a province dominated by the principles of the United States: life, liberty, and the pursuit of happiness. Yet, curiously, Albertans are among the most generous of Canadians with their time and their money. Maybe it isn't so curious, given that Americans are the world's most generous people, as long as they get to decide who deserves their money and, therefore, who receives it.

For one example of the dark side of the Advantage, travel to the other side of the province. On the highway from Grande Prairie, Alberta, to Dawson Creek, B.C., sits the small town of Hythe. It is the home of Alberta's most famous – or infamous – fundamentalist Christian and anti-oil protester, Wiebo Ludwig. Ludwig fancies himself next to Jesus Christ, who is next to God. At least, that's the impression he has given both his supporters and detractors.

Ludwig and the men, women, and children of his extended family live on a commune at Trickle Creek. Depending on who you question, they either have the courage of their convictions, or are nonconformist wingnuts who think they can recreate an Old Testament patriarchy in the rich agricultural land of northern Alberta.

A self-professed minister, Ludwig and his family could have lived out their isolated lives, raising their own food, carding the wool from their own sheep, rendering fat for soap, and making their own wine. Indeed, the Ludwigs have been successful in their attempt to distance themselves from the wicked reality of modern life, and they could have stayed that way, regarded as strange by the neighbours, if Ludwig and his friend and in-law Richard Boonstra hadn't taken up arms against Alberta's oil industry in a campaign of vandalism, including bombing a Suncor well head and pouring cement into another well.

Ludwig was eventually sentenced to three years, minus the time he had spent behind bars and in virtual house arrest. Boonstra received twenty-one days in jail for mischief.

The surprise wasn't that Ludwig was arrested, charged, and convicted, it was the anger he fomented in the hearts of his neighbours because he dared to do what few other Albertans have done – criticize the oil and gas industry and charge the industry with poisoning the air and endangering lives.

Ludwig, whose farm is surrounded by gas wells and is subject to regular flaring of sour gas – hydrogen sulphide – believed the flares released toxic chemicals, including benzene, into the air and caused multiple birth defects in the Trickle Creek livestock and at least three miscarriages and one stillbirth among the women. When he could get no satisfaction through legal complaints, Ludwig started his campaign of harassment and vandalism.

Ludwig isn't the first and won't be the last Albertan to raise the flag of environmental concern about the oil industry. But he and

less zealous opponents stand about as much chance as the prover-
bial snowball in hell in slowing down or derailing the oil and gas
juggernaut.

Many of Trickle Creek's neighbours signed a petition denying
that their health had been affected by sour gas. Their protestations
of vigorous good health sounded less convincing when it was
learned that many of them were employed by the oil and gas industry. It is this side of the Alberta Advantage that keeps the town of
Hythe prosperous.

The mood in the area was rancorous, and then it turned ugly:
a sixteen-year-old girl, Karman Willis, was shot to death by
someone on the Trickle Creek commune. Who fired the bullet that
passed through a nineteen-year-old man's arm and then killed
Karman remains a mystery. Part of the anger of townspeople and
farmers alike toward Ludwig rests on the fact that he showed little
remorse for the death, saying that two truckloads of teenagers were
racing across his property, tossing beer cans and yelling. A Canadian
Press story in 1999 quotes Ludwig as saying: "The emphasis ought
to be on the recklessness of these teenagers. . . . The focus ought
not to be on the fact a 16-year-old girl died on our property."

Whatever little support Ludwig had from the community evap-
orated with that callous dismissal of a young girl's death. The mood
in Hythe turned volatile, turned to talk of vigilante justice. The real
surprise is that nobody levelled a rifle at Ludwig and his family. This
is, after all, the heart of gun-totin' country, where varmints – like
foxes in the henhouse – are summarily dealt with. This may sound
flippant, but it is not. There were cries for the entire Trickle Creek
clan to be evicted from the area, completely ignoring the concept
of private property. Storekeepers posted signs asking the Ludwig
family to stay away. And in the parking lot of a downtown Edmonton
hotel, some still-unknown person placed a bomb under Ludwig's
truck. Ludwig was only a few metres away when it blew up.

Alberta, the last bastion of the fiercely independent, is the place
where fundamentalist Christianity finds a welcome home, yet the

nonconformist religious beliefs and strict adherence to his own brand of faith put Ludwig and his family – who first moved into the area in 1985 – at odds with their neighbours. If there is a message in this, it is that, above all else, there is allegiance to the oil and gas industry. It makes no sense, but there it is.

No scientist disputes the danger of sour-gas leaks. Persistent exposure at even low levels causes health problems. But it is going to take a lot more than a couple of academic studies to convince people dependent on the oil industry and, for example, its more than two thousand wells in the Hythe area, to demand that health and safety come before profits.

Not far from Hythe, between Grande Prairie and Edmonton, on isolated high ground served by only two roads, sits the Swan Hills waste treatment plant, the largest hazardous waste incinerator in Canada. It was an ambitious project begun by the Alberta government, which opened as the Alberta Special Waste Treatment Centre in 1987. A local plebiscite showed about 80 per cent of voters in favour of welcoming a hazardous waste facility. It would bring, said its supporters, 140 to 220 jobs to the area.

It also brought dioxin, furans, polychlorinated biphenyls (PCBs) fumes and accusations from environmentalists that, despite assurances of rigorous safety standards, the plant was leaking contaminants into the air, ground, and water. Unfortunately, for Treaty 8 aboriginals the Swan Hills are traditional trapping and hunting grounds. By 1990, PCBs were detected in the area's mice and vegetation and mercury was found in fish. Routine testing of employees showed higher-than-normal levels of PCBs in their blood. In 1998, the company operating the plant was fined $625,000, the highest environmental penalty ever assessed in Alberta, following an explosion that opened vents that are normally closed and spewed PCBs and dioxin into the air.

Alberta Health tested residents of Swan Hills and found no discernable difference in contamination levels between them and other Albertans. Nevertheless, people were advised not to eat wild game that roamed inside a thirty-kilometre radius of the plant.

The hazardous materials plant is still operating, under a new company with a long-term contract. Nobody but environmentalists are still making a fuss about contamination. Certainly not the people employed by the oil and gas industry, whose wages mean an average household income of fifty thousand dollars for 48 per cent of the residents of Swan Hills. The connection between the poisoning of paradise in Hythe and in Swan Hills hasn't been made. The area lacks a resident zealot like Wiebo Ludwig.

Determined though he may be, Ludwig should have found a welcome home in northern Alberta when he arrived. Albertans are largely conservative and Christian. Fundamentalists are welcomed and many Albertans consider the Bible a history book, to be followed word for word – except maybe some of the more gruesome aspects of the Old Testament, such as cutting off one's own hand if it offends, or selling your daughter into bondage. The rest of Canada laughed when former Canadian Alliance leader Stockwell Day insisted that evolution was a myth and that dinosaurs and humans roamed the earth at the same time, just after the world was created in six days, six thousand years ago. But in Alberta this belief holds, if not centre court, then a large chunk of the surrounding territory.

Ludwig's problem wasn't that he considered himself to be an Old Testament prophet at the head of an obedient family of modestly dressed women who covered their hair, strong and silent men, and obedient children, but that his continued battle with the oil industry could have threatened the livelihood of the district.

Given the prevalent attitude of an eye for an eye, it should come as no surprise that rural Alberta and its small towns are the most vocal opponents of the federal gun registry program and loudest supporters of tough justice. Support for capital punishment – and in some quarters, bringing back the lash – is strongest in Western Canada. This, despite all the statistics that show the death penalty has a major downside for the law and order crowd – juries regularly convict on lesser charges if the penalty for a guilty verdict is death.

That this simple fact seems to be consistently ignored by the supporters of the death penalty is nothing less than bizarre. These people are determined to exact the greatest punishments, yet the death penalty means fewer convictions. Nor does it deter crime: for the sick celebrity seekers of this world, it merely encourages it. For loners and misfits and monsters, the death penalty promises celebrity beyond their dreams – a place of brutal honour nothing in their pathetic lives, save whatever heinous act they committed, could deliver. We give such people, in death, the notice they never received in life. We remember their names. In effect, we celebrate them. His execution gave Timothy McVeigh, the Oklahoma bomber, the victimhood and celebrity he wanted. We focus on him, instead of the 168 innocent men, women, and children he killed when just after 9 a.m. on April 19, 1995, he ignited a two-ton truck bomb outside the Alfred P. Murrah Federal Building in Oklahoma City. It was, McVeigh said, retaliation for acts of the U.S. government, including the raid at Waco, Texas, and the showdown at Ruby Ridge, Idaho.

Ludwig's case caused one fervid reporter for the *North Shore News* to quote Ludwig as fearing "being wiped out like Waco."

Thus does any circle of violence continue.

Not for nothing have today's memorial services – those for the 2,081 who died in the terrorist attacks on the United States on September 11, 2001 – focused on the names of the dead, solemn recitations that serve more than any other words to remind us that in all brutal crimes our communities are robbed of lives that had every right to continue. While we cannot stop the shorthand of linking killers' names to violent acts, we can give their victims the same attention.

It is curious that even as Americans mourn their dead, they continue to contribute to the violence through capital punishment. Worse, we have Canadians who are envious of this irrevocable deed. There are plenty of Canadians who want the question of capital punishment revisited, even though Canada abolished it in 1976, after not having executed anyone since 1962. A national survey in the late 1990s showed the majority are still opposed, but support is regionally based: 61 per cent in favour of the death penalty in British Columbia; 36 per cent in Quebec – the two extremes. All other provinces are about evenly split. The numbers get skewed depending on the question. If pollsters ask about "capital punishment," the number supporting it rises; if the poll asks about the "death penalty," the numbers decrease. No surprise there – *death* is a more shocking word than *punishment*.

Those who would exact the ultimate punishment for criminals cite Clifford Olson and Paul Bernardo (or she of the stone-dead, ice-blue eyes, Karla Homolka) as monsters deserving of state-sanctioned death. Those on the other side are just as vocal, pointing to the wrongly accused and unjustly convicted such as Donald Marshall, Guy Paul Morin, and David Milgaard, all of whom would presumably have been executed long before anyone discovered they were not guilty of the murders for which they were imprisoned.

In any debate on execution, there are always the extremes: those who frankly don't care if a few innocents are killed by the state, as long as the guilty get the noose – or the chair, or even in a nod to the blackest kind of humour the "kind" and "humane" lethal injection. The other extreme are those who see the execution of anyone under any circumstances, for any crime, as reprehensible.

Because most Canadians sit somewhere in the middle, opportunists on the right continually seek to reopen the debate on capital punishment. They know passion often colours reason, and there is nothing more compelling – or more heartbreaking and emotional – than families visited by horror; ordinary Canadians who often can't or won't accept dispassionate justice based on fact, rather than on their personal loss.

Those who bring the Bible into the debate are inevitably more focused on the "eye for eye; tooth for tooth" provisions of Exodus 21: 24, than the caution of Deuteronomy 32:35 – "to Me belongeth vengeance, and recompence."

The need to feel in control in a world that seems increasingly out of control has reinvigorated the debate on the death penalty. The debate was stirred by the pro–capital punishment stance of the former Canadian Alliance, smug in its contention that in a referendum, the majority of Canadians would support a return to the death penalty. The reconstituted Conservative Party, an amalgamation of the Alliance and the Progressive Conservatives did not weigh in on the question before the last federal election, preferring to keep its more extremist views under a convenient rock.

In the unlikely and unwelcome event of a national referendum, here are some facts Canadians need to absorb:

An extensive national and state-by-state study of the death penalty in the United States – used in thirty-eight of the fifty states – showed that it had no deterrent effect, regardless of how statistics were crunched or manipulated. The rise and fall of the homicide rate were unrelated to the punishment exacted. Most murders are crimes of the moment, crimes of impulse – the consequences of an action are rarely considered. With few exceptions, killings aren't thoughtful, logical, and well-planned events. Most killers are stupid, scared witless, drunk, deranged, or mentally incompetent – sometimes all of the above. Bernardo and Olson are the exceptions, not the rule.

Remember also that it is impossible to write a law guaranteeing that only the guilty are executed. It is never a question of not killing the innocent. It is only a matter of how many.

But beyond all the facts and beliefs surrounding capital punishment, it is important for Canadians to understand what really happens in the courts when the punishment is death: the rate of conviction drops. The death penalty ensures juries will regularly convict on a lesser charge.

A study from 1941 to 1960 showed Canadian juries increasingly unwilling to convict in the face of the noose. The conviction rate for manslaughter rose as murder convictions fell to 33 per cent in 1960 from 37.8 per cent in 1941.

The real question is not how many killers we would execute, but how many we would set free.

6

Not Quite Citizens

They live among us, but are not quite of us, or with us. And all the fancy talk about the entitlement and aboriginal rights of First Nations does not make one whit of difference in the pathetic lives of so many natives in this bountiful country. In this regard, Alberta is no better, and no worse, than any other province, although Alberta's record of land-claims settlements puts others to shame.

We pay lip service to our "native brethren" but little else. The plight of urban aboriginals is well known, but surprisingly little acknowledged in Calgary and Edmonton. We look away. And my gut reaction is no better than others', and the sentiment it spreads through the community is toxic. I am ashamed that upon returning to Calgary from London and Toronto in 1977, when I passed an aboriginal out cold and face down in a flower bed outside a local restaurant, I thought: "Drunken Indian. I'm home."

Why would I admit to such racism? Because the polite fiction that there is equality here (or anywhere) in this country is just that – a huge lie.

Non-Indians are not the only ones at fault here. A rampant cronyism that is usually seen only in the boardrooms of corrupt multinationals exists on Indian reserves that would put most old-boy networks in downtown Calgary or Dallas or Washington to shame.

The lucky few – tribal chiefs and their best friends and relatives – benefit financially and emotionally from the money poured into reserves by Ottawa. The rest live in poverty, want, and despair, more frightened of retaliation should they complain, than brave enough to do so.

We continue the fiction of strong and silent, independent people living off the land and guarded by the Great Spirit. But the truth is far different: a story of displaced people resisting the continuing efforts of "white" people to force them to integrate into a wider society and thus disappear as a source of concern and cost.

If you live in Alberta, it is almost possible to forget native people, except for those who wander into the cities and find themselves alien and outcast and, unfairly, held to account for every case of public drunkenness. Everyone else drunk in public is merely drunk in public, not a sniffy example of ongoing problems that billions of federal dollars have failed to eradicate.

There is, as always, another side to the myth of the Indian as the traditionalist preserving an economically viable, communal way of life. Hugh Dempsey, in his 1999 history, *Calgary: Spirit of the West*, honours one side of aboriginal life, detailing their contribution to Calgary and calling the natives old neighbours. "They were neighbours long before there was a Mounted Police fort and they have left their mark in the uniqueness of the city, in everything from the naming of streets and bridges to the economic and social life of the community." Dempsey was partly referring to Calgary giving its major thoroughfares (no one caught in rush-hour traffic would call them freeways) aboriginal-inspired names – Crowchild, Sarcee, and Deerfoot trails. Then, there's the matter of the cursed bridge on Deerfoot Trail. Calf Robe Bridge has been the site of so many accidents that drivers believe (only half in jest) that it has been cursed by a native shaman. At least that reason excuses the human factor behind the wheel.

Dempsey, former chief curator of the renowned Glenbow Museum and a noted historian, chose not to linger on the problems besetting so many of Alberta's First Nations, but on their positive contributions, particularly to the Calgary Stampede as both an exhibit and as competitors in the annual rodeo.

A cynic would say that the First Nations in their colourful, beaded traditional costumes are trotted out for the wow factor they bring to the Stampede. They may be the single extant exhibit of the real life of the Canadian West, the Stampede having taken on the trappings of Hollywood fakery with six-shooters and gun-fights. But the Indians, at least, are real.

Still, they remained patronized. The Indian village on the banks of the Elbow River in the Stampede grounds, which includes representatives of Tsuu T'ina, Siksika, Peigan, Blood, and Stoney First Nations, is controlled by an Indian Events Committee, writes Dempsey, "which at one time was made up entirely of non-Indian Calgarians who supervised the programs, parade and other activities." Now, of course, that has been reversed, but it wasn't without a public scandal that left the Stampede with a black eye. Bruce Starlight became the first native chairman of the committee in 1989, after almost twenty years of volunteering. Dempsey notes that in 1991 "Starlight became the centre of controversy when he was passed over in an election for a seat on the prestigious Stampede Board."

Dempsey quotes an outraged editorial in the *Calgary Herald*. "For more than 70 years of Stampede history the board has worked with, and the Stampede has benefited from, the presence and participation of native Indians. Yet for all those years the Stampede board has managed to keep any and all aboriginals from joining its ranks."

The Stampede closed ranks, of course, just as the members of the Calgary Petroleum Club did when it was suggested that women be admitted as full members and be allowed to eat lunch with the boys. The Stampede board reacted to city-wide criticism by point-ing out the rodeo cowboys didn't have a seat on the board, either. They were loudly booed for that bit of dissembling.

It took only a year for the board to admit its mistake and appoint the chief of the Tsuu T'ina, Roy Whitney, to a non-elected seat. Later in the year, Starlight was elected to the board.

The Tsuu T'ina Reserve, hard up against the western edge of Calgary, is likely the most successful reserve in Western Canada, besides the oil-rich Hobbema Reserve. Yet most reserves remain a hidden nation folded into the greater community, coming to public notice only when tragedy strikes. The shooting death of a native woman, Connie Jacobs, and her young son, Ty, on the reserve in 1988 in an altercation with the RCMP raised public awareness of squalid conditions, but only briefly. Jacobs had fired a shotgun and an RCMP constable returned fire, killing Jacobs and her son standing behind her. Self-defence was the official verdict. The unofficial consensus was that if you get drunk and take a shot at a Mountie, you deserve what happens.

Access to reserves is limited, at best. Like any proud people, no aboriginal tribe wants its dignity affronted by the "usual" stories of despair, want, and living conditions that are – maybe – one step above the street.

Indian leaders, particularly the grand chief of the Assembly of First Nations, Phil Fontaine, are working slowly for change. Fontaine's supporters call him a diplomat, his detractors call him weak. During his 2003 bid to regain the leadership he had lost by eighty votes to Matthew Coon Come in 2000, Fontaine was characterized as too cozy with the Liberal government. (The prime minister, Jean Chrétien, had appointed Fontaine chief commissioner of the Indian Claims Commission after Fontaine's defeat. The Sagkeeng First Nations member and former chief had also worked for the federal government as regional director-general in the Yukon.)

After less than three years of Coon Come's confrontational style, which got his people nowhere, the assembly returned its votes to Fontaine in 2003. He still remains a shadowy figure to the general public, who are roused to notice native affairs only when there's a crisis.

Fontaine has two major tasks: to secure self-government and economic sustainability for the First Nations and to have his people accepted as equals by the rest of us. The latter will be, by far, the greater challenge. The former is formidable enough. What could tie the two goals together is the reconciliation of the "white" world with the native people, whose spiritual, cultural, and physical existence we have tried for years to eradicate. Many innocently think the residential school crisis over and done with – apologies from government and churches for a century or so of abuse having been proffered.

Too many of us believe restitution and forgiveness are comparable, failing to grasp the difference between being sorry and being forgiven. They expect once an apology is made, all will be well. Yet apology is only the first step. Regardless of whether the Canadian public is tired of what they see as outrageous demands on their Churches, demands that threaten some of them with bankruptcy, no Canadian can just ignore history. It is not enough to "get back" to preaching Christianity, as one Anglican bishop in Alberta suggested, falling back on the belief one mustn't judge history by today's yardstick. Fair enough, but even in the early years of the twentieth century, the sexual and physical abuse of children was not an approved standard of behaviour in any school or any community.

As early as 1921, one official described living conditions in residential schools as "a national crime," a phrase that John S. Milloy used as the title for his stunning investigation of the abuse of native children, published in 1999. Milloy – a professor of history and native studies at Ontario's Trent University – points out, as few have been brave or smart enough to do, that this history of abuse is not only the history of First Nations, but it is our story, too. Not to accept that is as Milloy writes: "To marginalize it as we did aboriginal people themselves, to reserve it for them as a site of suffering and grievance and to refuse to make it a site of introspection, discovery and extirpation . . . from which we can understand not only who we have been as Canadians, but who we must become if we are to deal justly with the aboriginal people of this land."

To expect or demand swift forgiveness isn't enough. If we are the inheritors of our ancestors' largesse, then we are also the inheritors of their mistakes. As Milloy writes: "The residential school system was conceived, designed, and managed by non-aboriginal people. It represents the intolerance, presumption, and pride that lay at the heart of Victorian Christianity and democracy, that passed itself off as caring social policy and persisted, in the twentieth century, as thoughtless insensitivity."

If the excuse used by our parents and grandparents is that of ignorance, more's the pity. It wasn't as if they didn't know what was going on. Official memos, reports, and complaints documented the outrageous treatment of Indian children from the beginning. That those same ancestors from whom we accepted a legacy of land and prosperity chose to ignore what was systematically being done to those they considered "savages" is our bill to pay.

I don't pretend to understand why so many First Nations people live in poverty, alcoholism, and despair amid such plenty and opportunity. After all, Ottawa funds their lives with more than $7 billion a year, and bands such as the Samson Cree in Hobbema are independently wealthy from oil royalties. I only know what I have seen in Fontaine's eyes and heard in his voice. Reading about the abuse that seems to have been widespread in residential schools can't compare with hearing one man talk about it.

Fontaine and I have met a few times – we have mutual friends – but the first time was in Toronto, just after the 1990 seventy-eight-day Oka crisis, which was ignited by something as innocuous as golf. The municipality wanted to expand its nine-hole golf course, first built in 1959, a move that would have partly encroached on traditional Mohawk burial grounds. Irate Mohawks blockaded the site, the Quebec Provincial Police arrived, and in the ensuing firefight, a policeman was shot and killed. To this day, no one has been held responsible. The Sûreté was swiftly replaced by the Canadian army. It was a summer of anger, heat, and violence, both real and threatened, until the standoff was resolved late in September.

Months later, Fontaine and I talked about the media's coverage of the crisis, all of which was heavily weighted against the natives. But that polite discussion paled in comparison to the bombshell Fontaine dropped in 1990 in a room full of mostly white, middle-class, privileged journalists. In his soft voice, he talked about his own experiences as a native in Canada, the reality he brought to his job of speaking for his people. He asked us to understand why it was that natives in Canada felt such a deep discontent, isolation, and despair. Why it was that some sought relief in liquor, drugs, and violence.

For the first time, Fontaine revealed his own horrific experiences as an abused child in a residential school, how he learned of the contempt in which natives were held by a white society, and how he came to fight for himself and others. He used his own life to help us understand Oka and its simmering hostility. Then, he asked us to respect his privacy and not to reveal he had been abused until he had a chance to do so himself, in public. Each of us honoured that request. Such is the respect this man earned from a tough crowd.

There are those who will still argue that Fontaine's diplomatic style of negotiation is too low-key to handle the needs of the diverse First Nations communities. Certainly the temperature of confrontation has been turned to below the boiling point beyond what columnist and author Richard Wagamese, himself a native, has called Indian Country.

Indeed, it is possible to ignore the reserves, except when visitors driving along the Trans-Canada on their way to Banff ask startled questions about the sudden appearance of huge, intrusive billboards along both sides of the highway. The reason is obvious – the natives can exploit their land any way they like. That they choose to litter the spectacular scenery as one approaches the Rockies is infuriating, and not a little ironic, something like a huge middle finger to all of us who have politely and ignorantly turned a blind eye to the First Nations, except when they please the tourists.

The difference between what Albertans want visitors to see and residents to believe about the First Nations is the difference between theme parks and reality. Nowhere is that more obvious and more devastating than on the Indian reserves that are our neighbours. But suburbia avoided the First Nations, as did much of the prosperity and for certain, the Alberta Advantage.

A number of years ago, Alberta's Indian Affairs minister, Pearl Calahasen, floated the notion of native "theme parks" in the four corners of the province – a suggestion that quickly fell with a thud into whatever black hole really bad ideas belong. The Indian Village at the Calgary Stampede – a working village of teepees and willing First Nations – is a huge annual attraction, but there was little enthusiasm for Indian World, or whatever the minister was planning on calling these developments.

Part of the lack of interest was probably caused by the serious, intellectual nature of the plan, which clashed with what people in the tourist industry know attracts visitors. Discussions about sentencing circles, the wisdom of the elders, and the spirituality of the land are far too serious, in truth, to be packaged into some banal display for tourists who long for the experience of being in the Wild West without being too far from a non-fat latte.

Calahasen announced she envisioned a sort of mini-Expo '67, in either Calgary or Edmonton, in which each "nation" that wanted to participate would have its own encampment – her word – with displays of the native Canadian ways of life, history, spirituality, food, and recreation. From that hub would spring various "parks" around Alberta where the traditional way of life would unfold 24/7. Presumably, there would be no roller coaster, hot dogs, or cotton candy in sight. Nor would there be any mention of the serious problems that plague Canada's natives – the alcoholism and addiction, the disconnection from the greater society, the clash of cultures, the entrenched racism that haunts their lives.

Perhaps the proposal went nowhere because we've already tried to package "Western" culture into a year-round attraction and failed. The Western Heritage Centre is an expensive reminder of the difference between history and tourism. The Centre, a $16-million interpretive development just off the Trans-Canada Highway, opened in 1996 on the site of Alberta's first large ranching operation, near Cochrane. It expected about 350,000 visitors each year, ready to celebrate the ranching heritage. It naturally assumed it would lure, on a side trip, some of the millions of visitors to Banff. Yet five years after it opened, it closed for good, $2 million in debt.

In its final year, the centre had only nineteen thousand visitors.

It failed, not because it wasn't real and earnest, but because it was all that and more. It was, as with so many other well-meaning ventures planned to celebrate the heritage of a country or a people, a one-trick pony. Nice, but nothing much to return to, unlike the interactive and always fascinating Royal Tyrrell Museum of Paleontology in Drumheller, which brings the history of dinosaurs to life for visitors, who can tour the exhibits and visit the sites of dinosaur fossils. The museum offers what the Heritage Centre didn't – the chance for visitors to be educated while having fun. The Heritage Centre was (as I suspect the native theme parks would be) what one friend refers to as a "prune danish": a little sweetness to lure in the unsuspecting covering, and a lot of prune filling designed to do you some good.

Disneyland and its clones are successful, not because they are authentic, but because they are only coincidentally, occasionally authentic. They appeal to the lowest common denominator of tourists: show me, entertain me, satisfy my prejudices.

If Alberta's First Nations bands want to dress up in feathers and war paint, whoop across the prairie, and maybe stage a fake raid for the benefit of the kind of people who believe the gunslinger show at the Calgary Stampede is the real West, that could be their choice. But at least let's admit what they would be doing is getting into the entertainment business, not into the native heritage business.

Theme parks only work when they build on prejudices, not when they are designed to smash them. Disney World and Disneyland are so successful because they exaggerate and build on the stereotypes of middle America and a kinder, gentler nation. They deliver, precisely and with flair, the fantasy that no longer exists in America's small towns and cities. Millions flock to the refuge that is a place without hunger, disease, fear, and crime; a place where the streets are clean, the entertainment safe, and the mood upbeat.

The Western Heritage Centre didn't deliver any such fantasy, and the reality of settling the Canadian West was that it was a fairly boring, arduous, back-breaking fight against weather and privation. Who wants to pay to find out how grandma and gramps really lived? Things have to be a lot older than that to get interesting.

Here in Alberta, we are only now recognizing that if we tear down all the unique buildings, we will have destroyed a valuable part of our history. In Calgary, the sandstone city hall was only saved by intense lobbying from the public, as were such heritage buildings as the old courthouse and the Burns building. Other valuable buildings – the original banks, for example – have survived only because they have been turned to other uses. The bank on the corner of 1st Street and 8th Avenue S.W. is an A&B Sound outlet; its companion across the street has become an expensive restaurant. When the new Hyatt Regency Hotel was built adjacent to the convention centre in Calgary, it had to incorporate a heritage site into its plans. And it did so by using an exterior wall as an interior decoration in the hotel. This is what commonly passes for heritage savings in Alberta – preserving the facade and ripping out the guts to put in something else. It is a start, at least, at preserving what might be valuable in a few hundred years.

At least in the major tourist areas of Alberta, those destinations inside the national parks, Ottawa has the last word, exercising its authority over the footprint of Banff to stop its expansion further into the wilderness.

That's the only real protection the First Nations – living and breathing Canadian historical treasures – have, too: the authority of the federal government, signed treaties, and guilt. They might first wish for something slightly less arbitrary and more permanent than mere promises. That is Grand Chief Phil Fontaine's ultimate goal.

7

Add Money and Stir

Alberta politics are a wondrous thing – part evangelism, part discontent, part tub-thumping. When all three parts come together in a wave of anger and rebellion over the federal government, one gets the Reform Party and its progeny, the Canadian Alliance, which was never allied with anything and was only Canadian in name. In October 2003, the two halves of Canada's political right stitched themselves back together under the title of the Conservative Party of Canada, without "progressive" in its name or its thinking.

The reunion was not without bitterness, particularly from the "old" Progressive Conservatives, who saw their party of inclusion subsumed by the hard-right members of the Canadian Alliance. The spring election of 2004 was the first test of the new Conservatives under leader Stephen Harper, who was perceived as a humourless, stiff ideologue. Worse, he was seen in Ontario (which returned the Liberals with a minority government) as having a hidden agenda for women's and minority rights. Harper's failure to immediately distance himself and his party from the perceived attacks on such fundamental Charter rights cost him the election. Canadians may have been discontented with the Liberals, but too much change was seen as too much.

If one of the goals of amalgamation was to convince Canadians there was little difference between the "new" Conservatives and the old, success came in one sense quickly and decisively. It took maybe a week for the media to begin referring to the new party as "Tory." That has continued unabated, and although real Tories from the old party resent it immensely, they are silent.

In Alberta, although the adjective is rarely used, the ruling party is Progressive Conservative. It differs from the federal party in two distinctive ways: how the public perceives it, and Premier Ralph Klein. While the newly constituted Conservatives labour under the accusation that the party is merely Reform in a new uniform, thanks to its hard-right faction, in Alberta the loonier right-wing is kept in check by a single man – the premier. It's not that the opinions of the hard right are silenced. Indeed, we are regularly treated to their screeds and diatribes: tough on crime, against the gun registry, opposed to gay marriage, anti-choice, and pro-religion, but Klein has such a firm grip on his caucus that the trial balloons never rise higher than the horizon. Those trial balloons, though, serve as a bellwether of the public mood, and have caused the government to back off many of its more radical notions for, say, health reform.

Klein recognizes (as so many of his ministers in the past have not) that Alberta is not a monolith of right-wing thinking. In fact, given the influx of newcomers, the right is being slowly diluted. Klein allows healthy debate in public, allows opinions to be aired, but behind the closed door of the caucus room, he imposes his almost unerring sense of what the public will stand for.

An excellent example of this is the continuing simmering question of reproductive rights. The range of opinions in Alberta is no more broad and the opinions no less fractious than in other parts of Canada. But in Alberta, the anti-choice opinions come from a wider cross-section than the province's pulpit. Having lost the war, the anti-abortion protesters continue to wage a losing battle. Between 2000 and 2002, when health-care reform was at the top of everyone's mind as three major commissions headed by former deputy prime minister Don Mazankowski, former Saskatchewan premier

Roy Romanow, and Senator Michael Kirby examined the Canadian health-care system, anti-choice Albertans were led to believe, more by their own hopes than by any hints, that the Mazankowski report, which focused only on health services in Alberta, would, in its 2002 final report, recommend the de-listing of non-essential services. At the top of the list was abortion services, the argument being that any girl or woman guilty of making such a mistake as to get pregnant and seek an abortion, should at least pay for it herself, rather than expecting the public purse to support her choice.

It was a popular opinion in rural quarters and in pockets of the province where religion is overwhelmingly powerful. It went nowhere in the larger cities. The proposed de-listing never did come to pass. Klein is too smart to fall into such a divisive trap.

Right-of-centre thinking prevails here, at least in catching the public's ear and the attention of the media, but the majority of residents hold pretty similar views as the rest of Canada. Yet politics in Alberta continues to be a thing of wonder and amazement. Where else would voters be so complacent, so happy with a single party for so long, only to turf it out summarily?

Social Credit, in power for thirty-six years under a succession of leaders since William Aberhart, didn't know when the end was coming, no more than today's Progressive Conservatives will be able to tell. Indeed, the hubris of politics is such that the Tories can be smug in their sinecure – thirty years and counting, a decade of that under the affable, gee-folks style of Premier Ralph Klein.

When people ask why Klein and his revolution are popular – so unlike in its outcome Ontario premier Mike Harris's Common Sense Revolution, which saw the so-called corporate elites support Harris while the ordinary people heartily disliked the man, his government, and what it did – the answer lies partly in the personality and inherent talent for pleasing people of Klein himself, and partly in the nature of Albertans.

Ralph Klein is, hands-down, the most popular politician ever to win an election in Alberta and probably in Canada. While he's never enjoyed the charismatic appeal of Pierre Trudeau, he's never frittered away the public's love, either. At least not yet. But there are signs people think he's been around too long: dinner-table conversations, when they get around to provincial politics, focus on Klein's increasing hubris and the growing idea that he needs to head off to a money-making career of sitting on corporation boards sooner rather than later.

Ralph Klein has been the most unlikely of politicians – a former television reporter, a hail-fellow-well-met type who was happier in a beer parlour than a meeting hall and who made a virtue out of his eccentricities. Late for a morning meeting when he was the mayor of Calgary? That's just Ralph. Three sheets to the wind and bumming cigarettes in some bar in Edmonton? Just plain Ralph. Indeed, if there is one politician who rarely – if at all – gets the honorific Mister, it is the Alberta premier.

Nobody calls him Mister.

Klein has never lost an election. Only one was even close, and that was just after he took over the Tory leadership and became premier of the province. His opponent, the late Laurence Decore (he was felled in middle age by a vicious cancer), was the only other politician with the status of Klein. Decore was the popular former mayor of Edmonton. He was openly a Liberal; Klein was only presumed to be. But Klein's party of choice when he went into provincial politics turned out to be the Progressive Conservatives, which, under a tired administration, was considered on its way out of office after twenty years. As if the mayors of Edmonton and Calgary needed a bigger arena to air their personal differences (mostly invented for the media coverage), Decore would go on to become the provincial Liberal leader and then almost premier. "Almost" in that he managed to lose the 1993 election – which the Liberals were widely expected to win – in the first few days of the month-long campaign.

Decore managed to alienate the modern women of Alberta and everyone to the left of the anti-abortion, anti-choice movement, which was most of the province, by attacking abortion clinics as "morally repugnant" and prime candidates for closure by his government. You could hear the groans of disbelief across the province, not because everyone disagreed with Decore – indeed, there is a loud and significant anti-abortion movement in Alberta, although they tend to be social conservatives and vote PC only because there is no provincial Conservative Party – but because it was politically stupid. That election was Decore's to win until that remark. In contrast, Klein said abortion was a decision made between a woman, her doctor, and God.

In the end, the Tories took fifty-one seats, the Liberals thirty-two, the largest opposition in recent Alberta history. The New Democrats failed to elect a single member.

Albertans – who had seemed poised to return a Liberal government to the province that hadn't had one since Charles Stewart, Liberal premier of Alberta from 1917 to 1921 – gave Ralph Klein his first of many majorities. Klein had taken over from Don Getty, remade the Conservative Party, and now he was ready to remake the province.

Only the foolish underestimated him. The former Tory cabinet minister Nancy Betkowski, who went head to head with Klein for the leadership of the party and lost on the second ballot, vanished into obscurity until she was reincarnated as Nancy MacBeth, leader of the Alberta Liberals. She had underestimated the power of the rural membership vote, on whose coattails and trust Klein rode, and she continued to do so in her brief tenure as the Liberal leader. She and her party were routed in the 2000 provincial election, reduced to seven seats, while the New Democrats kept the two they went into the election holding. MacBeth failed to keep her own seat, and her party lost whatever credibility it had built up with the Alberta voters. Klein's Tories romped to a seventy-four-seat majority in an eighty-three-seat legislature, not quite besting Peter Lougheed's seventy-four seats out of seventy-nine, but close enough to matter.

One would have thought Nancy MacBeth had the perfect, modern profile for Alberta. She was everything a province on the verge of sophistication could want – intelligent, educated, well-spoken, well-dressed, knowledgeable, charming, and sharp. All that mattered little to the Alberta voter, which is still for a large part more comfortable with a farmer than a philosopher.

Former senator Ron Ghitter calls this discomfort a legacy of Alberta's pioneer past, which in its spirit was an "intriguing blend of individual self-reliance and a strong work ethic," he says. That pioneer spirit "tended to a simple black-and-white approach to life still found in many areas of the province. Resistance to change there was and is (but with a dedication to the basis of existence built into it), as well as a distrust of everything sick and glossy and a deep sense of alienation from central Canada. Family, God, and hard work are what matter most."

The feminist red Tory turned Alberta Liberal never had a chance.

Perhaps she forgot author Robert Louis Stevenson's trenchant observation about politics: "Politics is perhaps the only profession for which no preparation is thought necessary." Not much has changed in two hundred years. Politics still has no prerequisites for admission; no aptitude test administered before the oath of office. It is only because the men and women who run for office are moved by a desire to make a better life for their communities that democracy limps along, not being perfect, but being, as Winston Churchill once said, better than the alternatives. That they get side-tracked from doing good into doing enough to get re-elected may be the fault of the system, not the quality of the people.

Nonetheless, my grandfather, Clinton James Ford, is likely the unwitting reason I hold so many of today's politicians and public figures in contempt, not because they are evil – they are not for the most part – but because they are so banal. Their qualification for a position of such public responsibility can be nothing more exotic than having won a popularity contest. Too often, they pride themselves on being "men of the people," which is code for holding education and intelligence up to the scorn of the ignorant.

That we live in a society that does not value intelligence, that believes the "self-made" man or woman is superior to the educated one is a strange quirk. The best example is the pride with which Albertans talk about our "folksy" premier, Ralph Klein, street-smart but not an educated man. That he can do his job without benefit of a university education is more a testament to his innate intelligence than to the fact he neglected to complete a formal education. One wonders how formidable a man and politician he would be had he done so first.

He didn't. So what?

It's the idea that not having an education is a compliment that so rankles; that politics is reduced to popularity over qualifications; promises over the ability and means to deliver.

If there were a single qualification that Grandfather saw as essential to each person, it was an education. In 1957, at the official opening of the elementary school in Calgary that bore his name, he said he was honoured "to have my name reduced to its simplest terms, attached to an elementary school."

Too bad that the deep thinkers in the Alberta government, when they decided one year to slash kindergarten because they believed it wasn't necessary (the decision was reversed the following year) didn't believe, as Grandfather did, that it was in the first years that curiosity and lifetime learning are developed.

It is the ultimate irony that of all the experiences in a citizen's life, elementary school is considered the least important. "There are two essentials that we need individually for success and happiness, and that a nation to be great and to stand in the world of tomorrow as of today must have," said Grandfather. "One is education in all its branches," but especially, an education in history in its chronological and connected whole. "How one movement in mankind followed another, one epoch after another, growing out of the former, as cause and effect; and to get the whole picture in one's mind gives a widened outlook and a better understanding of world events of today, that is otherwise impossible for one to grasp. With a good knowledge of history, one is better equipped for life."

Men such as my grandfather saw politics as a responsibility, a civic duty. In a radio address in 1952, on the fifth anniversary of the declaration of Canadian citizenship (we had all been British subjects to that point), he talked at length about the responsibility of citizenship. He talked, not about being an Albertan, about living in Calgary, but about being a Canadian.

> The real issue to be decided . . . is that of whether the verve and fibre of our citizenship will stand the test. . . . This depends on what we as a people understand citizenship to mean, and the nature of its responsibilities. Let us make no mistake, citizenship can exist in a democracy only. . . . We must take these matters of citizenship and democracy seriously if the day of our opportunity will be spent and the night be at hand. I say it with conviction that the day of our testing is the present; history is in the making, and it is for us to ask ourselves how much do we value our free citizenship. . . . We must pay the price of citizenship in a free country by an understanding of what it means and by undertaking our share in those activities of the corporate society in which we live and are a part.
>
> In short, it is in the home, the community, the school; in business, in the local and national governments; and even the international situation that we as Canadians must be vitally concerned. Our obligations and responsibilities extend to all these fields, and each will find his greatest opportunity for active work and influence in one or more of them.

It is rare these days to hear citizenship or politics described in such florid terms. Those who lament the death of debate and its replacement with insults and cat-calling; those who bemoan the paucity of intelligent repartee in any of our legislatures or the House of Commons and Senate are, in fact, seeking a return to this kind of thinking, this kind of passion, if not these particular words.

And these words were not spoken by a politician, but by an ordinary citizen, albeit one who in 1921 became one of five Liberal candidates in Calgary, coming seventh in a list of twenty competitors for a single riding. He was undeterred. Bob Marshall, the mayor of Calgary, was the winner. As Grandfather wrote in 1936 to his old friend and Member of the Legislative Assembly J.J. Bowlen, who would eventually be appointed Lieutenant-Governor of Alberta: "The second Liberal candidate was the late ex-MLA George Webster, who was also defeated in that election. He got just 100 more votes than I did."

Grandfather tried again in 1922, unsuccessfully contesting, he wrote, "for the vacant seat in Calgary created by the death of the late and justly famous Bob Edwards." Edwards was the irascible, drunken editor of the Calgary *Eye Opener*, a newspaper that revelled in pricking the pomposity of the self-satisfied and smug. Edwards had put his money where his mouth was and run for public office, despite his thinly disguised loathing for many politicians. "Why is it that all the rogues manage to get into the other political party?" Edwards wrote in the *Eye Opener* in 1920.

That Edwards was successful when he ran for office was probably more of a surprise to him than to his constituents. "It is a mighty poor politician who cannot promise his friends and supporters anything they want," he wrote. (After his death, Edwards was succeeded by yet another newspaper editor, W.L. Davidson, editor of the Calgary *Albertan*, the smaller and morning newspaper in the city.)

Eventually, Grandfather gave up trying for public office, but not public service – either politically or in his community. He looked back on those significant years of Alberta politics, the rise of the Farmers' Party and its eventual obliteration by Social Credit: "This was the time when the Farmers swept into power on a wave of enthusiasm that has sadly failed to prove a sound foundation for a real administrative and legislative success." Clinton Ford would, with those words, provide an ironic foreshadowing of the rise and sad decline of the Reform Party and its successor, the Canadian Alliance. The Reform Party would sweep into the Canadian consciousness on a similar wave of enthusiasm and would also prove not to have the right stuff for administrative or legislative success.

In the new world order, one of fear and mistrust caused by terrorist attacks, great store has been placed in a particular kind of citizenship: the jingoistic kind. Canadian voices who present a viewpoint counter to that of our neighbours and friends to the south are drowned out. A proud Canadian military is pushed and pulled by politicians who see a "war" on terror as an excuse to trot out whatever they believe is wrong and missing in the Canadian forces. That we, as a sovereign nation, decided forty years ago that we would not – we could not – mount a fighting force comparable to that of larger and more populated countries, was forgotten in the haste to be part of a war. At any time in the past four decades it has been within Canada's right to change that focus, to make the military a priority over other considerations. That we have not done so, over at least eight federal elections, says something that we are choosing to ignore. It says that the Canadian people are interested in a limited and specialized military. For the men – and they are mostly men – who prefer their wars to be violent and bloody and still object to the disbanding of the Airborne regiment after its despicable behaviour in Somalia, the aftermath of September 11 proved an irresistible opportunity to criticize and condemn Canada.

Such voices found a home in Alberta and in its politics.

Maybe to understand the curiosity that is Alberta politics it is necessary to be both onlooker and insider. There are likely many Albertans who could step into that role, but one would be hard-pressed to find someone more perfect than former Alberta senator Ron Ghitter. Ghitter is a born Albertan and has lived all his life in either Edmonton or Calgary, during a stint with the Progressive Conservative provincial government and his service as a senator in Ottawa. But Ghitter is also Jewish, raised in a province where anti-Semitism may have been of the gentlemanly variety, but was nonetheless overt to those Jews who found themselves politely but firmly barred from such institutions as the Glencoe Club or the Calgary Golf and Country Club.

Various ethnic communities in Alberta have been described as contributing to the bit-of-this, bit-of-that nature of the province, but the overriding ethic in Ghitter's earlier years – and still today – was of the white, Christian variety. And business and politics was overtly male. (It is not exactly a joke to remark that the largest "ethnic" minority in Calgary is the Americans. We just can't pick them out in a crowd.)

Ghitter knows all too well what he describes as "the cruel barbs one receives from being of a different culture." Albertans of all ethnic backgrounds seem to share some fundamental characteristics when it comes to politics. And, writes Ghitter, those are "perhaps best illustrated by their voting patterns over the years. The policies of the various however few governments reveal the consistency of Albertans in their commitment to certain principles."

Political scientists, sociologists, historians, theorists, and deep thinkers from one end of the province (and one end of the country) to the other have attempted to understand the monolithic nature of Alberta politics. The best way to describe it, in layman's terms, is to offer an analogy, notwithstanding the irritating inexactness of all analogies: If Alberta and its politics were a couple, they would be serial monogamists. Occasionally, there's a divorce and remarriage, but "infidelity" is not in the lexicon of Alberta politics.

On November 26, 1925, in the wake of the sweeping win in the provincial election of the Farmers' Party, Grandfather wrote the new premier of Alberta, J.E. Brownlee, addressing him, familiarly, as Brownlee:

> I have pleasure in extending to you my sincere congratulations on your accession to the premiership. In my opinion, you have earned the honour as a result of your able work during the past four years. As we are wont to say in our profession, without prejudice to my Liberal principles, I wish you every success in the new venture.
>
> As you know, I am not a supporter of the Farmer Government, of which you are now premier and therefore, I must make it quite clear that my best wishes are to you personally. As a former undergraduate with you at [Toronto's]

Old Vic and a later roommate in Calgary, under memories
of the old association which are strong, I would be a mighty
poor cad if I did not feel within me a sense of pride at your
success. I do, indeed, feel a sense of personal pride in what
you have achieved.

Whether or not you can hold the Government together
I am not going to say, but whatever may happen, I feel no
one else can hold it as well as you, and though you may have
heavy responsibilities and a difficult task, as I believe you
will, yet I am going to say here that I have confidence
you will succeed in the task, if anyone possibly can.

There is sad irony in those words, because Brownlee could have
been the most famous and successful of all of Alberta's premiers.
He out-slashed Ralph Klein, cutting the province's budget by nearly
50 per cent and letting almost half the civil service go. The Great
Depression was on. By 1932 Calgary had a population of 84,000, but
13,000 of them were on welfare.

Then, as now, hard times created new political parties. "Social
credit" economics were introduced by William Aberhart on his Back
to the Bible House broadcast. What would become the New
Democratic Party began at a meeting in Calgary as the Co-operative
Commonwealth Federation. But the key to Alberta's prosperity
would prove to be not on the land, or with the men who worked
it, but under it. And it was Premier Brownlee who had secured the
key, back in 1929. He had wrested control of Alberta's natural
resources from the federal government and returned in triumph to
Alberta and cheering crowds. Until Brownlee and Prime Minister
Mackenzie King signed the historic pact, all revenue from natural
resources went to Ottawa in exchange for an annual subsidy. What
was beneath our feet – eventually to prove the wealth of Alberta – was
now owned by the people. That most Albertans remain unaware of
Brownlee's coup is a result of the scandal that destroyed his reputation and defeated his government.

It was not politics that did Brownlee in, but his weakness.

She was eighteen-year-old Vivian MacMillan. He was the forty-seven-year-old married premier. When they met in 1930 at a picnic in her hometown of Edson, where her father, Allan, was the mayor, Brownlee was instantly attracted to the vivacious teenager. He persuaded her parents to send her to Edmonton to continue her education at a business school, promising he and Mrs. Brownlee would act as her guardians. Within months, she was a junior government secretary in the Attorney General's office, just down the hallway in the legislature from the premier. She was also a frequent visitor to the Brownlee family and would be driven home by the premier himself, even though he had a driver whose duty it would normally have been to escort the young woman.

Within months of arriving in Edmonton, the secretary and the premier were involved in an affair, usually carried out furtively in the back seat of the premier's Studebaker, but also in his office and even at his residence.

The affair continued for two years. Vivian believed the premier loved her. Brownlee clearly believed he could get away with it. And he almost did.

When Vivian tried to end the affair, after she had met a young medical student, Brownlee became enraged, she said later, refusing to let go. Eventually, she confessed to her mother. Her mother immediately told her father who launched a lawsuit against the premier, charging him with seduction.

It went to trial in June of 1934, before a jury of six men. It took that jury less than five hours to find Brownlee guilty, despite all his protestations of innocence, which were backed up by his attentive wife, who sat by her husband's side for the six days of the trial.

That wasn't the end of it: for the next six years, the case wound its way through appeals, finally reaching the Privy Council, which upheld the trial court judgment.

That was just the final note to a ruined career and reputation.

In 1935, a record 82 per cent of Alberta voters turned out to defeat the Farmers and bring in Social Credit. Brownlee had resigned in disgrace and returned to Calgary and private practice as a lawyer.

He would die in 1961, at age seventy-eight. Both Grandfather and Brownlee clearly would have moved in the same small legal circles in Calgary for all those years after the scandal, but as a child I never heard his name mentioned. (Grandfather would die in 1964 at age eighty-two.)

I suspect a polite but firm snubbing of a former friend who had so violated the principles of accepted, moral conduct. No family record exists of any further correspondence or contact between the two men who had been near lifelong friends and former roommates. Why would I presume a genteel shunning of a disgraced man?

Because Grandfather and his like-minded associates lived by a simple moral code, one Grandfather copied from a church sermon, and wrote in his diary in 1910, as a young man just heading West: "Live your own life, and make the most of yourself in every way; and mind your own business. . . . It is not what you hate, but hate itself that is destructive. So, do not hate evil, love good. Do not work against wrong; work for righteousness. Do not try to drive darkness out of the world, try to spread light. Do not try to stop other people's bad habits; show them good habits. Do not crusade against vice; spread virtue.

And as for injustice, wrong, crime, sin, vice, liquor, tobacco, profanity and so on; forget them."

A Social Credit government ran Alberta as a tightly controlled quasi-religious fiefdom for thirty-six years, beginning with William Aberhart and ending with the little-known Harry Strom. By the time the end came, Social Credit was an embarrassment to the growing urban nature of Alberta.

This was the government that passed a law permitting (if not actively encouraging) the sterilization of "mental defectives." As would be proven long years later, that classification included rebellious, hard-to-handle, or disobedient young women, whose only "defect" was to fall into the clutches of a fundamentalist government's thinly disguised efforts at genetic manipulation. A number of these damaged individuals would later successfully sue the Alberta government.

It was a Social Credit government that passed such outrageous legislation as the Communal Property Act, discriminating against the province's growing Hutterite colonies. That law, too, was eventually repealed as an embarrassment, if not because of its downright religious discrimination.

Voters' support for Social Credit all those long years also included buying into the crackpot economic teachings of Major C.H. Douglas, an anti-Semite who believed there was a conspiracy of Jewish bankers determined to undermine the economy of the world. To prevent it from being taken over, he argued, Alberta should create its own money, its own banks, regardless of the Constitution. The ensuing battles between the province and Ottawa will have a resonance today. When the dust cleared, Alberta was still using Canadian money, but a quasi-bank, the Alberta Treasury Branches, had sprung up under 1938 provincial legislation. Now Canada's ninth-largest financial institution, still a singularity of Alberta life, still living in some parallel, albeit legal universe, the ATBs are an $8-billion business with almost 150 branches and more than 125 agencies across the province. A little more than sixty years after a bit of imaginative legislative high-stepping, the constitutionality of this bank-which-isn't-a-bank has still to be settled.

Well, if this "banking" system isn't constitutional, why has it lived and prospered all these years? Call it Eastern bias and Western guile. Ron Ghitter says that the Social Credit "was a government narrow in focus and it rarely faced any meaningful opposition but had little impact on the national scene." So the answer is a simple: the law flew under Ottawa's radar.

Social Credit was a rural-based government, and it made sure that country voters enjoyed a distinct advantage over the more numerous city voters. They still do. The government might have changed, but the disparity between the power of the declining rural vote over the growing urban population continues to this day.

If the imbalance were to be addressed in a logical fashion, the number of rural seats in the legislature in Edmonton would be reduced while the number of urban seats would grow to outnumber the rural vote. That's the rub for a conservative government that has allied itself philosophically with the right-wing Conservative Party: urban voters are more likely to be turned off by social conservatism and the anti-gay, anti-feminist agenda it supports. Ralph Klein's real support – from the time he won the leadership race by sweeping through the rural ridings with his just-plain-folks style – has come from the farming, ranching, and mining communities, where "social assistance" means the neighbours get together to help each other.

That rural spirit of self-reliance, admirably suited to communities where one can grow a year's supply of vegetables and slaughter a hog for meat, seems quaint and irrelevant in a high-rise in Edmonton. But it is still the overriding attitude of a government whose strongest support comes from rural areas and the business/development community.

The underlying reasons Albertans repudiated the only political party many of them had ever known remain a mystery to political scientists. Nobody has ever quite managed to explain what it is about Alberta politics that makes the voters suddenly turn on a party they have supported for decades, nor why any party thus defeated – neither the United Farmers nor Social Credit – has ever been given a second chance. The man who took over as premier from Ernest Manning, Harry Strom, went into deserved and unlamented obscurity, overtaken and overshadowed by Peter Lougheed and his Progressive Conservatives.

Social Credit has been followed by thirty years and counting of Progressive Conservative government, although the government of Ralph Klein is farther to the right than the government of Peter Lougheed could ever have imagined. Indeed, the Klein government with the exception of the premier himself, looks more like Social Credit in its attitudes.

When Peter Lougheed's Progressive Conservatives were elected in 1972, they rapidly changed the tone of government from one of stern, unbending morality to something more modern. Their first legislation – the Bill of Rights and the Individual Rights Protection Act – were welcomed enthusiastically by a new Alberta, rapidly changing from an agricultural economy to one based primarily on natural resources. The Sterilization Act and the Communal Property Act were quickly repealed.

Alberta would no longer be seen as a backwater. As Ron Ghitter, an MLA and cabinet minister under Lougheed, writes:

> The 1970s seemed to propel Alberta onto the national stage. The personal dynamism of Peter Lougheed, the rapidly growing significance of our oil and gas industry during a period of high prices, and the growing prosperity of the province boosted Alberta into national prominence.
>
> It was a time of great wealth, the Heritage Trust Fund, burgeoning revenues and increased recognition of Alberta's potential. It was also a time of confrontation and distrust between Alberta and the East, of the National Energy Program, Pierre Trudeau, the Federal Investment Review Agency, [Allan] MacEachern budgets and the struggle for the right to govern our own resources and keep them from the greedy grasp of the Liberal mandarins in Ottawa. It was also a period of philosophical shifts in Alberta.
>
> The Lougheed government was a government of inclusion. It took great pains to provide programs that were representative of all Albertans, even those who did not typically vote Conservative such as the membership of labour unions and those of more liberal or even socialist inclinations – although there were very few of those in Alberta.
>
> It was a time of low taxes and no sales tax . . . when financial institutions were encouraged to locate their decision makers in Alberta. The government was doing whatever was possible to capitalize on the growing influence of this province so that decision making could occur in Alberta rather than Toronto.

With inclusion came intervention and interference in the marketplace. The Lougheed government got into business with the vague idea of encouraging development. So Alberta ended up with Pacific Western Airlines – we called it Peter's Western Airlines – and businesses as diverse as canola plants. The government created the Agricultural Development Corporation and the Economic Development Corporation. But most obvious to the ordinary Albertan was the rapid decentralization of services, a sort of seeding of goodies throughout the province. Incentives were offered to encourage businesses to locate in Alberta. Hospitals and schools went up, it seemed, wherever there was a Tory voter. Twenty years later, we lost all that brick and mortar, when Ralph Klein began to slash services. Across the province, small communities that had enjoyed the benefit of a local hospital, for example, found the "legacy" of the Lougheed years closed, shuttered, sold off to private interests, or, in the case of the Calgary General Hospital, blown up.

The Lougheed government was bold in its vision of a government concerned about all aspects of Alberta life. The government backed innovative early childhood education programs, passed a new mental health act, revised the sexist policies of the matrimonial property act. At the same time the province put money into the growth of universities and colleges and made a strong commitment to the public-school system.

"Underlying this inclusiveness," writes Senator Ghitter

were the economic policies enunciated by John Maynard Keynes, that it was totally acceptable for government to assume "manageable debt," to invest today for the benefits of tomorrow, to spend on universities to train our youth and provide the infrastructure, hospitals and schools. It was a concept that declared that government must accept some debt as any family must, as a fundamental investment to ensure the maintenance of a way of life in the future. It is an approach that assumes groundwork must be laid and foundations built for times to come.

Alberta was to have a blueprint for a society compassionate for the less fortunate, and economically feasible for all, a good society supporting personal liberty, basic well being, racial and ethnic equality with opportunity for a rewarding life for all, not just the fortunate few.

I lived through those years, never realizing we had it so good. Maybe it is the combination of the man and the timing that makes Peter Lougheed the most respected former politician around. He was good, but he was lucky. He came into power at the right time and left with the same unerring sense. When Lougheed retired from active politics in 1985, things were starting to change and not for the better.

Alberta was headed straight for a fall, and the man who took over from Lougheed never could read the signs, even though they were there in front of Don Getty's face. All that infrastructure and those programs brought in by Lougheed were money pits. The interest revenue from the Heritage Fund – rainy-day savings from oil royalties and one of the major causes of interprovincial jealousy – was redirected to general revenue and no new money was invested. Deficits ballooned, but no new sources of revenue were tapped. When Don Getty became Alberta premier in 1985, he faced disaster: rising costs and reduced revenues; rising interest rates and failing businesses. Some ventures, whose debt had been guaranteed by the government, were expensive public embarrassments when they crashed. Probably none more so than the high-flying Principal Savings and Trust whose collapse stripped small investors of their life savings while leaving the company's executives rich. Other companies such as Gainers and Novatel became public symbols of government failure.

Did the Getty government move swiftly to stem the bleeding? No. It went along as if nothing much was happening and the results were predictable. After recording surpluses in 1984 and 1985, the deficit began to mount. Provincial debt, almost zero in 1986, rose to more than $17 billion – almost $7,000 for each Albertan – by the end of 1992. The deficit that year was a choking $3.4 billion. Alberta was up to its neck in debt and the provincial government seemed incapable of understanding the problem.

If Ralph Klein wasn't exactly the image of a knight on a white charger, if his prescription was brutal and abrupt, nobody can take away from him and his style of Conservative government the fact that he slaughtered the dragon. But, like Lougheed, Klein was lucky in his timing. The next boom was just around the corner.

It would be reasonable to assume that the miracle of slaying the deficit and the debt brought happy smiles around the cabinet table, but it didn't. These people seem not to know what to do with success.

Then came September 11, 2001. The aftermath and subsequent economic downturn following the al-Qaeda attacks returned the Klein government to what it does best – a sort of Scots Presbyterian gleeful dourness. That's not as much an oxymoron as might be assumed. Think of Scotty, the chief engineer of the *Enterprise* in the first *Star Trek* series, and his insistence the ship could not do Warp 9 for any length of time: "She canna take nae more, Cap'n." It is this same kind of happy pessimism – the *Enterprise* may shake a bit and the dilithium crystals work a little harder, but the ship always came through in the crunch and earned a fond pat or two on her engine cowling – that characterizes the attitude of Alberta's Conservative government.

It is never so happy as when the outlook is gloomy and tough decisions must be made. Throughout the autumn of 2001, the avuncular premier talked unceasingly about how poor Alberta was and how there would be no further spending. Indeed, much was made of more than $1 billion (yes, that's a "b") in cuts to the year's budget. The anomaly was the promise that none of the cuts would affect consumers – or citizens, if you prefer – leading more than one of those consumers to wonder how effective the Alberta budgeting system is if that much money could be taken painlessly out of expenditures.

Meanwhile, residents of other provinces could be forgiven for believing Alberta was, indeed, broke. Klein is nothing if not a compelling communicator. If he says we're broke, gee, we must be. Well, this is not dissimilar to the down-on-his-luck millionaire insisting he has been forced to buy twelve-year-old Macallan, instead of the twenty-five-year-old single malt. Everything is relative, and the poor-mouthing in Alberta is just that. (The *Calgary Herald*'s front-page headline the day after the provincial finance minister's budget prediction was: 'Surplus plummets to $12 million.' Only in Alberta.)

The government's announcement of hard times a-comin' is as philosophical as it is practical. Governing in good times doesn't give a right-wing politician nearly the frisson of excitement that managing in bad times does. After all, people such as me are fond of pointing out that roasting the fat goose is easy; making a satisfying meal from an old hen is something else.

So the government of Alberta promoted the belief spending must end and belts must be tightened, and when we all come through more or less bruised instead of battered, we, too, will get a friendly pat on the engine cowling.

We're still waiting. We're wallowing in money, profits are in the billions of dollars, the province is spending like a sailor on shore leave, but the myth of bad times just around the corner, beyond the next hailstorm, after the next drought, continues. We Albertans are nothing if not predictable in our pessimism, even as we gamble on natural resources.

Perhaps the most disingenuous statement made by the premier – the provincial finance minister has been notably less visible and mostly uninspiring, except for announcing her retirement from politics and the collection of a $500,000 severance package – is his insistence that deficit financing is "against the law." The predicted reaction is for Albertans and other Canadians paying attention to nod sagely and murmur assent. The fact remains that the law against running a deficit, this much-quoted law against spending (because that is essentially what it is), is a law of the same government that quotes it at arm's length. Changing that law is exactly as easy as a majority government deciding to do so. This, after all, is not the Criminal Code of Canada. It is provincial jurisdiction. It doesn't make it less viable, but it certainly should give the intelligent person pause. There are good and valid reasons for not driving the province into a deficit. There are sound arguments for not eating more than you kill. The weakest is to say, as if you have nothing to do with it, is that there is a law.

Today, convincing Albertans they must tighten their belts, while not simple, is considerably more acceptable than it was at the beginning of the Klein era. We've been beaten into shape, and arguments against the user-pay, market-driven system of life get little air and less light. The coup was the 2000 provincial election, held during times of exploding energy royalties. If ever there was a time for Albertans to turn away from the dour face of government, it was then. And what did we do? We returned the Klein Conservatives with an even stronger majority, bare percentage points away from the record majority set by Peter Lougheed.

We have, indeed, been weaned from the welfare state. And, instead of continuing to fight for the people most affected by government cutbacks, we have, like so many abused family members, chosen to side with whoever holds the power. As University of Alberta sociologist Claude Denis writes in *The Trojan Horse: Alberta and the Future of Canada* (1995): "Albertans must forget what they were used to, and they must acquire a new sense of what is normal."

Welcome to normal, twenty-first-century style.

Denis notes:

> Anywhere else in Canada, a government that undertook this kind of program would run into very stiff opposition. The peculiarity of Alberta in this respect is that those elements of the welfare state that were developed directly by the provincial government (e.g., the proliferation of small rural hospitals) were not connected to a corresponding state-oriented ideology, and were not financed with taxpayers' money, but rather with oil royalties. This made the Alberta welfare state unusually vulnerable to attacks couched in the self-reliance discourse that remained the dominant political language in the province. . . . [T]he originality of the Klein restructuring is that, through the strenuously argued

attack on welfare-state budgets and government structures, it is attempting to accomplish the second task ordained by capital: to create the kind of conditions required for the return of easy profitability.

This is exactly what has happened. Easy profitability occurred and allowed the premier to envision a province with the lowest tax rate in North America, and muse about eliminating provincial income taxes altogether.

Any sociologist or political pundit who predicted when Klein first came to power that the new-style conservative government of Alberta would alienate its own citizens in the long run would have been seen as mad. After all, the politics of political action is re-election, and if you alienate enough of the electorate, being elected again is impossible. Klein's Conservatives have rewritten such accepted wisdom by getting themselves re-elected in the face of criticism and all the political pundits. There are many examples of what could be seen as voter deal-breakers, but one should suffice – video lottery terminals. In his essay called "The New Normal," Denis postulates: "The Klein government may yet come to grief, in fact, over the VLTs, the proliferation of which is opposed by a good majority of Albertans."

Denis was correct in his thesis, but wrong in the outcome. Indeed, a good number of Albertans did and do oppose the proliferation of gambling. In a 1995 poll, 49 per cent of Albertans were strongly opposed to increasing the number of VLTs in the province. If those who were moderately opposed is factored into the mix, a whopping 68 per cent are against proposed increases. But argue those numbers against an even more impressive one: $1 billion. That was the total profit on VLTs recorded by the Alberta government in its 2003–04 fiscal year.

Despite the Calvinistic opposition (or so it would seem) to the wages and profits of "sin," Albertans heartily endorse its ease of access. When asked about the privatization of liquor sales – often considered an example of the Americanization of Alberta by those who don't consider that a compliment – no less than 65 per cent of Albertans were in favour.

This should come as no surprise to anyone who tipples even occasionally. The idea of being able to buy liquor with the same convenience and choice one buys groceries is not only popular, it's profitable for small business. In the years since Alberta privatized such services as licence registries and liquor stores, the level of service and ease of access still stuns most adults, long used to lineups, surly or non-existent service, and restricted hours. Actually, only one government regulation stands in the way of real free-market enterprise for booze – the grocery giants are still prohibited from adopting the marketing techniques of their American and European counterparts with aisles of liquor right next to the soft drinks and designer water and cases of beer stacked in coolers across from the butter and cheese.

Why wide-open gambling and not wide-open liquor sales? The answer seems to be as simple as it is banal: small-business owners fear their mom-and-pop liquor store will be put out of business if consumers can add a litre of Scotch to their grocery cart alongside the coffee and steaks. This restriction does not sit well with consumers who believe privatization doesn't mean only so far, and no more. But it has not deterred the marketing gurus of giant retailers such as Safeway, who have put up independent liquor stores right next to its supermarkets, awaiting the inevitable repeal of government regulations before knocking out the wall.

No less a well-known Albertan than Jim Gray, head of Canadian Hunter Exploration and part of Calgary's powerful oil establishment, led a widespread campaign against VLTs. The campaign resulted in a referendum in the municipal elections of 1998, after the premier promised that any community that voted against VLTs could have them removed immediately. Across the province, the split was roughly fifty-five to forty-five between those who voted for and those who voted against VLTs.

In the small central towns of Sylvan Lake and Rocky Mountain House, local plebiscites in 1997 resulted in about sixty machines being pulled out of bars and lounges. A year later, Coaldale, Canmore, and Lethbridge County in southern Alberta; and Stony Plain, the County of Opportunity and Wood Buffalo Region, which includes the booming oil town of Fort McMurray, all in northern Alberta, voted to follow the lead of the two towns in central Alberta. But they're still waiting in at least seven Alberta towns. The government was saved from having to act by a court injunction requested by about a dozen business owners with VLTs, who argued the province's constitutional right to remove the machines. Another municipal election has come and gone and still the people of those communities wait to see their democratic decision acted upon.

Nobody's holding his breath this situation will be resolved soon, even though Gray believes the machines should be pulled out and, if the communities lose the court case, returned. Agreeing with him is the mayor of Canmore, who echoed popular opinion when he said the town voted as a community, and rightfully expected the government to act on that vote.

Hotel owners whose bars have the machines aren't in a flap about the vote. Years have passed and nothing has happened. In the words of one owner, if the court challenge goes against them, there is always an appeal or two to launch. By the time that winds its way through the system, we'll probably have forgotten all about it.

Albertans don't seem to care any more, other than the social workers who deal with gambling addicts and the families who face the consequences. It didn't arise as an issue at all in the municipal elections of 2001 and was barely above the radar in 2004. (There's the $1-billion profit to be considered.) As long as the court injunction stands, it's business as usual in front of the machines, which, with the combined profits of other forms of gaming, provides more than $300 million to charities and non-profit groups each year and another $700 million to other organizations. That is a long way from church basement bingo.

The government's not following through on a promise to its citizens seems a prime example of alienation. But it's not. Ralph

Klein's government, as long as it exists under his cloak of popularity, can't seem to do any wrong – or at least not enough wrong
to jeopardize its rule.

The Klein prescription for prosperity meant the hoax of better living
through tax cuts, the return of the long-disproved Reagan-era supply-
side economics. High taxes are presumed to discourage investors. Tax
cuts, which in the United States amounted to 25 per cent over three
years, had the predictable result there of increasing the deficit to $200
billion and the debt to $3.5 trillion by the time both Reagan and
George H. Bush left the White House. They, too, had been unlucky
in their timing. Bill Clinton was luckier and enjoyed an unprece-
dented run of economic good fortune and prosperity.

When George W. Bush came to power after the disputed 2000
federal election, his country's finances were enviable. So, one of his
first acts (after stripping federal funding from international family
planning and medical clinics supporting birth control and abortion)
was to bring in yet more tax cuts, which mostly benefited the
wealthy supporters of the Republican Party. They were promoted by
a public-relations campaign to convince people that having more
money "in their pockets" would increase consumer spending and
thus result in higher productivity as the manufacturing sector geared
up to produce more goods for people with more money to spend.

In Alberta, a campaign to introduce a flat tax was couched in
similar trickle-down language. Yet tax cuts do not produce higher
productivity, as can be seen by the huge debt, the results of cuts, in
the States. Still, the economic policies of the rich prevailed, at the
expense of the common weal. And, in January 2001, Alberta brought
in a 10.5 per cent flat tax, justifying its inherent bias toward the
wealthy by the pompous assertion that a flat tax is a fair tax.

Few Canadians would argue against tax reform. But a flat tax is
an easy solution that seems fair, but is not. As currently constituted –
leaving in available deductions and other tax avoidances – a flat tax
is a godsend to the rich. If there are questions why it is so enthusiastically supported by people with money and clout, look no further

than their enormous savings realized under a flat-tax system based on taxable, not on actual income.

Such a dramatic change in how taxes are assessed is seductive in its simplicity. It benefits the top tax bracket the most, not that there's anything intrinsically wrong in giving the rich back some of their money. But the numbers don't add up, and it behooves the government to be up front about where the money lost in revenues is going to come from.

Economic growth is supposed to make up for the more than $500 million in revenues that would be lost through such a system. But even rosy predictions see less than half the forgone monies being recouped.

The trade-off may be dropping the promise of fairer taxation for everyone, in favour of a bonus for the rich and the prospect of having to make up the shortfall in other ways. Those other ways can be conjectured, but logic says somebody will make up the shortfall and that "somebody" is the middle class.

Nobody likes taxes. But Canada's system of progressive taxation supplies the incentives for corporations and organizations to support charities and political parties; to provide benefits to their workers; to invest in Canadian business; to create jobs; to pay for research and development; and to provide the framework for medical care and the rest of the social safety net.

But the big lie of flat taxes persists. Why? Because we all believe that we, as individuals, will be in the favoured group that will pay fewer taxes. And here in Alberta, we are infused with American-style thinking and optimism. (One American writer referred to poor Americans as believing they are merely "pre-rich," which accounts for the lack of jealousy in the States about the widening gap between the haves and have-mores and the have-nots and have-nothings.)

The notion the people at the top with the money will let enough of it trickle through their grasp to nourish those lower on the end of the economic scale was a feature of Ronald Reagan's administration in the United States. It didn't work. The rich are rich because they don't let much slip through their grasp.

Yet the people of Alberta know there is money in the province's bank account and they rightfully want some of it back. And therein lies the problem – not everyone in the province wanted it back in their pocket. Many people wanted it poured back into the services and programs that benefit all of us, particularly health and education.

The Alberta government believed tax breaks would do the job. The presumption was that when all of us had a couple of hundred dollars more in our jeans, we would distribute it to where it would do most good. This is charity at its personal best. Unfortunately, it's the kind of charity that throws money at sick and irrepressibly cute kids and ignores the homeless bum who may be just as in need of medical attention, but isn't considered "deserving" enough for people to spend their own money to help.

A universal system seeks to eliminate that kind of charity. It seeks to replace emotion with equality; the Lady Bountiful model with humanity and dignity. It respects the admonition we are responsible for "the least of my brethren." There's nothing about helping only those whom you like, which could be construed as tax policy in Alberta.

The flat tax isn't an Alberta creation, it's been hanging around for decades waiting only to be adopted. I first met it in a church in San Antonio, Texas. It was not a religious experience.

The church was no longer holy, but served Mammon, having been de-sanctified and reborn as the banquet area of a crafts centre. There were no religious icons left, save the stained glass windows, yet the metaphor of a sacred setting for a profane task was used for emphasis by the man we'd come to hear. Dick Armey, a Republican congressman from Dallas–Fort Worth, who was then the majority leader of the U.S. House of Representatives, was addressing an annual meeting of the National Conference of Editorial Writers, a gathering of editorial-page editors and writers from across North America. We weren't his favourite audience. He despises the press.

During one question, Armey cast his eyes upward to the apse, opened his arms wide, and invoked the "Lord who hath delivered mine enemies unto me." It got a huge laugh, larger than his eventual answer. He dismissed the question – whether investment income would be subject to taxation – as "obnoxious sophistry." Some of us believed what had come before the question was the real obnoxious sophistry – the kind of fervent, pulpit-pounding message of tax reform designed to make the rich wealthier while it pretends to make taxation fair.

The Canadians in the audience weren't just casual observers. What we heard from Armey was the gospel of the flat tax that had recently arrived as an idea in Alberta and was being touted by the Reform Party. Armey called it fair, simple, and progressive. "So fair it might even restore your faith in the government. So simple," he said, "you could do your taxes on a postcard."

It looks simple, sounds simple, and on the surface is fair. But taxation is never simple. And fair is in the eyes of the beholder.

Armey's proposal taxes each dollar only once. The catch is in the wording, which suggests that if the dollar comes to your pocket after it has been taxed at source – through investments or a business – it comes tax-free. "What I don't do is tax it the second time," said Armey. (In Alberta, the single-rate tax – the so-called flat tax – is 10 per cent of taxable income, instead of provincial income tax being calculated as a percentage of federal tax.)

The result of a flat tax is obvious: A further widening of the gap between the rich and the rest; a serious problem for charities that depend on tax deductions to attract money; and a possible revenue shortfall for all levels of government. Middle-income earners, under such a program, could well find themselves sending more, not less money to Ottawa or Washington, although the time it takes to calculate the amount would be less.

What the tax represents, in terms of Armey's self-appointed revolution, is one part of the systematic dismantling of all the reforms that distinguish Western democracies – the social and government programs that extend help to the less fortunate and less advantaged. Armey and his followers would bury the legacy of Franklin

Roosevelt's New Deal. Their toadies in Canada who see the United States as having all the answers would follow right behind.

And Alberta did just that.

Here it is heresy, living as we are with the Alberta Advantage, to question both tax cuts and debt repayment. The simplistic idea that a provincial economy can be run like a private household with a hand-held calculator and a computer spreadsheet is so entrenched that nobody questions the reasoning. We accept that it is good political household management to pay off one's mortgage – even if you starve a couple of your children while doing so. Because that is the real analogy: not that Alberta can be run like your house, but that it is possible to decide between your children's welfare and paying off the mortgage. No parent would do so but a government can because the people it is "starving" are deemed unworthy of love and care.

This, too, this political manipulation, is a face of the Alberta Advantage.

Politics never interested me until Grade 9, when Beth Maynard, whose father, Lucien, had been a Social Credit cabinet minister, took me to a sitting of the legislature in Edmonton. We walked across the High Level Bridge, were shown to seats in the Speaker's Gallery – thanks to Beth's connections – and proceeded to flirt outrageously with the page boys, one of whom I developed a full-blown crush on. It was the kind of crush only a barely teenaged girl could develop and caused me, for months to come, to take the long way home from school, necessitating a walk past the front of Courtney Breckenridge's house. (When he finally got the message and called for me at home – we lived a few blocks farther south on the same street – I wasn't around. My mother couldn't understand my dismay. He was just another boy, wasn't he?)

While the name of that page boy has remained with me for more than forty years, the names of the cabinet ministers, the government, or the debates have vanished from memory. (Although the premier must have been Manning, as he stayed in office from 1943 to 1968. To put it more personally, Manning's term as premier of

Alberta lasted from two months before my parents were married until after their oldest child – me – was born, went all the way through school, including university, and was on her third newspaper job in London, Ontario.)

What remains is a child's curiosity, an abiding interest, and a healthy skepticism that has only been exacerbated by long years of watching government and oppositions behave no better than ordinary men and women. Which, of course, is what they are. Except they have the power to affect our lives, which means I hold them, like police officers and other public servants, up to a higher standard of behaviour. More fool me.

The most honourable politician I've ever met was William Davis, former premier of Ontario, followed by Dr. Stuart Smith, who wanted to be premier of Ontario, but who was too erudite, too Jewish, and too educated to appeal to the heartland of that province. I never heard a whiff of scandal about either man's private life, as opposed to just about every other male politician who's ever been elected, including some who've made it fairly obvious that good things would happen if I'd agree to a more "private" kind of interview.

If politicians wonder why journalists hold so many of them in contempt, they might consider the fact that we watch every aspect of their lives, whether anything is ever actually printed or broadcast. The politician who thinks he can cheat on his wife with impunity is sorely mistaken. Its a small world, even in Toronto, but especially in Edmonton. The whispers, who gets into whose car late at night, who's seen in a bar with whom – all this we notice. Mostly, we're not impressed.

There is no such thing as being successfully discreet. One is always found out. And the rumour mill takes less than a day to disseminate information from Edmonton to Calgary and all points beyond. That the gossip never makes it into print is more a case of it being gossip than good manners or any desire to save a public official from public embarrassment. If we could prove it, we'd print it. And that has nothing to do with whether we believe the gossip or not.

I never wanted to be a political reporter, but one can't be in journalism and escape it. And over the years, stuff sticks; memories accumulate, the institutions with which you deal become part of your life, too.

I didn't realize on that spring day in 1957 that so much of my life would centre on what was happening in the Alberta legislature. Had I taken a job with the *Edmonton Journal*, rather than the *Calgary Herald*, I have no doubt I would have spent the past years immersed in Alberta politics, instead of being just a dabbler.

One man who did immerse himself in the politics of Alberta, without ever running for public office, was J. Patrick O'Callaghan, known to all as Pat. An Irishman who'd spent years as a journalist with the Liverpool *Post and Echo*, Pat came to Canada in 1959 (stopping in Ontario for six months to learn about Canadian newspapers from the *Peterborough Examiner*'s editor, soon-to-be-famous novelist Robertson Davies), before moving into the editor's office at the *Red Deer Advocate*, a daily in central Alberta owned by the English newspaper company. Pat settled in Alberta and stayed in Canada, eventually retiring to Toronto, until his death in 1996.

There have been few newspaper publishers like him in this country, certainly none still remain. He was passionately involved in what he thought was the real work of newspapers, that of finding out, writing, and reporting the news. He was one of the last modern publishers to come from the editorial side of this business. His newspapers – the *Advocate*, the *Edmonton Journal*, the *Windsor Star*, and the *Calgary Herald* showed that.

When he took over as publisher of the *Edmonton Journal*, Pat hired consultants to find out, as he writes in his unpublished memoirs, "what sort of newspaper our readers wanted . . .

"The responses were instructive, numbing, confusing, belligerent, outraged, destructive, edifying, devastating, passionate, indifferent, angry, kind, cynical, bemused, predictable and even flattering."

That would also encompass just about all of the responses Pat would ever bring upon himself. He was an engaged publisher, a man who loved words, their power and their effect. His targets ranged from politicians to hockey players – and their owners. When the owner of the Edmonton Oilers bounced an *Edmonton Journal* sports reporter from the locker room, Pat responded with an editorial, which he later said was "full of stirring words on preserving the independence of the paper and embellished it with a passionate defence of freedom of speech."

It was Pat's nature to fight, but in Edmonton he had silent encouragement within his own office. On the wall behind his chair hung the only Pulitzer Prize ever awarded outside of the United States. The Pulitzers honour the best of American journalism and the *Journal* won its award for, writes Pat: "The stirring battle it led to fend off government control and censorship of the press in 1937."

The Alberta Social Credit government, led by Premier William Aberhart, who harboured an irrational hostility to the provincial newspapers, had passed the Social Credit Act, to deal with public credit, but also to control the press. Writes Pat: "Before it was all over, there were a flock of court judgments and appeals, imprisonment of two ranking Social Crediters, and a threat of jail to a reporter. . . . When the federal government disallowed the Social Credit Act, the Alberta government responded with an Act to Ensure the Publication of Accurate News and Information."

The *Journal* editorial said: "The Alberta government would turn back more than 200 years the clock of liberty and progress . . . the machinery of dictatorship and censorship is outlined clearly in the bill . . . [it would] place in the hands of a few men such power . . . as no British monarch or government has presumed to assume for the past two centuries."

Eventually, the Supreme Court ruled that the legislation was beyond the scope of the powers of the province.

The newspapers of Alberta won that round.

Forty years later, Pat O'Callaghan would confront the government again, when he took it upon himself and his newspaper to be the "unofficial" opposition to Premier Peter Lougheed's government.

This wasn't a popular stance, except in our business, where the idea of a monolithic Alberta government seemed so anti-democratic, regardless of the mandate. Every government needs an opposition, every high official, a burr under its saddle. O'Callaghan became that burr when Lougheed won the largest majority ever recorded – seventy-four of seventy-nine seats in the Alberta legislature in March 1979.

In his unpublished memoirs, Pat recalls the time: "The size of that Tory majority gave many true democrats heartburn, no matter how proud the premier himself might have felt at the sight of all those blue-bottomed Tories arrayed in their legislative splendour and conveying the image of unparalleled voter approval." Within days of the election, Pat not only congratulated Lougheed on his victory, but warned that the *Edmonton Journal* had a responsibility to act as a voice for all those who are, as he wrote Lougheed: "silenced in the legislature by lack of representation." The opposition may have been swamped by the Tories, but that merely made Pat O'Callaghan determined to be his own voice of dissent to "autocracy and paternalistic dictatorship by default of the voters."

"I declared the *Journal* to be the 'unofficial opposition,'" he wrote.

> There were mostly Tories who regarded this as an arrogant assumption on my part. They may well have been right. But my fear was that the newspaper, supposedly the surrogate for the public, had no other choice without running the risk of letting Alberta drift through that period of government with no more than yawning tokenism where democracy was supposed to be.
>
> Some Tory supporters – then and now – look upon all journalists as mavericks who refuse to be corralled. But Tories, by nature, tend to be humourless, glaring apoplectically at the world out of countenances permanently afire because of collars that fit too snugly around their bull necks.

Pat O'Callaghan's reflections could well have been written to Klein after his first success at the polls. Like Lougheed, he faces no real opposition in the legislature. Who would have thought Klein, another Calgarian, would achieve the same success as Lougheed, despite a lack of education, erudition, and just about everything else that drew the public's admiration?

Klein shares, with Lougheed and Ernest Manning, that sure touch in leadership, that personal ability to draw voters into his vision and to make them trust him. His personal popularity, now years into a new century, is stronger than Lougheed's ever was, even if his overwhelming mandate in the 2000 election didn't quite score the percentage majority Lougheed did.

Klein has something Lougheed never possessed – the common touch. Ralph's supporters can consider that a compliment, and it does have the advantage of drawing in all those folks who would not feel comfortable having a draught beer and a tomato juice with the elegantly suited and mannered Lougheed.

More's the pity – Lougheed's conversation is infinitely more interesting.

Yet there is one trait Lougheed, Klein, and Manning share – they became the right men at the right time for their province.

8

City of Mushrooms

There are fourteen cities in Alberta, ranging from Wetaskiwin, with a nearly stable population of a little over eleven thousand, to Calgary, at one million and counting, but the only two with any relevance to the rest of the country are Calgary and Edmonton – the former having the money; the latter, the provincial government. Both cities are waiting like bridesmaids who can see the altar in their future, for both have the real prospect of success. The future of Canada lies in its cities, and the future of Alberta is in its two largest municipalities, both of which are expanding at an astounding rate.

They are also suffering from what Jane Jacobs in her new book, *Dark Age Ahead*, calls a bad case of "dumbed-down taxes."

"The disconnection between public treasuries and local domestic needs drawing upon them does not exist within taxpayers' pockets or bank accounts. The same taxpayers supply money for all layers of government. Rather, the disconnection is purely administrative and governmental. It is a political artifact with the strength of bureaucratic traditions. That being so, the dumbed-down result should theoretically be simple to mend; but, if experience in Canada is a guide, it can't be mended," writes Jacobs. Why? Because, she says, it's not necessity, but opportunity that is actually the mother of invention. Alberta's two largest cities – along with the country's

richest (Toronto) and the poorest (Winnipeg) – have lost the opportunity to finance their own existence, have lost the benefits of subsidiary and fiscal accountability.

Subsidiary, as Jacobs explains, is the "principle that government
works best – most responsibly and responsively – when it is closest
to the people it serves and the need it addresses." As for fiscal
accountability, every Canadian over the age of reason knows what
that means – tell us what you did with the money.

Where our tax money goes is almost impossible to discern
through the welter of bureaucratic doublespeak and the cost and
time of freedom-of-information requests. We trust the government
to tell us, and it is passing strange that Albertans think the federal
government can do no right and the Alberta government can do no
wrong. Neither one is accountable to the people who face potholes
on their streets, crumbling infrastructure, starving arts and culture
agencies, litter and garbage sharing the streets with the homeless,
beggars, and squeegee kids.

It doesn't have to be this way. Calgary and Edmonton are rich
cities and should be capable of providing for their own municipal
needs. But the money is "shared" with rural areas in a misguided
notion of "fairness" that is nothing more than an attempt to woo the
rural vote. No politician will say it, although it is true: you can't
live in a rural area and rightly expect the same level of public service
that you would get in a city.

As New Democratic Party leader Jack Layton writes in
Speaking Out, published only weeks before the 2004 federal election was called: "Canada's cities generate enormous revenues to
the federal and provincial governments. What they get in return
is a pittance." Municipalities control less than 5 per cent of the
monies taken in taxes.

"By law," writes Layton, "with very rare exceptions, cities don't
have the authority to collect income taxes, fuel taxes, sales taxes, or
most other kinds of tax except property tax. So when the federal
government wants to wrestle the deficit to the ground, it does so
by passing on costs to provinces, which pass some of them on to

municipalities, the level of government with the least capacity (by far) to pass them on to anyone else – or to raise money to backfill the fiscal excavations. The result? More potholes."

Conservative Canadians, particularly those living in a rock-ribbed conservative province like Alberta, see Jacobs and Layton as little more than whiny socialists, who'd spend our hard-earned tax dollars on such fripperies as daycare or English as a Second Language teachers or subsidized housing for the homeless or poor. We have been lulled into believing the myth that lower taxes will benefit all. Yet we can see, with our own eyes, what happens when taxes are lowered: something else increases, and in Alberta that means municipal property taxes and user fees for services.

Alberta's cities have no choice but to raise taxes and fees to make up for the shortfall between what they get from the province and what they need. The result has been a double-edged sword, because along with increasing costs to the ratepayers living in cities have come decreasing services. Even Alberta's first post-debt budget in April 2005, promising more cash for cities and infrastructure – $3.1 billion over five years – did not stop increases in property taxes. This hit especially hard in Calgary, where increases in market-value assessments in a hot real-estate market had already meant higher taxes.

But it isn't just so-called socialists who are crying foul and warning us that as our cities crumble, so does our way of life. It is all the people who must drive our city roads, negotiate the potholes, deal with traffic headaches, and face rising costs for all city services. Thanks to the lack of secure financing from the "upper" levels of government, Alberta's cities have to be creative with the money they have. Something as unforeseen as a July flood in Edmonton or a May blizzard in Calgary can knock a huge hole in their budget.

Edmonton, because it owns its public utilities, is more secure financially than Calgary. But when the two cities talk about their so-called woes, their mayors and city councillors concentrate on the serious issues of traffic and roads, public services, and declining finances. Meanwhile, the ordinary citizens of the two places taunt each other in an age-old rivalry.

There's no doubt the cities are practically and philosophically different. Take the mundane matter of the layout of city streets. Calgary decided to orient itself by quadrants, with Centre Street running north-south and the Bow River that flows west-east acting as the axis. The only anomaly came when city planners suddenly "remembered" the Bow takes a sharp curve to the south just east of what is now Deerfoot Trail. To keep the east-west axis straight, it was necessary to invent a Centre Avenue about where the river would have been if it didn't turn. As a result, there are a number of streets north of the river that have south-east street addresses, causing confusion for everyone. The *Calgary Herald* is one such building (along with Bridge Brand Foods and a city works yard). All are clearly to the north of the river and east of Centre Street. But the perfidy of nature gives these few streets a "south" designation, and as the city expands eastward, more confusing addresses come. At least in the city if you get yourself in the right quadrant, finding an address is simple; it's not in the new suburban subdivisions, where some cretin decided every street should have the same name – except for street, avenue, close, circle, crescent, and a host of other "imaginative" designations. Try, I dare you, even with the aid of a city map, to find an address in the suburbs. To make it more fun, you'll have to search without much help from street signs. Apparently, there isn't enough money in the budget to actually light them up – when there are any signs at all. Why, I often muse, do cities never hire a couple of strangers to find their way around what we call home, and then make their suggested changes to the signage?

Edmonton also has a quadrant system, although you'd be hard-pressed to find a majority of citizens who know so and even fewer who realize it has been in place for the past twenty years, necessitated by an oops! factor. When Edmonton (which was founded in 1795 as a Hudson's Bay trading post and a century later became a town, and in 1905, a city and the provincial capital) got around to the business of street designations, it went for what the city fathers thought was practicality. Unlike Calgary, which gave names to its earliest streets (still confusing visitors in Mount Royal who can't know except through maps that Dorchester intersects with Carlton, and Vercheres connects Premier Way to Council Way), Edmonton chose numbers. Who would have thought in 1914, when the city elected to go with a numbered street and avenue system, that giving the centre of the city the designation of 101 Street and 101 Avenue, the latter retaining its name of Jasper Avenue, would be a recipe for planning disaster.

By the 1980s Edmonton was down to single-digit designations, and was running out of descending numbers to the east and south. The city adopted a quadrant system to eliminate having to descend into the minus numbers. The not-yet-built 1 Avenue (Quadrant Avenue) and 1 Street (Meridian Street) divide the city into an urban oxymoron – a quadrant system with only three parts. (There is no city to the southeast.)

Edmonton also differs from Calgary in less amusing ways. Take the attitude to security, for example. Even prior to 9/11, security in Calgary was, let's say, more American in flavour than it was in Edmonton. This is a description of attitude, not a criticism. It can be loosely characterized as the difference between the British presumption that most people will act decently (Edmonton) and the American one that most people won't (Calgary). The former attitude presumes a society doesn't need a whole list of laws to stop illegal behaviour, the latter presumes that, unless a law is specifically written for the occasion, anything goes.

Consider two events held on the same weekend in 2000, one in Edmonton, one in Calgary. While the two "conventions" aren't mirror images, either in the importance of the delegates or the possibility of trouble, they bear looking at. And it's likely that the delegates to the Jesus 2000 Festival in Edmonton thought their mission, message, and attendees just as important as did the three thousand delegates attending the World Petroleum Congress. In Edmonton, they gathered in the hundreds – cheering and chanting – in Churchill Square, adjacent to City Hall. There wasn't a barricade, truncheon, or black-visored riot helmet in sight. Meanwhile, three hundred kilometres to the south, Calgary was closed up tight. We were showing the world how tough we were.

Calgary barricaded its streets. Calgarians had to produce photo identification to get to work behind the barriers. Officials closed an LRT station and removed post boxes to stop bombs from being mailed. Maybe the worst part wasn't the lockdown, but the lack of protest on the part of Calgarians. As we have discovered post-9/11, whipped-up fear will silence even the most vocal of citizens. And Calgary officials looked back to the disruption, rioting, and violence on the streets of Seattle during the World Trade Organization meeting in November 1999 and took that to mean Calgary would face the same mobs. That there was no indication of impending riots, indeed there was a promise of only peaceful protests on the part of the usual suspects, made little difference.

We locked down a city that every year controls drunken yahoos on its downtown streets, day and night, for the ten days of the Calgary Stampede. About a million people pass through the gates of the Stampede grounds each July. But, apparently, a city that can handle such revelry could not handle three thousand people in suits on the inside of its downtown hotels and convention centre and a few fists waved by protesters outside. So, we locked down a city that welcomed, without incident, thousands of people for the sixteen-day Winter Olympics, including a few crowned heads of state and heirs to monarchies. This despite the very real spectre of terrorism and mass murder at the 1972 Olympics in Munich.

Security at such events is tight, but not obtrusive. The steel-mesh barricades and riot police that cordoned off downtown Calgary were anything but. In his opening address to the congress, Alberta premier Ralph Klein talked about Calgary's hospitality and friendliness. I'm certain no irony was intended.

My criticism is not aimed at the police, who did a wonderful job when asked. It is aimed directly at the civic officials who undertook this overreaction and the citizens who didn't complain.

We were praised for our peaceful city. It would have meant more if officials hadn't presumed we were ready to run riot and vandalize stores and businesses.

Calgary and Edmonton will continue to compare and contrast just about everything, including the size of their municipal egos. Edmonton has the West Edmonton Mall; Calgary has the Stampede. Edmonton calls itself the City of Champions; Calgary tells everyone it's the city of winners and that Calgarians know the difference.

Edmonton has been cashing in on the glory years of hockey's Edmonton Oilers and the prior glories of football's Edmonton Eskimos (named before the advent of political correctness) for so long that the city's motto – City of Champions – has been seriously questioned only in the past few years, out of a sense of embarrassment.

Former Calgary mayor Al Duerr (the only municipal politician to record a plurality better than Ralph Klein's) forever named Edmonton the City of Mushrooms. Champignons. Champions. Guess you had to be there with a passing knowledge of Canada's other language to appreciate the joke. Maybe you had to actually be at Duerr's speech to appreciate how unusual it was for Calgary's mayor to get a spontaneous laugh at any of his presentations. There was nothing wrong with Al Duerr's sense of humour, it just didn't translate well in public. He was branded a "serious" man and that sobriquet lived with him. He simply couldn't match the folksy personality of Ralph Klein when he was mayor of Calgary.

Edmonton's mayors have never had quite the panache of Calgary's, with the possible exception of William Hawrelak who, like Don Mackay in Calgary, let a 'colourful' political life get cut short by questionable dealings. Between 1949, when he was first elected alderman, and his death in office in 1975, Hawrelak was Edmonton's mayor three times, resigning twice in the face of inquiries into what were called suspicious land sales. As for Mackay, the man who instigated Calgary's White Hat ceremony, who put the party in Grey Cup weekend, left office in disgrace after "borrowing" bags of cement from the city and never quite getting around to paying for them. It is still bizarre that such popular mayors – Mackay was the Ralph Klein of his time – could sully their names with such minor chicanery.

Every so often, some serious-faced mayor of one or the other city pretends there is no rivalry. Nobody believes them. Why kill the fun? What we do believe is that most of the jibing that goes on between the cities is friendly. It didn't start that way.

Edmonton became the capital city of Alberta in 1905, along with the creation of the province. It was awarded the University of Alberta, much to Calgary's chagrin. This was achieved through a bit of trickery by the first provincial premier, Alexander Rutherford. He mollified Calgarians who complained that for Edmonton to get both the designation as the capital and the university would be unfair by agreeing the university would be located south of Edmonton. How far south? Just spitting distance, as it turns out – in Strathcona, on the other side of the North Saskatchewan River. By the time I attended the U of A in the early 1960s, Strathcona had long been subsumed into the city of Edmonton; in fact, it was practically downtown.

Calgary did eventually get its own university – it started petitioning the legislature in 1910 – but it took many long years. Calgary wasn't appeased by a provincial act creating Calgary College, especially since the newly created institution was not given degree-granting status. The college idea was abandoned during the First World War and a technical college for the training of servicemen was started after the war. What was to become the Southern Alberta Institute of Technology didn't get its own buildings until 1923. Talks that lead to the establishment of a "branch" of the University of Alberta in Calgary weren't held until the Second World War. Eventually, the University of Calgary began life in 1945 as the University of Alberta at Calgary and spent the next twenty-one years as a bridesmaid before becoming autonomous in 1966. It still rankles in Calgary's academic world that the U of A is considered the more mature and serious of the schools.

Edmonton became my home in 1955 when my father, a provincial court reporter, was transferred there. I left Edmonton to work in Calgary, after junior high, high school, and university, less than ten years later. Another transfer saw my family move to Red Deer in 1962, after my first year at the University of Alberta, forever allowing me to say I never left home – home left me.

I left Edmonton right after school, not because I didn't like the city, but because of geography and my father's overwhelming love of Calgary to the exclusion of any other city. The geography part was easy: I figured in order to get anywhere else in civilization, one first had to get to Calgary. So I moved.

The north still remains mostly a mystery to me. But there's no mystery to why my immediate impression of Edmonton wasn't favourable. I was only ten years old, but first impressions, regardless of age, are lasting. I had a sour taste in my mouth from the first day of a new grade in a new school in a new city.

A privileged student in Calgary, in Edmonton I entered the nightmare of being bullied. It was a complete turnaround to be the bullied instead of the bully. And if anyone ever challenges how I presume to write with more than arm's-length knowledge about the state of bullying in schools, regardless of my never having had a child in school, I merely point to personal experience on both sides of the divide.

I wasn't bullied by the other students, who having all been together since kindergarten did what all other closed groups do – ignored me – but by the teacher. I was her pet bully project, and there was no escape. Neither charm (which all ten-year-olds know about from years of wheedling things out of parents) nor submission made any difference. Nothing did. It did teach me one valuable life lesson: that anyone can be bully or bullied; all that normal, ordinary kids – and thus adults when they grew up – need is the opportunity and a victim.

For whatever reason, and it will remain merely conjecture, St. Paul's Elementary School in north Calgary had handed me off to the ministrations of the Edmonton Separate School Board with a glowing report card and an advance from the first half of Grade 5 to the second half of Grade 6. Perhaps I foolishly believed I deserved it.

The Ursuline nun in charge of the Grade 5/6 split at my new school (whose name, for the life of me, I cannot remember – nor can I remember the name of the school) believed otherwise. She made it her personal mission to disabuse me of the cocky self-esteem and self-confidence I had managed to engineer through five years of school, and she was aided, unwittingly, by a classroom of children. I was the outsider, and she and they were determined to bring me to heel, academically and socially.

I had, of course, missed a half year of Grade 6 school work which I was expected to catch up on while keeping up with the rest of the class. I could have learned what I missed. Instead, what I learned was the power of the bully, especially a bully with power. A student I could have handled. The teacher was beyond me. And so, every day, the kid who had loved school and the teaching sisters in their long black habits in almost equal parts grew to hate and fear both.

I was stupid and lazy and backward, according to the teacher, and I would never pass Grade 6 if she had anything to do about it.

My rescuer was my mother who didn't need a psychology degree to figure out that a big, strong child – one of hers – arriving home from a new school in tears every day might have something to cry about. What was surprising in an age when parents automatically blamed their children for problems at school, siding with the teacher if problems arose, was my parents' belief that I was not making things up.

I was too young to know the machinations necessary to have me transferred into another school's jurisdiction. I just remember sitting for what seemed like hours on the lawn outside the Edmonton Separate School Board offices, having summarily been taken out of class. The next day I was attending another school from which I was sent happily onward to junior high, at which I re-encountered all those stolid faces I had left months before.

I've told this tale of schoolroom angst only to point out that my nose for bullies – of the management or political variety – is not only born out of my long years as a journalist, but of even longer years of living. At the beginning of every school year, when the issue of bullying is reprised in the press, I remember. Each year there is hand-wringing and calls for zero tolerance. That's what we want in our schools. Too bad, that's not what we promote in our lives.

In the real world, bullies are often the winners. They are the so-called tough bosses who have pushed their way to the top over the heads of their weaker and less aggressive colleagues. They are an archetype. They are the bulldogs, the pit bulls, the take-charge guys. They are the Donald Trumps of our lives. We've all worked for bullies. They are the most emotionally draining of bosses, sometimes physically threatening, and always intensely disliked by the people they treat so shabbily. To a man (although they are not always men) they are stunned to discover they are loathed by their staff, albeit they are rarely told that to their faces. Bullies don't take kindly to being told the truth, either about their management style or their personalities. Worse, for any business, they set up such a climate of fear they often don't know when the business is going seriously wrong, because nobody wants to be the bearer of bad tidings.

In the business world, bullies are rewarded. They are lionized. They are imitated and toadied to. Too often, the men and women who report to them adopt the same attitudes toward their staffs, and so it goes down the line until you have a toxic work environment. Little wonder schools are incapable of routing bullies; the world around them can't and won't.

Bullying is tough to stamp out because we secretly admire it. We don't say so, but we act so.

Maybe the biggest surprise to a fully fetched grown-up is the level of bullying in teenage movies and music videos. Presumably to teens, the dialogue and sexism, the objectification of people, but especially women, is hip, cool, and with-it. To adults, it's just plain mean, cruel, and wrong. As for the sexism, young girls today seem to believe it's empowering. It is just bullying by another name. If this is what passes for entertainment, little wonder the real school corridors are so scary for kids.

And bullies can smell scared, just as animals can smell fear. As a species, we dislike weaklings, we regard them as burdens. Were we a less evolved species, we'd let the weak and whimpering be eliminated by whatever natural predators abound.

Yes, I have passionate opinions about the two faces of bullying. And they come from a deeper well than my forty-year career.

That career started when I moved back to Calgary. I didn't even consider staying in Edmonton.

Twenty years later, in 1985, writer Ron Marken would put all the reasons why I moved in his lighthearted and funny take on Edmonton vs. Calgary, *The Easterners' Guide to Western Canada*. (The book came in two halves. Turned upside down, the other half of the book was *The Westerners' Guide to Eastern Canada*, edited by Don Gillmor.)

"The world loves Calgary and hates Edmonton," wrote Marken. Actually, that isn't true. The shopping mavens of the world love Edmonton and the West Edmonton Mall. Unless you have experienced the size of this sucker, you may think it's just like any other shopping mall. It ain't. It is enormous. It is scary. It has maps to help the uninitiated get around. Anyone with mild claustrophobia and a habit of losing her car in a parking lot needs to stay away. The attraction of the mall isn't the shopping, it's the idea that a full-sized NHL rink, a water park with a giant replica of the Santa Maria, and a complete hotel are included. It's an attraction in and of itself, and unless the owners are hiding the interesting stores in some corner I failed to traverse, what's for sale is the same stuff that's available in other, smaller malls. So, go to say you've been there. But make sure you have the kind of car, as I do, that will honk its horn and flash its headlights when you lose it.

The rest of us prefer Calgary.

"What irritated Edmonton the most," wrote Marken, "was that it had the legislature, was the capital city and was home to the provincial university. Still, no one beyond Wainwright had heard of it. Meanwhile, Calgary was famous as far as Fort Worth. Even Montrealers knew of its existence; they thought men wearing high heels and big white hats were chic.

"Edmonton writhed again. So it bought fifty-five young Americans, called them 'Eskimos' and used them to beat up on the rest of Canada all through the '50s." (There are no real Eskimos in Edmonton, of course, but the name suggested it was cold as hell in Edmonton and, therefore, that Edmontonians were really tough.)

Actually, the word *eskimo* is only ever used by Americans and in reference to Edmonton's football team. In polite company, the word has the same squirm effect as referring to Squaw Valley. Yet no move has been made to change the team's name, unlike the successful campaign to change a mountain in Canmore from Chinaman's Peak to Ha Ling Peak.

Continues Marken: "Although Calgary didn't really want to, it also bought fifty-five young Americans with some petty cash. . . . They were called the 'Stampeders,' naturally. They proceeded to lose all their games – with style. Everybody still loved Calgary.

"Desperate by now, Edmonton went all the way. It tried to rival the Calgary Stampede with a forced extravaganza called Klondike Days. The real Klondike, in the Yukon, thought it was pretty ridiculous and Calgary ignored it completely. It was too busy putting on the one show that every man, woman and child on earth wants to see: the Calgary Stampede. . . .

"Edmonton got so angry it bought fifteen Quebecers, ten Saskatchewanians, and a gawky kid from Ontario . . . I've got you at last! I have an NHL team and they are going ta kick the ass of everyone on this continent. . . . Calgary, puzzled by this challenge, absent-mindedly bought an entire NHL team from Atlanta, Georgia (famous for its hockey players) and continues a losing sports tradition."

Almost: the Calgary Flames won the Stanley Cup (in Montreal) in 1989, and the Calgary Stampeders won the Grey Cup in 1948, 1971, and 1992 and hosted the party the following year. Unfortunately, the Stampeders weren't there in 1993 – having been beaten in the semi-finals.

The Edmonton Oilers – that "gawky kid from Ontario" was Wayne Gretzky – won five Stanley Cups in the six years from 1984 to 1990. And the now-retired Gretzky still holds the NHL record for most goals, most assists, most points, and most points as a centre in a single season. In fact, Gretzky is still the greatest hockey player ever to lace on skates, and I remember Bobby Orr. The sad reality about sports is in the "what-ifs," where brilliant athletes like Orr reside. What if Orr's knees hadn't given out? There were no what-ifs in Gretzky's career. He just did his best for the length of his time on ice. And he continues to do so. It was Gretzky who put together the 2002 Winter Olympics gold medal Team Canada, enduring the scorn of those who thought too many of his choices were too old to face the young bucks. Gretzky and team captain Mario Lemieux proved the critics wrong.

But while Gretzky was with the Oilers, the team was merely following in the tradition of the Edmonton Eskimos, who dominated Canadian football for what seemed like the better part of the 1950s. The names on those teams live in Canada sports history: Jackie Parker, Normie Kwong, a.k.a. the China Clipper, Johnny Bright, and Rollie Miles, together dubbed the Four Horsemen by sportswriters, although my husband insists he has never heard of the moniker. Of course, as a Calgarian he'd prefer never to have heard of any of the wildly successful Edmonton sports franchises.

Calgary almost got its sweet revenge in the spring of 2004 when the hapless Flames, having not managed to get anywhere near the playoffs for seven years, took the city – and the country – on a ride through the Stanley Cup championships. Calgary didn't win (who cares who did?) but you'd never know it from the hooting and hollering, drinking and cheering that went on in the city. Sometimes losing a championship matters less than how you play for it.

The first flush of the City of Champions – although Edmonton won its first Alberta Rugby Football Championship in 1895 – happened to overlap with my six years there. When the club flagged late in the '50s, Jackie Parker kept us feeling like winners, picking up three consecutive Schenley awards. That winning feeling really began in 1954 when Parker recovered a Montreal fumble and took the ball ninety-five yards to a touchdown, a Grey Cup tie that was subsequently converted for the win and became a Canadian football legend. The feeling for me lasted through three consecutive

Grey Cup victories until my move back to Calgary and my switch in allegiance to the Calgary Stampeders. (So much for girls not being sports fans. I still remember the stunned look on the face of the sports editor in Calgary when, without looking, I correctly spelled the name of Tony Pajackzkowski.)

My interest in sports comes directly from a relatively unknown member of those winning teams – Gino Fracas. He was the football coach at St. Mary's High School in Edmonton the year we met Victoria Composite in the city high-school final. We lost the sudden-death playoff game 21-7. But that's not the lesson of the story.

Vic Comp was the city's biggest, most bloated, and most arrogant high school, with more than one thousand teenagers crammed into a sprawling white stone edifice on the north side of Edmonton. It even had a swimming pool. St. Mary's was the smallest school in the city, a two-storey brick building in the industrial south side that had, maybe, four hundred students and if memory serves me correctly that included a couple of junior high grades. We were lucky to have a gymnasium, let alone a football squad. But have one we did. Actually, there were two teams, junior and senior, and the roster consisted of every able-bodied teenage boy in the school, irrespective of size, ability, or interest.

If this was a Hollywood movie, it would be *That Championship Season* and would be filled with lessons about how size doesn't matter, about how sports is all about heart. But Edmonton is a long way from Los Angeles, and there wasn't, on that bitterly cold Friday night at Clarke Stadium, a championship at the end of the game. We were quite simply outmanned. Vic Composite's Redmen were able to field an inexhaustible supply of large hulks without necks. They handed St. Mary's its second defeat of the year. It isn't that final, losing game I remember, but the spirit of community and the effort expended by everyone in the school. What we lacked in size we made up for in sheer spirit and lung power.

If that small community of kids from disparate backgrounds who were thrown together in the school only by virtue of our shared religion and the fact there were only two Catholic high schools in

Edmonton, one on either side of the North Saskatchewan River, well, if we had a football hero beyond the obvious one – Jackie Parker – it was the coach. Gino Fracas.

He played for Edmonton for eight years, from 1955 to 1962, and he was the first football player I ever met when he came one autumn afternoon of 1956 to visit Mount Carmel Junior High. He was mobbed by screaming kids in the hallway. I was one of them.

When he coached our football team he gave Edmonton's smallest high school its most exciting season and instilled in all of us a sense of community and a fervour for the game that transcended interest and ability. His lessons to his players were focused on spirit, intense desire, the will to win, and grim determination. All in all, not bad lessons for just about everything.

Fracas's counterpart at the other Catholic high school, St. Joseph's, was the late Bernie Faloney. Faloney, too, played for the Eskimos. He was the quarterback who got Edmonton to the Grey Cup where Jackie Parker returned a fumble for the win. Faloney volunteered to coach the St. Joe's senior team, and when St. Joe's completed the season without a loss, they travelled to Calgary to compete in the provincial championship. Like St. Mary's, in the final game, they lost. The students still believe had the Eskimos given Faloney permission to go to Calgary with "his" team, they would have won.

When the Eskimos returned to Edmonton after that Grey Cup win, instead of Bernie Faloney being there to receive the adulation of the crowd, the entire St. Joseph's football team, says one of its members, "proudly carried the banner with Bernie's name on it."

I am sure there are still lots of sports figures who are role models to young people. Somewhere, in the world of multi-million-dollar salaries and bonuses and adulation, there are still the men – and women – who willingly and without recompense deliver back to their communities. I just can't find them in modern sport amid the welter of egos and Corvettes and money. I just can't find them in the cult of celebrity.

I should be able to find them in politics. But, in Alberta, you don't find many in the Edmonton legislature. You find them in business. Men like Jim Gray, who fought a losing battle against video lottery terminals for no other reason than he believed them wrong. Like Sheldon Chumir, the late Liberal MLA, taken by cancer at too young an age. Chumir went into politics to protect the public school system and stayed to be a voice of reason in an unreasonable and fractious legislature. His legacy to Canada is a foundation devoted to ethics in leadership. Women like former New Democrat leader Pam Barrett, possibly the only woman in politics, especially on the "socialist" side of the legislature, who earned the public admiration of the Tory premier. Like Gray and Chumir, Barrett was a fighter. There are hundreds of such people in Alberta, people who are visionaries. These are the people who have propelled this province into prosperity, even if few remember their names.

Call them role models or heroes or visionaries, they occupy a place of pride that even the highest-paid celebrity only gets to visit. Many are unknown outside their field. But they all share a common value – daring. They dared to do things differently. In Alberta, we celebrate the panache of the mountain climber and the audacity of the skier. (It isn't coincidental that the Crazy Canucks came from the high mountains of Alberta, and that both the first Canadian man and first Canadian woman to climb Mount Everest were Albertans: Laurie Skreslet from Calgary and Sharon Wood from Canmore.)

We're even the kind of people who believe that the mere fact of being landlocked is no bar to becoming a sailor. Conventional wisdom is that Westerners make better sailors than other landlubbers. Boys from Saskatchewan are considered the best of all, as growing up in a province where nothing obscures the line of the horizon trains them well for the equally wide expanse of the ocean.

It took a visionary Calgary lawyer to challenge the real sailors at their own game.

Marvin McDill, who died too young in 1988, decided that not having large lakes or oceans was no barrier to challenging for the

America's Cup, the world's premier yacht race. And he had us believing we could win it. That's the kind of vision Albertans celebrate. We didn't win, but the enthusiasm of McDill and his backers is just one example of the values Albertans bring to their lives and their hobbies.

Winning isn't the Canadian way, as years of pathetic Olympic performances, spiked by the rare gold medal that has us giddy with glee, have shown. Canada is the perpetual best friend, the selfless guy who gives his all for his friends and his family and is happy to be second-best. Not that this is necessarily bad, but it would be heartening to, just once in a while, bring to our endeavours the kind of determination and self-confidence that characterizes Americans. Marv McDill was just such a guy.

Yachting – particularly the twelve-metre variety – is a rich man's sport, regardless of what its supporters want us to believe. Poor men and women don't own yachts. And the richest of the rich – those habitués of Newport, Rhode Island – considered the America's Cup their property, so much so that the ugly silver cup was bolted to the floor of the New York Yacht Club, where it had resided since 1851. That was until the Australians successfully challenged the wealthy clique in Newport in 1983 and unbolted the cup from the floor to take it to Perth.

Canada had rarely considered entering the race, even though yachting and races are a fixture of places such as Toronto and Kingston, where the Great Lakes offer the water, the wind, and the opportunity.

Until McDill launched Canada 1's challenge in 1980, the last Canadian entry had been in 1881. That was the second and last time that Toronto's Royal Canadian Yacht Club entered the race. It fared dismally both times – so much so that fresh-water yacht clubs subsequently were banned from the race. So, in 1986, when someone from the dryland prairies put together a syndicate to try again, there were a lot of noses out of joint in Toronto.

"We can go out and beat the world," McDill told me at a fundraising cocktail party. Then he added: "By three minutes." The time it takes to soft-boil an egg was the Calgary lawyer's prediction. How good was his pitch? I believed him. McDill's attitude was that the America's Cup wasn't about sailing, it was about winning.

Of course, it's also about money. Had the syndicate not lost its prime mover, suddenly, a couple of years later, perhaps Canada would have managed to drag itself out of its bridesmaid's mentality and come to believe we're as good as the rest of the world. That's essentially what always rankled McDill: not the lack of money, but the lack of positive thinking and the national inferiority complex. You don't win races of any variety by thinking in maybes and keeping your fingers crossed for luck.

If Canadians as a nation don't want to take chances and are the kind of people who wear both a belt and suspenders, we are not like that as individuals. We have heroes by the score, including ones ordinary people rarely hear about, men like Edmontonian Lawrence Lemieux, a Canadian sailor who had piloted his Finn-class boat to second place in the Seoul Olympics. He had a medal in his view, but he saw another boat in trouble – his competitor from Singapore had been swept overboard. Without hesitating, Lemieux left the course and rescued the sailor. "There was never any decision to make," Lemieux commented to the press afterward. He did what he had to do.

In the words of another staunch Canadian, the Calgary liaison for the Council of Canadians, Michelle Stanners, the sign of a Canadian is that "we show up." Regardless of the challenge, we show up.

All of Canada may not know Lemieux's name, but the entire sailing community in Canada, if not worldwide, knows what Lemieux sacrificed to rescue a rival. Lemieux was in second place in the competition when he chose to rescue the downed sailor, rather than continue the race. The International Olympic Committee awarded Lemieux a medal for heroism.

In some ways the very concept of hero seems to conflict with traditional views of what it means to be Canadian. Marshall McLuhan described us as "the people who learned to live without the bold accents of the national ego-trippers of other lands." Even though our history is full of great acts and great people, Northrop Frye contended that we are "a country which has manifested a great deal of courage but has never responded with much warmth to charismatic leadership." Well, maybe we did once, to Pierre Trudeau.

While, as a nation, we have been notoriously reluctant to elevate ordinary individuals to the realm of myth and heroism, our literary and cultural artifacts reveal a rich tapestry of historical and fictional figures who have at some time captured the public imagination, and who reflect the dynamism and diversity of the Canadian mosaic in general, and Alberta in particular.

9

The City That's Always Halfway

Red Deer is a city in which I have always been a visitor, even though it was my parents' home until my father died in 1974 and my mother's for years after, until she moved out to Sylvan Lake. I had already completed one year of university when Father was transferred, so while my parents and younger sister and brother became part of the community, I remained only an occasional visitor. I did, though, spend one summer living at home and selling shoes in a store on Red Deer's main street, an occupation that forever embedded in my soul a lust for shoes and taught me two valuable lessons: you can tell a great deal about a person's character from the way he or she deals with sales clerks, and unless you want to spend your life being treated summarily by bullies, get an education.

There was also an unintentional third lesson: beware of snoops and gossips. My family had lived in Red Deer for just less than a year when I came home from university to sell shoes. Because my father worked downtown, I would ride to work with him in the morning and, likely as not, meet him for coffee breaks at the restaurant midway between us. It took barely two weeks for one of the small city's more prominent Nosy Parkers to telephone my mother to report, although it pained her to do so, she said, that Mr. Ford had been seen regularly with a young blonde downtown. "I thought you should know," said the gossip. Mother, knowing just how to handle such "consideration," did not explain the blonde was her oldest child, she merely thanked the caller for telling her and hung up.

Red Deer had about thirty thousand people when my parents moved there and built a new house on Stanley Crescent, within walking distance of downtown and just as close to the edge of the city. Over the past forty years, the population has almost doubled. The whole of the population of central Alberta has boomed, from the older generation looking to retire to the "lake district" – Sylvan, Pine, or Gull – to employees of the Joffre petro-chemical plant.

But Red Deer remains a kind of halfway station, in the shadow of the two main cities that are connected by the four-lane Highway 2. From the time my father was a child and a trip from Calgary to Sylvan Lake (just west of Red Deer on Highway 11) took five hours and four flat tires, to today, when getting to Sylvan Lake takes no more than an hour and a half, even if the highway is crowded, Red Deer has always been just a pit stop on the way to either Calgary or Edmonton. Before the highway bypassed the city itself, stopping for gas and an obligatory piece of fifteen-centimetre-high flapper pie at the Peacock Inn downtown was part of the driving experience.

To the people who live there, Red Deer is the ideal small city in which to raise a family. Its citizens have the best of both worlds – whatever Edmonton or Calgary offers is available equally to people who live in Red Deer. Both international airports are equally accessible, Calgary's being on the north side of that city and Edmonton's being a thirty-minute drive south of the capital. But, even as it grows and expands, Red Deer still lives in the shadows of its larger neighbours, offering the young and single little to do but drink and dance. At least in the summer, the lakes are only a half-hour drive away.

I have a soft spot in my heart for Red Deer and the key is held by two very different men. My only blind date, arranged by a neighbour when my parents moved to the city, was an Air Canada captain. I was seventeen; he was twenty-three and an air force instructor at Penhold, the air base just southwest of Red Deer. He was everything all those old war movies had led me to believe pilots should be –

handsome (of the blond and blue-eyed variety), fit, smart, and funny. The smile that broke out on his face when I opened the door to his knock that first date did more than anything or anyone else in any situation to bolster a chunky teenage girl's hope that she was attractive. (Smart and mouthy was fine, but good-looking – then as now – was more important.) To this day, I owe him a debt of gratitude.

My life is no movie, so the instant attraction did not translate into a long-standing relationship – other than as friends. He was transferred, as members of the Canadian forces often are, to overseas duty.

And then, for one glorious summer, there was the tall, dark, and manly agriculture student who worked for the city. He was everything that Red Deer and rural Alberta stood for, despite his university education. He personified the idea of a rugged, rural city: the pickup-truck, blue-jean-and-workboots capital of the province. I sold shoes, he sprayed the weeds along the road allowances, and we spent the summer driving back and forth to Sylvan Lake. To this day, the smell of weed killer, which seemed to have permeated his clothes and his skin, can still cause a sweat to break out on my upper lip.

Red Deer today has a large and thriving post-secondary college and probably more churches per capita than any other city anywhere. The overwhelmingly Christian make-up of Red Deer and district contrasts with Alberta's more secular major cities and makes it more like some southern U.S. Bible belt town.

Red Deer is the home of the first commission accepted by the celebrated Canadian architect Douglas Cardinal, whose Museum of Civilization in Ottawa is one of the premier architectural expressions of the Canadian landscape, with its undulating facade of stone that seems to flow into the land and the sky simultaneously. Before that commission, before he was a national name, he was a young architect who convinced a Roman Catholic parish in south Red Deer to accept his vision of adoration in built form. That vision came in the shape of St. Mary's Church, an edifice like no other and as different from the existing Catholic church, Sacred Heart, as Holt Renfrew is from Wal-Mart.

The existing parish church was as traditional as they get – peaked, spired, ornate, and designed for an era when churches were meant to inspire awe and reverence in the parishioners. It emphasized the notion, as old as the Church itself, that church-goers are supplicants in a ritual that is done to them. When Pope John XXIII and Vatican II shook up the relationship between church and faithful in the 1960s, it lead to a new concept of worship: that the people had a vital role to play in their faith and in the churches designed for their celebrations.

St. Mary's in Red Deer was one of the first designed on that philosophy, and a thing of awe and beauty it was. The congregation, who had been attending church functions, including Sunday mass, in a school auditorium, was led by Rev. Werner Merx, a parish priest of vision and ruggedness, who convinced skeptical parishioners to commit to a kind of church nobody had seen before. Parishioners who remember the negotiations to build a new church on Red Deer's south side, and the four years of construction before it opened in 1968, still shake their heads. "All this beauty," said one, "but you couldn't do anything in the church. It wasn't functional."

First, there was the vision. In *The Architecture of Douglas Cardinal*, author Trevor Boddy writes about the happy combination of an artist with a vision and a priest with faith. Between Cardinal and Father Merx, there was a synchronicity of spirit and expression. Between the two of them, they convinced the diocese of Edmonton and the parishioners to spend the outrageous sum of $350,000 on a new church.

It would be not just new, but a church that was innovative. It would have an irregular poured concrete roof; walls that would curve around the congregation in an embrace; an altar made out of a single, five-ton block of Manitoba tyndall stone; and light streaming onto the altar from a cannon-style skylight. But "the skylight leaked from Day One," wrote Boddy, "which Merx merrily accepted as a demonstration of the building's flawed and mortal humanity."

Worse, there was no place to meet, no church basement and kitchen, no room for any of the minutiae of parish life that happens in a church building. There was just this awesome beauty, a structure that soared with the spirit of God but couldn't put on a parish dinner.

At times the physical limitations didn't matter. The church in which my sister and brother were married, the church of my father's funeral, has a spirituality unmatched in other buildings. But spirituality proved not nearly enough. By 1995, parishioners, who had spent more than $1 million over the years on repairs, decided their architectural miracle was no longer a work of art to be preserved. They wanted a living church that could serve a growing, changing parish. An addition to the east side of the building would be built.

Douglas Cardinal believed destroying the integrity of his first – and, some say, archetypal – public building would be like painting a moustache on the Mona Lisa. St. Mary's Church "laid the foundation for my self-expression as an architect," he said. He had designed the church to be "a prayer to our Creator and [it] shows the best of our human endeavours." Twice he appealed to the courts to stop what he saw as a desecration of his work and his spirit; twice he failed.

Still, parishioners tried to enlist Cardinal to design the addition. His price was too high and after protracted negotiations, he was excluded from bidding on the addition. Duane Pickle, the chair of the parish council, told the local newspaper, the *Red Deer Advocate*, "We still believe some of the problems we have had to date arose because of the original design of the church."

In the end, it was Cardinal's own words from 1985 that opened the door to the Philistines: "As soon as you finish the building and turn it over, it's up to them to do with it whatever they wish." Even if it is painting a moustache on Mona.

Until you have stood in the centre of a Cardinal building, felt the life in the stone and the design, felt bigger and stronger as a human spirit because of the beauty and inspiration of your surroundings, it's almost impossible to explain why anyone would be so passionate about a building. What the Museum of Civilization accomplishes on a grand and sweeping scale, St. Mary's achieved within a small space. I haven't had the courage to look at the church since the addition was completed, just in case that spirit has been squashed flat.

Since my mother moved to Edmonton a number of years ago, there hasn't been any reason for me to stop in Red Deer to visit St. Mary's.

Today, now the highway bypasses the city and a jumbled and unattractive strip of service stations and fast-food restaurants has grown up on either side of the highway, few travellers actually venture into Red Deer. I haven't stopped there for longer than it takes to give a speech (it's a logical convention centre for companies with offices in both Edmonton and Calgary) for at least ten years. I went back just the once to see if I felt any emotional attachment to the city. I don't. My mistake was to go back when the entire province was in the middle of a recession. Red Deer depends on good harvests to give the farmers money to spend in the stores, on vehicles, and other large purchases. It has no real business or industrial base except that of servicing farms and riggers and other oil-industry offshoots, and it was hit hard by the recession of the mid-1980s.

I went back to the family house my parents built in 1962 to find it unloved and uncared for. Perhaps it was best there was no one home when I knocked on the door. Who knows what I would have said to the owners? The front steps had listed and the ugly green indoor-outdoor carpeting that had been installed to cover the cracking concrete was itself ripped and water-damaged. The front door was scratched and marked, and through the wide front window I could see the reason – a drooling, tail-wagging English sheepdog was scrabbling its front paws against the window where, on the outside, the paint was peeling off the shutters and windowsills. The back fence that took an entire summer to paint was broken, the gate hanging drunkenly off its hinges. The trees my mother transplanted from the road allowance near Lacombe, each one carefully uprooted and carried back to Red Deer, were in desperate need of pruning.

That was the only time I smiled, as I looked up and down the crescent at the canopy of trees. My mother and her friends (and commandeered children) decided to "steal" trees the spring after the house was built and landscape the entire six-house crescent. Mother would scan the *Red Deer Advocate* for public works notices of road widening. Because the trees on the road allowance would have to be removed, she didn't think it was stealing if she and her band of helpers got there before the road crews and rescued the smaller trees.

Like most prairie settlements and the people who fight for them, Red Deer came back from the recession even stronger and more determined. When your good times depend on something as impermanent as the price of natural resources, when the quirks of the weather can mean the difference between a bumper crop and an agricultural disaster, when the third leg of the economic tripod is the fickle tourist dollar – you accept setbacks with equanimity. At least true Albertans do. It isn't as if we haven't been through this before.

In the thirties, the Depression coincided with drought and savage winds to turn the prairies into a dust bowl. We fought back. In 1932, an Ontario-born Calgary high-school principal who was also head of his own Prophetic Bible Institute became convinced that a new economic order was needed. William Aberhart's doctrine of Social Credit took hold of the province in 1935 and didn't let go until 1972. (In central Alberta it wouldn't let go at all, and it is no surprise that the biggest support for the erstwhile Reform Party came from these farming and rural communities.)

There was a downturn in the early seventies as well, when the bottom seemed to drop out of the oil exploration market. Engineers and geologists who had spent twenty years with one company suddenly found themselves out of a job. Albertans hunkered down and went headfirst into the storm with the stolidity of farmers facing a prairie blizzard when the cows have to be milked.

People who have seen snow cover the peonies in June, who have sat on their front lawn in shirtsleeves on New Year's Day (I have a picture as proof), and who have watched a relentless August hail beat the heavy heads of wheat and barley into the ground are not going to be deterred by a flattening of a boom. It's just another cyclical swing. After all, this is Next Year Country. We're not only resilient, we're optimistic.

In the summer of 1999, that optimism failed in the face of nature's awesome power. Up to that sunny day in mid-July, the only natural disasters in Alberta that would come easily to mind would be the Frank rock slide more than one hundred years ago, when half of Turtle Mountain crashed down and buried the town of Frank in the Crowsnest Pass, and the tornado in 1987 that touched down in Edmonton and killed twenty-seven people.

But in July 1999, a tornado ripped through a popular campground at Pine Lake, laying a swath of destruction through tents, campers, and recreational vehicles. Twelve people were killed; a thirteenth died later. In the aftermath of a minute's fury, two human traits came to the fore: the need to help and the need to communicate.

My nieces were visiting with their maternal grandparents in their cabin on another part of Pine Lake. Thankfully, they had the presence of mind to telephone just after the news broke, to reassure us they were unharmed.

For families of the dead, for the injured and traumatized, it will be years – if ever – before they can look at a lowering sky and rolling black clouds without memories rushing back.

No one who has never been caught by the fury of weather, by its power, can ever quite comprehend what swirling winds are capable of doing. According to Environment Canada, damage assessment at Pine Lake suggests a five-hundred-metre-wide central corridor in which winds reached three hundred kilometres per hour. The vortex was of such power that windows were sucked out and large trees snapped off like dead twigs, not unlike the effects of a bomb. Hailstones as large as baseballs were reported, blasting through roofs and cars like bullets.

About twenty tornadoes touch down in Alberta each year – around eighty in the entire country – but most hit uninhabited areas. Since statistics were compiled, less than a hundred Canadians have been killed by these fierce summer storms.

We are fragile creatures in a hostile environment, dependent upon natural resources and modern technology to keep us alive. That is the privilege of civilization, but every once in a while, nature intercedes to remind us exactly how tenuous our hold on a spot of ground can be. Nature's fury also serves to remind us how dependent on one another we are. Too bad it takes a disaster to bring out the best.

Red Deer deserves more than to be considered the way station for Alberta's major cities, more than a blue-collar and agricultural town, but no campaign can make it so. It is destined, forever, to be halfway.

Had train service been upgraded and continued, were a high-speed rail link between Calgary and Edmonton (presumably stopping once in Red Deer) ever to be more than just a passing fancy, maybe Red Deer would stand a chance to be more. For years, driving from Calgary to Edmonton has no longer entailed a slow trip through the heart of Red Deer. The turn off has become merely the halfway point for hurried drivers.

It is possible, on a sunny, dry day with no recreational vehicles driving in convoy in both lanes, to drive to Edmonton from Calgary in two hours. It's not recommended, though, given the Mountie who usually parks just outside Ponoka and delivered into my hands one August a speeding ticket that looked like the national debt. No, I don't know how fast I was driving. My car at the time had the first – and apparently last – digital dashboard readout, which would not register a speed over 140 km/hr. The speed limit is 110. The ticket said I had been going 50 km over the limit. Were Highway 2 an *autobahn*, nobody would turn a hair at that speed, given the straight road and the flatness of the land. I now let my husband do the highway driving, at a stately 120 km/hr. Legally, that is speeding, but on Highway 2 it barely keeps you abreast of the traffic.

There is a tendency while driving to bemoan the loss of the train link between Edmonton and Calgary, although it was slow and inefficient at best, and deadly at worst. The Dayliner, the supposedly high-speed express train that stopped en route only in Red Deer, was regularly late, slow and sloppy. I once paid full fare to stand every minute of the way from Red Deer to Edmonton because the train was full. My futile requests for a refund under the circumstances were treated with a mixture of boredom and contempt. It was this kind of careless service, combined with a crumbling infrastructure, that eventually led to the death of the Dayliner. The idea it was an express train was a joke. I will never forget one journey when the train took four hours to make the ninety-minute trip from Red Deer to Calgary, stopping sporadically and often in the middle of the prairie fields.

The railway, we are reminded, first linked this country together. As wonderful as that little bit of truth and nostalgia is, the CPR was also well-bribed with land and leases to run its twin rails across the country. None of the subsequent development was altruistic. And when the end of the road came for train travel as a mode of transportation for people, it already went unlamented. Who needs a train link when driving is so easy?

It was the CPR's greed that determined much of the development of the West, including both Calgary and Edmonton. To be fair, while both Calgary and Edmonton owe their beginnings to matters other than the appearance of the railroad – Edmonton to the fur trade; Calgary to American whisky traders, buffalo hunters, and mountebanks – civilization arrived at the same time as the train in the form of the North-West Mounted Police, created by the federal government specifically to bring order to the wilderness. It was they who established a fort at Calgary in 1875, at the confluence of the Bow and Elbow (then called the Swift) rivers. The Bow Valley presented the Mounties with a panorama that still stops the heart, although the modern traveller has to imagine a lush valley under the pavement, the houses, and the development that threatens to extend to the mountains themselves.

But what Constable George King, the first policeman to crest the valley, saw was paradise. He wrote in his diary: "Never will I forget the scene that met our eyes – the confluence of the two winding rivers with their wooded banks, the verdant valley, and beyond, the wide expanse of green plain that stretched itself in homage to the distant mountains. . . . [A]t last we had received our reward, that this was . . . a Garden of Eden."

The troop built their fort on the east side of the junction of the rivers. The railroad, having been deeded the right of way and, for some reason, the odd-numbered sections of land, put their "station" on the west side, since that was Section 15 and the east side was Section 14. The company, a private eastern concern, tried to buy Section 14, but considered the price too high. Eventually, as has been the history of the railroad in Western Canada, the world bent to its wishes and the city of Calgary moved to accommodate the railroad. Calgary became the first town in what would be the province of Alberta in 1884 and a city in 1893, giving enthusiastic city officials a century later two reasons within ten years to proclaim centenary celebrations. (By the time 1993 rolled around, there was scant interest in another party.)

Edmonton was passed over as the site of the main CPR line because there was more profit to be made on the southern route. While Edmonton thrived, the towns along the North Saskatchewan, the original route for the railroad, were deprived of what they believed was their promised prominence.

As Pierre Berton wrote in *The Last Spike*, when the task of building a transcontinental railway was turned over to private interests, it was assumed the main line would follow the valley of the North Saskatchewan, a route that led northwest from Winnipeg to Edmonton and the Yellowhead Pass. That route had taken years of argument, political manoeuvring, and millions of dollars to build. Then, in a hotel room in St. Paul, Minnesota, three of the four-man executive committee of the CPR changed the course of the railroad and in doing so, the fortunes of the country.

Writes Berton: "That decision affected the lives of tens of thousands of Canadians. It ensured the establishment of cities close to the border that otherwise might not have existed for another generation, if ever – Broadview, Regina, Moose Jaw, Swift Current, Medicine Hat, Banff and Revelstoke. It doomed others. . . . It affected aspects of Canadian life as varied as the tourist trade and the wheat economy. In addition, it gave the railway company something very close to absolute control over the destinies of scores of embryo communities along the right of way."

Why the change of plan? Because the decision makers were convinced by an enthusiastic explorer that the desert that was the southern part of the Northwest Territories was a myth, despite expert testimony that the southern plains were an extension of the American desert. Within the hour, the CPR decided to build through Calgary.

And Calgary blossomed. As did the CPR.

Maybe that explains why we're not nostalgic about the railroad out here. We know the history of the CPR has nothing to do with the whitewashed version of singing iron rails and happy settlers brought to a new land.

The last Dayliner limped to a halt, ironically having yet another accident on its last run, in late 1985. Having spent a goodly portion of my student days on that train, I knew it deserved a merciful end. But there was much whining and carping across Canada about the cancellation, convincing me that most people who talk about the train as some sort of national symbol never actually took one. An Ottawa-based consumer group, Transport 2000, spent much time, effort, and breath urging the Canadian Transport Commission to review its decision to cancel the Dayliner six years short of its hundredth anniversary.

But Albertans knew the train service was crappy and there was little chance of improvement. We knew it because we travelled, and we marvelled at the service across Europe, and even at the much-maligned U.S. train service and, inevitably, in what was offered to Eastern Canada. What made me realize how abysmal the service really was was being whisked through the Ontario countryside by rail, in comfort.

The year the Dayliner was finally cancelled, by happenstance I took the train from Toronto to Kingston, a trip of just over two hours. It wasn't quite as long as Calgary to Edmonton, but long enough to understand that the difference between VIA Rail 062 and whatever that rolling stock was puffing and tooting up the line in Alberta was, was the difference between a Cadillac and a cattle car. The train left on time, the track bed was smooth, the club car quiet, the service efficient and attentive. And the reason the two lines were different was just as obvious: passengers. People. Bums in the seats. Alberta could never consistently deliver, day after day, the kind of passenger load available on the Toronto to Montreal run.

Passenger train service in Alberta – freight trains to the spur lines servicing grain farmers and small towns had already disappeared – ended in September 1985, killed by apathy, disuse, profit margins, and disgruntled customers.

For prairie folk, the train's last run wasn't the end of an era. That had come years before, when the freight trains to their towns, the vehicle on which their parents and grandparents had travelled to Alberta, lured by promises of land and a new life, were cancelled.

And there's the crux: before airlines, before automobiles and paved roads, taking the train was how Canadians got from one end of this country to the other. We cling to the notion that the train means something other than a way of getting wheat to Thunder Bay or coal across the mountains or cars from both coasts to their markets. It doesn't. It doesn't mean anything to Canada as a nation any more.

The automobile has rendered the train redundant over most of this country. Your car leaves when you want, allows you to stop on the way, doesn't drive through the Rockies in the middle of the night because the coal and freight trains get the prime hours, and never attempts to feed you dead sandwiches in shrink-wrap.

Every so often, the notion of a high-speed train link between Calgary and Edmonton resurfaces, especially since Edmonton closed its municipal airport, forcing Calgarians who were used to getting into downtown Edmonton from Calgary in less than an hour and a five-dollar cab ride, to rent a car from Edmonton's outpost of an international airport, or bear the exorbitant cab fare.

I find it richly ironic that after cancelling the Calgary-Vancouver link, closing the Calgary train station, the CPR turned around and set up an expensive, exclusive tour modelled on the Orient Express that starts and ends in Calgary and takes up to twenty-two passengers on a circuitous, thousand-kilometre leisurely ride through the Rockies in meticulously restored rolling stock – including an observation car. The *New York Times* called the three-day trip "travelling like a magnate," in a vintage train "luxurious enough for a robber baron," and raved about the service, the view, the food, the luxury, and the side trips in the all-inclusive package priced at US$4,995 each – or about CAD$8,000 – the usual charge for double occupancy. It is the only passenger service CP still runs. Poor Canadians need not apply.

The experts point out the success of high-speed trains in France and Japan, but what they don't tell us, is that the population base in those countries is able to support the cost of such service. It's all in the numbers. The U.S. can afford to subsidize a national railway network. We can't. So Albertans rely on the highways, and we drive back and forth between our two largest cities and we play Let's Trash Edmonton/Calgary on the way. It's fun, it's harmless, and it keeps your mind occupied when all you can see is rolling fields of grain and baled hay to the horizon, or the ass end of yet another recreational vehicle driven by some mouth-breather who can't read the signs that clearly say: Slower Traffic Keep Right.

And if the RVs in convoy prove too vexing, there's always the halfway haven of a stop in Red Deer.

10

Everybody Needs a Gimmick

In real life, Vulcan, the mythical planet home to *Star Trek*'s Mr. Spock, is an unprepossessing town on the dry southern Alberta prairie that saw an opportunity and seized it. The *Star Trek* franchise gave the small town of Vulcan – population 1,800 – a natural opportunity to attract visitors, and the town burghers took full advantage. In 1995, the town put up a thirty-one-foot-long, nine-foot-wide concrete "spaceship" on top of a nine-foot-high base, and in keeping with the spirit of the original *Enterprise* on the television series, painted the underside with the appropriate Federation starship identifiers: FX6-1995-A. (The letters and numbers identify the airport designation for Vulcan, the year the starship was unveiled, and the A because it was the first of its kind.) On the base, plaques welcome visitors – alien or otherwise – in three languages: English, Vulcan, and Klingon. (For anyone not conversant with *Star Trek*, Vulcans and Klingons developed from the same ancestors.) Vulcan wants everyone to feel welcome.

Three years after the ship took, er, flight, the town put up an earthbound Tourism and Trek Station, designed to look like a landing spaceship. In the summer of 2004, a Calgary couple held their *Star Trek*-themed wedding in Vulcan, complete with fake foreheads, federation uniforms, and vows in both Klingon and English. It was all legal, imaginative, and completely silly.

If nothing else, the *Star Trek* link brings much-needed revenue into the town and – if such a fancy concept can be applicable in this case – represents the diversification so necessary for any town's future life.

There's no word whether the people of St. Paul, two hundred kilometres northeast of Edmonton, population 5,300, appreciated being outdone by Vulcan. Nearly thirty years before Vulcan's tourist-friendly venture, or about the time the original *Star Trek* was just going into reruns in 1967, the town of St. Paul erected a forty-foot, sixty-five-kilogram UFO "landing" platform as a Canadian Centennial project. Go figure. At least Vulcan can claim a certain kinship to its *Star Trek* theme – if only by name.

Less bizarre, at least to the large Ukrainian population of northern Alberta, is the world's largest painted Easter egg, which is set in a park in Vegreville, population 5,400. The first Ukrainian settlers homesteaded near Vegreville in 1898, and the uninitiated might presume this gaudy and intricately patterned attraction was put up in honour of those first settlers. That would be wrong. The pysanka was erected in honour of the RCMP centennial in gratitude for the Mounties' law enforcement in the district. No, indeed, there is no logical explanation.

That's not the only giant foodstuff on display for visitors: in the village of Mundare, with a population of only 653, a giant forty-two-foot, six-ton fibreglass ring of kielbasa, a popular Ukrainian sausage, was erected in 2001 in honour of Stawinchy's Meat Processing, whose most popular product over its half-century of business has been, you guessed it, kielbasa. The village of Vilna has three twenty-foot mushrooms, and Vauxhall – the Potato Capital of the West – has, naturally, twin seven-foot fibreglass potatoes, Sammy and Samantha, looking like a child's nightmare versions of Mr. and Mrs. Potato Head.

More in keeping with the reality of Alberta, there are towns with giant animals guarding over parks. The hamlet of Andrew, population less than five hundred, features the world's largest flying duck, a mallard with a twenty-five-foot wingspan. It is outdone only by the town of Hanna, population 3,100, which sports three giant concrete geese – one landing, one taking off, and one "flying." Edson has an eight-foot-high squirrel named Eddie, Beaverlodge has a fifteen-foot-tall beaver, and Beiseker has a skunk named Squirt.

Large concrete and fibreglass mascots are a common enough feature of small-town life in Alberta, and in many other small towns across the country. It is only the outsiders, the so-called sophisticates, who laugh at the pretensions of a giant sausage or a landing pad for unidentified flying objects. Each of these attractions has been erected to sell the features and attractions of small towns that are facing extinction, as children leave for the cities and businesses shut their doors.

If it takes a gimmick to keep the town alive, then bring it on. And if the outsiders laugh at the locals then at least let them come and spend money as they snicker. But it is a curious factor of small-town Alberta that its pride and dignity remain intact even as they know they are irrelevant to an urbanized society except for the food they produce. They can't even set a fair price for their agricultural products, pinned to the wall, so to speak, by international trade and subsidies. A bumper crop doesn't necessarily promise a full larder in the farmhouse, and in small towns across the West, people watch politicians and trade delegates talk endlessly about their livelihood and the subsidies that support European and American farmers. The modern concept of "fair trade" goods doesn't seem to extend to our own farmers who, like just about every other endeavour, are being Wal-Martized out of business.

Yet these are not stupid people. No farmer today can be and stay in business. They know they have a right to be heard and have been largely denied that outlet.

It's little wonder that feelings of being ignored and being irrelevant led to the Reform Party of Canada. The subsequent fifteen years have not ameliorated their lot of farmers or their anger. The rural areas of the West provide the backbone support for neo-conservatism, but the diehards there are manipulated and controlled by an elite cadre of intellectuals. (Curiously, when the Reform Party first fulminated against "the elites," the target of the anger was liberals and Liberals; the elite of conservatism was ignored.)

Small-town Alberta grew to supply surrounding farms with the dry goods and essentials that couldn't be produced by the land. As the crops prospered, so did the towns. As they failed, they produced a domino effect of closings across the face of the province. It isn't necessary to be a farmer to know how the agriculture sector is faring – just drive down the main street of any Alberta town. You can almost taste the economy in the dust, and rank the local portion of the GDP by the number of people walking down Main Street laden with shopping bags.

Alberta's towns, regardless of the industry that underpins them – ranching, farming, mining – are held in thrall to the vagaries of giant businesses they don't own, don't operate, and can't control. Lack of diversification means a community is dependent upon a single industry for its livelihood. Drought, grasshoppers, and hail are all familiar enemies to Alberta's agricultural communities and the small towns that depend on them. And when a single cow was discovered to be carrying bovine spongiform encephalopathy, the bottom dropped out of an entire section of the economy. The ranchers and farmers watched as their livelihood dried up or was sold off, even as the price of beef in the supermarkets fell not one whit. They have a right to be angry when they are being driven by closed borders into poverty, while meat packers and retail merchants maintain a healthy profit margin.

The mad-cow crisis is only the latest in a long list of grievances that small-town, agricultural, rural Albertans hold in their hearts. They are proud people, and having to ask for help is demeaning. Worse is asking for help and being ignored. That's as good as any an explanation for the rise of Western populist political parties. Preston Manning's Reform Party was only the most recent in the history of the politics of discontent.

If a philosophical reason for this unhappiness is needed, look no further than the family in the next house, the next section, the

next rural route: We are all newcomers. We are all outsiders wanting
to fit in and feeling we are denied inclusion. The story of Alberta
is the story of those outsiders – people who came to the West fleeing
pogroms in Russia, racial and religious discrimination across the face
of Eastern Europe, the second sons and spinster daughters, the land-
less and the desperate. The comfortable bourgeoisie of Europe did
not arrive looking for a free quarter-section of land. The people who
came were pioneers. Tough. Uncompromising. Determined. Why
would anyone think that their great-great-grandchildren have
mellowed, after being raised on family histories of escape, personal
sacrifice, and hard work?

More than anything else, that background explains the rise of
Reform, its subsequent morphing into the Canadian Alliance, and
now the Conservative Party. Reform had hopeful beginnings and a
disastrous evolution, because it was the politics of protest, the politics of the outsider. All these long years later, the newly minted
Conservatives (conspicuously lacking the adjective Progressive) are
no longer outsiders. That brings its own particular problems. When
"they" become "we" it is difficult to promote the notion of the outsider wanting a place at the table. The place has already been set and
the first course has already been finished. A political party based
on the rallying cry "The West wants in" should have been better
prepared for the inevitable invitation. The Reform Party, its supporters, and the angry neo-conservatives simply weren't prepared for
the view from the inside.

They have become – almost, and that's a big "almost" – just
another mainstream Canadian political party. The "almost" is the
party's inability to appeal to the mainstream Canadian electorate.
And within the party itself, there is reluctance to become what it
must in order to be elected – a party in the middle of the road that
appeals to the majority of voters. The Conservative Party has yet
to rid itself of the hard-right social conservatism that sets it at odds
with the majority of Canadians.

Particularly in Alberta, particularly to urban Albertans, the
angry voices of protest ring hollow: those doing the most public

protesting about their treatment by various governments don't seem to be those with the most to complain about. The loudest voices don't come from the needy or the disadvantaged, but from opportunists who see in the politics of anger and discontent a chance to remake Canada. Small-town Alberta may support any protest against, for example, gun registration as yet another attempt by loafer-wearing city slickers to make life difficult for them, but the architects of their rebellion aren't out on the back forty shooting coyotes that are preying on livestock. No, the protest is led by well-educated opportunists who believe might, right, and money will buy anything. Despite bumper stickers to the contrary, what is being protested is not just gun-control legislation, the Kyoto Accord, same-sex marriage, and all the other right-wing bogeys, but Canadian values themselves. Of course, supporters of neo-conservatives don't say that they are protesting values the majority of Canadians hold important, but insist that they are fighting for "freedom."

Much of the anger and resentment that echoes through small-town and rural Alberta is based on a very American ideal – that money should always be able to buy a bigger voice in society. Yet that attitude runs smack into the more widespread Canadian notion of privilege and power being earned with something other than a bank account.

And while rural Albertans were arguing pointlessly about guns and the GST, their world was changing faster than they could realize.

Former Canadian senator Ron Ghitter warned years ago that technological changes doomed the simple rural lifestyle from which many Albertans are merely a generation or two removed. With the triumph of technology that virtually eliminated border and boundaries came a recession that hammered both rural Alberta and the younger generation who had left the farm for a city job.

Ghitter said: "Technological change in the way of the Internet, cellphones and the like, further additions to the new lexicon such as Generation X, ozone layer, acid rain, became common topics. On the negative side were growing numbers of unemployed graduates, increasing family violence, or so it seemed. Attention was becoming focused on youth crime, attitudes were hardening toward new Canadians, particularly those of colour, all of these things were uncovering a more fearful, cynical and sometimes mean-spirited side in previously tolerant Albertans."

It may seem, to Ghitter – and certainly to a large number of equally well-meaning Albertans – that Albertans were changing before their eyes into some kind of different species, forced to by some outside influence. I think it's more basic than that – that the growing intolerance to "the other" was merely a process of uncovering the real nature of far too many Westerners: a nature of us versus them. This nature was on display in the hard and uncompromising attitude of the former Conservative cabinet minister and MLA Connie Osterman. She took the political pillorying for the financial collapse of the provincially regulated Principal Group in 1989. Pundits would have us believe she "took it like a man," as if that were a compliment. Taxpayers footed the million-dollar bill for this fiasco but Osterman was fired from her cabinet post. Three years later, she resigned from the legislature. Tougher than the boys who let her take the fall in their stead, her attitude was one of steel-jawed acceptance and silence. She took her strength probably literally from the land. Osterman once remarked that she and her husband weathered bad times with the help of neighbours and they had, in effect, pulled themselves up by their own bootstraps. This is still the attitude of the Alberta government – that those who are homeless or poor, needy or disadvantaged are just not trying hard enough. (This is the government that suggested single people on welfare could "double-up" if they couldn't afford accommodation in downtown Edmonton or Calgary.)

In the face of huge technological changes, the men and women Premier Ralph Klein calls the "severely normal folks" reached enough of a critical mass, were frightened enough by the loss of jobs, and thanks to a growing hardening of attitudes toward social assistance of any form (which cost money that any recession makes a precious commodity), became emboldened enough to start to speak the language of discrimination they had hidden for years, if not generations.

The resentment and anger that once could not be spoken in polite society gained currency in the heartland, where somebody had to be made to pay for the shock of lost jobs, bad investments, and declining personal opportunities. Albertans looked to "the other."

As long as the blue-collar and working-class Albertans – not a few of whom were resentfully walking away from houses they could no longer afford to live in – could be guaranteed jobs, then there was room at the bottom of the economic ladder for immigrants. Once the declining fortunes of the province robbed these people of their guarantees, they blamed "them," who were taking jobs away from "us."

It was so easy to identify "them," the foreigners with their darker skins, strange religions, and curious cultures. It wasn't just that immigrants from around the world were taking the lowly jobs considered beneath a white Canadian, it was that they had the effrontery to skip to the middle of the ladder, even to the top – into the universities and professions long considered the purview of Anglo-Saxon Canadians and Europeans. Those who resented immigration, whose mantra of entitlement through a European name and white skin extended to loud complaints that "we" couldn't even get on the list to come to Canada while "they" were streaming in through the loophole of refugee status.

It was, of course, mostly a lie. Canada was not being overrun. Indeed, any fast look at the real statistics would still show that the most-favoured status for any Canadian was – and still is – to be white and male. But perception became reality. In a province where the only differently shaped and coloured faces belonged to aboriginals or the French (or the combination of both, the Métis), the sight of an Indian nurse or a Pakistani teacher was notable.

A related example of what standing apart in the crowd means was once carried out in a company for which I was working. There was a growing backlash against what was perceived to be the number of "feminists" who were "taking over" the business. As an employee, a feminist, and an executive, I knew this wasn't true. But the heated words and angry attitudes had poisoned the office, forcing people to take sides.

Our actions did not address the systemic discrimination that would encourage the men employed in the office to resent women being promoted – after all, the women in the office had had more than 100 years (the age of the business) to swallow the continuing insult that men automatically deserved promotions, were ready for them, and more willing than women to work for them – but it had the virtue of showing the men their perceptions were utterly wrong.

Using numbers from our own human resources department, we drew a chart of all the jobs, showing the president at the top of the pyramid, followed by the executives who directly reported to him, and so on down the chart. The bottom lines were the support staff. For each position we used the universal bathroom pictograph for male and female.

The chart shut the complainers up.

It showed two women in positions of authority, a few in the professional ranks, far outnumbered by their male colleagues, and, at the very bottom, two lines of dresses. What was characterized as a feminist takeover was two female executives. Why this happened is as simple as why some people believe white men are now in a minority – visibility. The two women in the executive suite were simply more visible than all of the men around them.

The question of discrimination based on gender or any other difference still besets employers and their workers, whose energies, in an atmosphere of rank discrimination, are too often used to fight battles they could rightfully have presumed over and done with, and in the past. But it remains difficult to convince people who for generations have harboured hatred and suspicions that, now they are in the New World, they must change.

Alberta wasn't the last place chosen by immigrants, but it was close. It isn't that we didn't have immigration, it's that most of our immigrants walked under the radar of visible minority. Alberta's most populous immigrant group in the south was American ranchers and entrepreneurs and in northern Alberta it was European peasants. On the streets of Edmonton, for example, the Europeans were no different from anyone else, as long as they didn't speak in their distinctive accents. And even then, their colour ranked them higher than non-Europeans.

Asian migration stayed mostly on the West Coast. French-speaking blacks from Haiti went to Montreal; English-speaking blacks from Jamaica or Trinidad headed for Toronto, as did the bulk of Asians. For those from warmer climates, Ontario seemed to offer a less-harsh winter. For those from non-English- (or French-) speaking countries, a city the size of Toronto – or Montreal or Vancouver – offered a cadre of countrymen and the chance to ease into a new life and new language inside the bosom of familiarity. Eventually, though, Alberta's booming economy made it a destination. And second and now third generations stayed here, for exactly the same chances and good life that whites did. But they could not disguise their heritage as the Americans and Europeans had done. A dark skin cannot not be dispensed with, as an accent can.

They became the brunt of ugly attitudes and racist opinions. And all of a sudden, their tormentors had a political movement that would support them.

The Reform Party did not set out to be a haven for racists and sexists. But, as with any movement of rage and resistance, it collected them. And in many ways, the party's neo-conservative policies encouraged them.

Members and supporters of the Conservative Party will vigorously deny all of this. They will point to female members to prove the party is not sexist; they will point to Indian and Sikh members to prove the party is not racist. What they cannot point to is the positive actions made to refute the charges.

On the other side of the sea change in Alberta came new pressure groups who were just beginning to speak up: ethnic communities, homosexuals, immigrants, restless young people, and women. "The result was the inevitable clash of attitudes between traditionalist God-fearing Albertans and these newly emerging groups," said Ron Ghitter. "Fuelled by certain influential media, building circulation on the fear and cynicism inherent in these clashes and best exemplified by a publication such as the *Alberta*

Report and the shout-in radio shows, the social disquiet in the province was growing, and a new entourage of faddist right-wing writers were making their living from this blip in Canadian history."

The conflicts of transition and acceptance brought populist politics back to Alberta. Populism preached economic reform headed by elimination of the debt and deficit, a return to what was defined as family and religious values, and a host of other simple solutions to complicated problems. Populism, as it had at the beginning of the twentieth century, was selling the mood of the moment. Albertans bought into it and the Reform Party's membership mushroomed. In the 1993 October election the new party seized the Progressive Conservative base.

Meanwhile, a similar "revolution" was happening in the United States, although the two-party system of America has meant the extremists on both sides of the political spectrum continue to find a home in either the Republican or Democratic parties. In 1994, two years into the first Bill Clinton administration, the mid-term elections brought Newt Gingrich and his band of Republican moral reformers into Washington, determined to rid the landscape of liberals, feminists, illegal immigrants, repeat offenders, anyone who was "soft" on crime. Their campaign of moral outrage and religious evangelism was rooted in a fictional past of secure family values. At the time, a senior U.S. official whose grasp of grammar was shakier than his convictions, told Senator Ghitter: "Anyone other than white Anglo-Saxon, Chamber of Commerce Christians had better watch out, because if you happened to be an environmentalist, an immigrant, one of the needy or a senior citizen, a train was coming straight at you." It was clear that the politics of exclusion, of cynicism, and meanness toward anyone who was not "us," as defined by Gingrich followers, would find no welcome in the so-called new America.

A new and "righteous" government was supported by a so-called moral majority whose definition of righteous and moral would exclude just about anybody who believed in the equality of rights. This moral majority movement was encouraged and led by Pat Robertson and other evangelists with large television audiences, the modern equivalent of tent revival meetings. There might be a Democrat in the White House, but there would be righteousness in the land. The country's most popular president, Ronald Reagan, had been followed by George H. Bush, and he was only defeated by Clinton because of a faltering economy, high deficit spending, and inner-city violence. So Republicans endured the eight years of Bill Clinton's administration, considered by the right wing to be an unfortunate blip in the natural order of things. The contested election of George W. Bush in 2000 was seen as a return to the true Christian values of the United States and his re-election in 2004 was proof to the neo-cons that they were right.

The return to "family values," the security of the past, and the large dose of religious evangelism in the States echoed the expressed values of Reform as outlined by Preston Manning.

Says Ghitter: "It was and continues to be a political force feeding off the fears and uncertainties of the voter, built on a basic obsession with debt and deficit. But it is a political movement fraught with danger, short-term gain for long-term pain. It is a political approach that is often mean, cynical and over-simplistic, feeding off negatives, hatred and disguised racism. It is a political movement that presents itself, both in Canada and the U.S., with clear and forthright statements, but statements that are based more on emotion and hoax than reality."

By the time of the disastrous failure of Canadian Alliance leader Stockwell Day to make a breakthrough in the rest of Canada in the fall election of 2000, the fiscal complaints of the Alliance had been addressed. The Liberal government had managed to end-run the party by simply usurping its fiscal policy. Ottawa was now on firm financial footing. That left the neo-conservatives with nothing but their social conservatism to fall back on, and it became obvious the majority of Canadians repudiated it. They were not prepared to advance rapidly into the past. The religious, ethnic, and social make-up of the country had changed and with it, the country itself. We like universal medical care. We support multiculturalism and we definitely want French and Quebec.

The results of the 2004 federal election show the rest of Canada, excluding Quebec, is far more willing to accept a united Conservative Party, notwithstanding the thorny issue of social conservatism. And since he became leader of the new party that supposedly unites the right, Conservative leader Stephen Harper has gone a long way to cure the political disaster left him by Stockwell Day. But the thorny issues of gun control, law and order, and constitutional reform still remain, albeit less of a sore point with other Canadians than Albertans. Eventually, Harper will have to deal with them.

Looking at Alberta from the outside, you'd be forgiven for thinking the entire province has its collective finger on the rifle trigger, ready to shoot whatever city parvenu agrees with the gun law. Curiously, this isn't the case. The opponents of gun control, while vocal and as persistent as a swarm of mosquitoes on a summer evening, don't represent the majority. (The level of support for gun control in Alberta, as a surprised former attorney general discovered when he disputed the public's opinion on the matter, reaches as high as 72 per cent, depending on the question asked.)

In the debate about gun control and justice, the loudest voices in Alberta take their tone and attitudes from the United States. But in Canada, there is no inherent right to own and use a gun. It is a privilege. And it is one that Canadians across the country have decided should be regulated. Regardless of the inappropriateness of the argument, regardless of the overwhelming support of the majority of Canadians – and a majority of Albertans, also – debate has not diminished as the federal government continues its approved course of taking guns out of the hands of ordinary citizens.

There is, of course, sympathy for the farming and aboriginal communities, in that they alone have a reasonable case for owning firearms for hunting, food-gathering, and killing predatory wildlife. Yet even in those two cases, it should be impossible to argue against registration and licences. I am not the only person who sees the irony in a government that purports to listen to the people – Ralph Klein's campaign slogan one election was "He Listens; He Cares" – yet ignores the majority of its constituents in favour of challenging gun control.

Federal Justice Minister Anne McLellan – herself an Albertan – saw the irony in the specious challenge launched by the Alberta government and followed in sheeplike fashion by Ontario, Manitoba, Saskatchewan, and the Yukon. During a visit to Calgary, she said: "The battle over the substantive policy is over." Few gun lovers were listening to her. They still aren't.

"I work on the basis that until the Supreme Court of Canada tells us otherwise, the law is constitutional. And we're moving ahead to implement it," McLellan said. Not only to implement the legislation, but to get it right, she added, for all of the Canadians who have vociferously indicated their support.

The provincial governments that launched the legal challenge against the legislation (that's your tax money and mine) and refused to link gun registration to driver's licences, have been given a free ride. If the scheme has become a "billion-dollar boondoggle" as opponents claim, no one seems willing to place some of the blame for cost overruns and the necessity for a separate bureaucracy on the intransigence of the provinces. Want to save a billion dollars? Link gun registration to the owner's driver's licence. No fuss, no muss, no separate bureaucracy. Did the federal government overspend? Yes. Was it a mind-boggling financial snafu? Indeed. Could it have been avoided? See above reference to driver's licences.

Through all this furor, the law stands. Yet individuals and groups continue to carp about gun registration, pulling out all the tired shibboleths about private property and government intervention, about law-abiding gun owners and non-compliance. The protesters, wittingly or otherwise, take their cue from the U.S. National Rifle Association, as vile a lobby group as ever tried to impose its misguided will on a public begging to be duped.

The myth of the rural redneck lives only in song and story, and in hamlets and gas stops, where bragging rights are secured by the size of your rifle and the length of your spurs. Yet the NRA persists in fighting to keep the United States an armed fortress where thousands die by gun violence each year. It is money, not public opinion, that buys support for the NRA and its Canadian counterpart, the National Firearms Association.

Ordinary Canadians would do almost anything to prevent the kind of thinking that permeates American society where guns are concerned – the crocodile tears and mawkish sentimentality as people tie ribbons on trees and themselves into knots explaining yet another mass shooting as being the fault of something other than a gun-loving, gun-toting, gun-permitting society.

It has become conventional wisdom among gun lovers and their supporters that maniacs who amass an arsenal and then slaughter people have nothing to do with the issue of gun control, but are merely deranged individuals out to kill. These are called crimes of hate or rage; crimes of passion. The thinking is the acts would happen with or without the easy availability of guns. It is the person who commits the act, not the weapon.

Fair enough, if disingenuous. A crazed killer can attack his next-door neighbour with a banana, but all that brings to mind is the Monty Python skit. Attacking with a weapon that requires little involvement other than pulling a trigger brings no laughs at all.

If the human toll isn't persuasive, perhaps cold math is: gun violence costs Americans $100 billion a year. Medical expenses and lost productivity are only part of the cost, write economists Philip Cook of Duke University and Jens Ludwig of Georgetown University. As they go on to say, the real total involves: "The devastating emotional costs experienced by relatives and friends of gunshot victims and the fear and general reduction in quality of life that the threat of gun violence imposes on everyone in America, including people who are not victimized."

Few Canadians, except misguided gun supporters, even want the dubious freedom to keep a handgun in their car or their bedroom. Most Canadians don't need, don't want, and don't use guns. Those that do must be willing to tell the rest where and what kind they are. Yet, we continue to compare our gun-control laws to those in the United States, instead of other countries, where the prohibitions against owning and using firearms are far more aggressive. In England, France, and Australia, for example, the laws go well beyond anything we have, as Anne McLellan says.

Less than a quarter of Canadian households have a gun. In Alberta 40 per cent do. Most of those firearms are the shotguns and rifles owned by farmers and hunters, none of whom McLellan is interested in ticking off. "If you are a lawful gun owner who main-tains his or her guns in a safe and secure manner you have nothing to fear from this law," she said.

In the face of a campaign that insisted that the hidden agenda of the government is to confiscate legitimate weapons, she was adamant that this was not the case. Her concern was safety, she said. Law enforcement agencies must have the information necessary to police communities and deal with various kinds of crime, particu-larly domestic violence. "Urban Canadians . . . want an enhanced culture of safety in their communities," she said.

That doesn't sit well in the heartland of rural Alberta, where community safety means the vigilance of neighbours who know each other.

Whenever the subject of guns arises, I remember how my father, uncle, and grandfather enjoyed hunting. In my den are a stuffed pheasant, a grouse, and a partridge bagged by Grandfather. Mostly, we just ate what they killed, being careful in case there was any shot still in the bird. None of the men in my family were bloodthirsty hunters, rather merely ordinary men enjoying an ordinary pursuit. Their shotguns were cleaned and stored with care. I have no doubt they would have complied with the simple requirements of the Canadian law: registration and licensing. They would do it, because it is the law, not because they liked the law. None of them would have had the effrontery to flout federal law and cloak themselves in righteousness. They wouldn't have used bureaucracy as an excuse; complicated forms as a reason not to comply. They could smell liars a mile away. Of course, such law-flouting citizens are not many in number. They receive more attention than they deserve, because they are making news with what they think is a principled stand.

They even have the gall to call it civil disobedience, as if fancy words and Thoreau can disguise contempt for a law of which the majority of Canadians approve. And that's the real offence: They have such little respect for others, they believe they have a right to break the law and consider themselves justified in bragging.

The issue of gun ownership in Canada largely centres on rifles and shotguns, although there is a small coterie of people who believe handguns should be legal.

I never understood the sheer fear a handgun could engender until I met one in the middle of Warsaw's old town square. It gave me a visceral understanding of why weak men and scared women would want to own a gun and keep it handy. It is an object of terror. It is an object of death. It puts the power of life or death in the hand of the user.

Nothing much happened in that split second I looked down the barrel of a handgun, except I finally understood what the phrase "my knees turned to water" really means. Luckily, I wasn't alone. My companion, a Russian-speaking American ex-spy, caught me as my knees gave way. It was, he said, just an old revolver. Russian-made, he thought. Probably unworkable.

My friend's soothing voice, as he took me by the elbow and led me away from the town square in Warsaw, almost cleared from my mind the harsher words I'd heard moments before uttered in English in a thick Polish accent: "No, I not kill you today. Maybe I kill you tomorrow."

Why, of all the people in that square that sunny spring day in Poland, did the man with the handgun pick me? I'll never know, just as I'll never know if the gun could have been fired, and if so, why he did not shoot me. Probably even more unnerving, in retrospect, is the awful realization that he could have pulled the trigger, and nobody could have stopped him. It happened that fast – in time units so small they would have to be reckoned in Olympics-like hundredths of a second. I was surrounded by people, including my friend, whose training and build would have enabled him to handle any threat to my safety but this random, unplanned act done without provocation and without warning. He could not have saved me from death. Nobody could have.

It is easy to dismiss this story as the impulsive action of a drunken madman. To that I reply, Come back, after you have had the business end of a handgun held five centimetres from your nose. Come back then and tell me how there was nothing to be frightened about. Then you can talk to me about permitting guns in our town squares.

All of my adult life, I have been unalterably opposed to the private ownership of any guns, but the incident in Warsaw made it personal, instead of merely emotional. I'm inordinately pleased to still be here – able to recount the story, capable of being unreasonable and rabid about gun control. Because, there was one moment there, when the chance of never being unreasonable again was very real, and very close.

It was a rifle in the hands of a disturbed teenager that killed the beautiful seventeen-year-old son of my friends, one of his teachers, and injured more than a dozen students long years ago in an Ontario high school. We have case after case of the deranged, the angry, and the out-of-control suddenly and dramatically taking out their frustration with the world, their pitiful failures in life, by substituting a gun for personal power and real fortitude.

It isn't a brave man who takes to a gun, it's a coward.

Gun-control legislation makes it a labour born of intense desire legally to get your hands on a pistol. Yet for those who are willing to jump through the legalities, handgun ownership is still possible. It remains a ridiculous privilege to bestow on citizens. There is no inherent right of handgun ownership.

There is nothing brave and macho about handguns. They are terrifying weapons meant to kill, and if anyone should be permitted to own them, he had better be a police officer. Even at that, I believe even the police should not have handguns. But that would be truly unreasonable.

There is no purpose in the private ownership of handguns. No, sir, it does not matter to me that you wish to collect handguns, that you have a collector's interest in the weapons. That is not sufficient reason, unless, of course, you render them useless. Funny how all the arguments about merely wanting to own the guns for their intrinsic beauty – never to shoot them – so rarely translates into taking out the firing pin.

There are dozens, hundreds, thousands of people like me who do not wish to live in the fear of being presented, as I was that day, with the small, black hole that constitutes the end of a revolver barrel. But we are not as forceful or loud as those who wish uncontrolled ownership of guns. They use an inordinate amount of breath to denounce anyone who dares speak for gun control.

Perhaps we should start by eradicating the notion that the handgun had a role in the settling of the Canadian West. It did not, and it is a dreadful, stupid lie to let children believe Western Canada was settled by the marshal and his gun. I cannot prevent Americans from filling their own children's heads with lies and canards, but I can rail against the importation of this nonsense north of the border. It is bad enough that there are "Wild West" shootouts during the Stampede. They are offensive. They are just plain silly. But at least nobody pretends they are history.

Bill C-68, on gun control and legislation, took effect January 1, 2001. If you don't have a gun licence, you are in violation of the law. You don't have to like it one whit. You can rag on to your buddies about freedom and the traditions of the West all you want. But you are no longer a law-abiding citizen. And you know what? I hope they throw the book at you.

Arguments about freedom and choice don't just rage when the issue of gun control is raised. Consider the case of fluoride, an additive to drinking water that prevents dental cavities. The lucky cities and towns have naturally fluoridated water. Calgary is not one of them. As a result, the same kind of self-appointed expertise and attendant emotion that surrounds gun control raged in Calgary during the fluoride "debate." Even after the municipal plebiscite that finally brought fluoridated water into Calgary's system, the "experts" still predicted dire consequences, including death from poisoning, for all of Calgary's citizens.

The orthodoxy of this thinking is rooted in the concept of zero tolerance, the bane of public schools where the child who brings a table knife to school for his lunch and the thug with the switch-blade are treated the same; where an Aspirin is considered as harmful as heroin. It is the same kind of silliness that believes a whiff of smoke causes lung cancer; aluminum pots will give you Alzheimer's; talcum powder causes ovarian cancer; cellphones and overhead power lines cause brain tumours; and vaccinations and inoculations are more dangerous than the diseases they prevent.

Those who opposed fluoride being added to Calgary's water – even though every other major municipality in the province has natural or artificial fluoride in its drinking water – were willing to risk the dental health of Calgary's children because of the possibility of a rare condition known as dental fluorosis, a discolouring or (at worst) pitting of tooth enamel.

They would use their fear-mongering to harm those children who should least be penalized: children whose parents don't care or can't afford regular dental checkups or fluoride treatments. As a child who grew up drinking Calgary's non-fluoridated water, who spent what seemed like most of my early childhood in dentists' chairs, having the effects of non-fluoridated water dealt with, I wouldn't wish that on other people's children.

In a climate of fear, where people want absolutely risk-free lives, the anti-chemical campaign sucks in people who want the best for their children and only hear of the evils of additives. The problem is that they have lived safe from harm. They are often the same people who have never actually seen the devastating, life-threatening complications of any childhood disease such as polio or measles. They only hear the risks associated with vaccinations and inoculations.

Because so much of the fresh water in North America is naturally fluoridated, or has been artificially fluoridated in the past fifty years, worriers fail to see the differences between children raised with fluoridated water and those raised without. They should consider the evidence before their eyes – the millions of North

American children whose teeth have been protected from cavities. It's not the toothpaste, it's the water.

Because a couple of generations of parents haven't had to face the diseases that used to kill children, there is an ignorance about protections from vaccinations to additives such as iodine in salt or fluoride in water.

In the end, the fluoride debate is an instructive model for the changes taking place in Alberta. We eventually get around to moving on issues that concern the public; it's just that we're so, well, conservative about them.

The issue of fluoride has arisen in Calgary repeatedly since 1951, when Calgary's health officer W.W. Hill urged council to move cautiously on the question, saying its health effects hadn't been determined. About that time, while Dr. Hill was fretting, I was making one of a series of childhood visits to the dentist. Fluoride might have helped. It certainly wouldn't have hurt. But caution, and not common sense, ruled.

In four separate plebiscites since then, Calgarians voted against putting fluoride in their water. Finally, a fifth vote succeeded. (This was the only way of changing the bylaw. Once a plebiscite, always a plebiscite.) But the argument wasn't over. The opponents managed to get enough support for a sixth plebiscite. But this time common sense prevailed. Fluoride is still added to Calgary's water.

While the fluoride debate was rancorous, it wasn't nearly as bizarre as the debate over moving to daylight saving time, during which well-meaning farmers wanted to know why they'd have to wake their cows up an hour early. Unlike their Saskatchewan colleagues, the farmers of Alberta – and all the city dwellers – finally voted in favour of daylight saving time. Now it's unimaginable that a vote could take away that extra hour of daylight after work during the summer months. Or take the fluoride out of the water. Or make owning a gun as simple as walking into a gun show and buying one.

This is also part of the Alberta Advantage – that enough urban voters are exercising their numerical might to move the stubborn and stolid rural vote into something close to the twenty-first century.

11

The Bishop, the Bride, the Bereaved

Medicine Hat is one of those small prairie cities – population about fifty thousand – that people come from. Along with Moose Jaw, Saskatchewan, Medicine Hat is one of those knee-slapper names that provokes remarks along the lines of "What kind of a name is that?" usually voiced in tones of deep sarcasm masked as humour.

Medicine Hat's place in the lexicon was set when the British writer Rudyard Kipling remarked in 1907 that the hot and dusty city had "all hell for a basement," after learning there was a nearly four-hundred-square-kilometre natural-gas reservoir lying underneath southern Alberta.

A hundred years later, the gas reserves still lie under Medicine Hat, albeit about half depleted, and people who have never visited the Hat, as it's called, still boast of Kipling's comment with a kind of Canadian delight that anyone "famous" would think twice about us.

One of Kipling's more famous poems, "The Ballad of East and West," written in 1899, the year Medicine Hat was formally founded, begins with the sentiment that is drilled into the hearts of Albertans: "Oh, East is East and West is West, and never the twain shall meet." I have bored countless friends to tears with a recitation of the complete poem, having learned it in its entirety from my father, who was given to reciting epic, florid Victorian verse on long car trips. (Passengers were encouraged to join in on alternate lines, as we were with the "legal logic" lesson of American jurist Oliver Wendell Holmes in *The Deacon's Masterpiece Or, The Wonderful One-Hoss Shay: A Logical Story*, written about the same time as Kipling's and sharing similar overwrought sentiments.)

About the same time Victorian poetry was flourishing, so were the colonies. While Alberta was named for Princess Louise Caroline Alberta (all three of the princess's names were given to Alberta sites), Medicine Hat gets its name from the First Nations who were driven off the land by the railroad, European settlers, and the extinction of the great buffalo herds. There is an aboriginal legend of a fierce battle between the Blackfoot and the Cree, during which a medicine man lost his headdress in the waters of the South Saskatchewan River.

Not too long ago, aside from news of the occasional street ruckus between local yobs and off-duty soldiers from the huge Suffield army base nearby, Medicine Hat didn't often rate a newspaper headline. Most people only knew the city from the signs as they drove past on the Trans-Canada Highway.

Then came the bishop.

When Roman Catholic bishop Fred Henry was appointed to Calgary in 1998 from Thunder Bay, he was preceded by at least two rumours: his golf game was wicked and his sensibilities liberal.

During his two years in the Northern Ontario city, the bishop had spoken out against cost-cutting measures instituted by the Ontario government under Mike Harris. Such measures, called fiscally prudent by supporters and draconian by others, the bishop believed only made unemployment, homelessness, labour unrest, and child poverty worse. Writing in the local Thunder Bay newspaper, Henry said: "I never perceived myself as an agent for social justice. But the poor and unfortunate have no voice. So I think of what Jesus would do for them and he would speak up. I have a voice – so I do."

Such apparently liberal sentiments caused more than one Alberta neo-conservative to dub him "Red Fred." It was amusing, but it was dead wrong.

It soon became obvious that Rt. Rev. Frederick Henry was cut from sterner and more fundamental cloth than wussy liberals assumed. Just because he was identified as a champion of social justice didn't mean that he was prepared to speak up for the so-called liberal agenda of free choice and free will. Nope, his faith, at least in his public pronouncements, is of the fire-and-brimstone variety, and he isn't shy about making his feelings and his Church's teachings known publicly.

The bishop told Jean Chrétien while he was prime minister that he didn't know what it was to be a good Catholic and he was risking his soul. Burning in hellfire was evoked. He suggested to former prime minister and then-MP for Calgary Centre Joe Clark that should he die, the Church and its bishop might not bury him.

As if Canadian Catholic politicians weren't a wide enough target, Henry took a poke in the *Western Catholic Reporter* at John Kerry, only the second Catholic to seek the presidency of the United States. Kerry's "sin" was to be, in the bishop's words, "offside" on the issue of abortion and same-sex marriage, having voted pro-choice throughout his political career, as had the two Canadian politicians.

The ugliest threat he made, albeit not obvious to non-Catholics, was to deny those politicians access to the sacrament. Henry wrote: "I believe the question, 'If a dissident Catholic leader obstinately persists in opposing fundamental Church teaching should he or she be turned away if they present themselves for Communion?' has to be answered, 'yes.'"

How to frame an analogy to make this threat understandable to non-Catholics? Consider being banned by your Church and its clergy from walking your daughter down the aisle at her wedding because the minister doesn't believe you are sufficiently in God's good graces to be given such an honour. Consider being told this as you and your daughter are standing in the vestibule waiting for those first chords of the processional.

Religion may be a public matter in America, but in Canada, it's considered personal and frankly, nobody else's business. Here, with few exceptions, religion has never been an issue in politics. Thanks to Canada's two solitudes, which not only include French and English, but Catholic and Protestant, the faith of politicians is of little concern. (Indeed, most Canadians would be surprised to discover the majority of Canadian prime ministers have been Catholic.)

Religion, at least in the rest of Canada, if not Alberta, is a matter between a man or woman and God. But in the twenty-first century, the separation between church and state is getting thinner and more tenuous. Various special interest groups – and yes, religions are special interest groups – want to bring back prayer to public schools and public meetings. Personal religious beliefs are being trotted out in public as if the fact of belonging to an organized religion makes one a better person. As we all know, it doesn't. Some of the world's most famous Christian evangelists are guilty of many of the Deadlies, as we call the seven deadly sins, which purportedly endanger a person's eternal salvation: pride, covetousness, lust, anger, gluttony, envy, and sloth. Lust, pride, and anger seem to be the favourites. But I am not the judge of the extent to which the sins have replaced the second heavenly virtues in their souls – faith, hope, charity, fortitude, justice, temperance, and prudence. Still, it would make an interesting debate on whether charity trumps anger or temperance banishes lust.

The media loved Bishop Henry. He was uncompromising. He stood on higher moral ground than we poor mortals, and he wasn't above telling us so. He made good press and headlines. Saying the prime minister of the country "doesn't understand what it means to be a good Catholic" was certainly a headline-grabber.

But it's not just politicians, who are used to being targets, who have come under Henry's stern, unforgiving gaze. Ask Celina Ling, a young Medicine Hat woman whose grave error, in the eyes of her church, was her job as volunteer coordinator for Planned Parenthood.

Ling told her parish priest who her employer was nine months before her planned wedding to Robert Symmonds, a non-Catholic, and she admitted to "living in sin" with her fiancé in direct contradiction to the teachings of her church. None of this was a problem until a newspaper article quoted Celina and Planned Parenthood in the same breath.

All hell broke loose. The parish priest refused to marry the couple and his decision was upheld by his boss, the bishop. Bishop Henry was eloquent in his condemnation. He said that Celina was violating one of the canons of the Church and could be automatically excommunicated, a rather harsh fate for a young woman whose biggest so-called sin was to organize the volunteers for an organization that offers counselling. But there was no quarter given, no consideration that Planned Parenthood counsels any person who comes to them, regardless of his or her spiritual beliefs. The organization presents all the options available for any woman facing an unplanned pregnancy, and that includes abortion. That alone, in the eyes of the anti-choice, pro-life movement – there is absolutely no such creature as someone who is pro-abortion, regardless of fiery rhetoric – condemns the entire organization. Bishop Henry told the *Calgary Herald*: "She is involved in actually counselling and facilitating abortions by reason of her position." Maybe worse, in the eyes of the bishop, was Celina's refusal to act penitent. No sackcloth or ashes for this young woman: she simply said she didn't care if she was excommunicated, automatically or not, that she no longer wished to practise her faith. She paraphrased the Bible for the newspaper reporter: "He who has never sinned can cast the first stone." John 8:7.

There is no word whether the Roman Catholic Church will ever figure out that among the reasons people no longer practise the religion is its uncompromising attitude toward human frailty. Do priests look out from the altar on Sundays, survey their flock, and presume none of the women praying and witnessing has had an abortion? Or used birth control?

We all know the answer to that question. Modern Catholic women make their own choices and then, if they think they have sinned, go to confession and continue their lives. The church considers that "healing."

Celina is made of stern stuff. She wasn't about to be bullied by anyone, particularly not her Church, in whose faith she was raised and educated. "They said if I quit my job they'd marry me." Instead, Celina asked for her money back, the two-hundred-dollar deposit she'd put down for the wedding itself and the fifty dollars for the marriage preparation course she and Symmonds went through, actually *had* to go through before the church would marry the couple. What seemed to rankle her more than anything was how the parish balked at paying back the fifty dollars. You took the course, she was told. We had no choice, she replied, and got her fifty bucks back.

Celina and Robert were married by a justice of the peace, not quite the wedding she had planned, but marriage nonetheless. A year later, she still hadn't returned to the church of her childhood, even though she says the local priest has telephoned her and invited her to come back. His explanation for the invitation? She had made her choice with a clear conscience and thus the church would welcome her back, she said. The onlooker might be moved to remark that since Planned Parenthood had closed its Medicine Hat office for lack of funding and local support, Celina was no longer in a religious conflict of interest.

Celina snorted at the notion that what she did in private didn't concern the church, but what she did in public was another matter. "How hypocritical of me" would it be to go back to a church "that treats women the way they do?" she asked, adding that not only did the church cancel her wedding, but she was also told, while she was "bawling and crying," that if she died the next day, the church wouldn't bury her.

The church hierarchy picked the wrong young woman to threaten, a faithful Catholic who believes in a God of love and care. "I believe He looks into your heart," she said. And what would God find in Celina and Robert's hearts? The kind of love that has welcomed into their home three foster children, two boys and a girl. The kind of love that caused the couple to adopt an infant – Dylan, they named their son – who was born only a week before the couple was married.

Celina has put most of this behind her – one would say she's far too busy, with four children to care for – but she is faced with a conundrum: What kind of religious education will Dylan have?

It is passing strange that here in Alberta, admittedly the heart of the so-called Bible belt, God and religion inhabit so high a place of concern, not just in people's private lives, but also in public life. Years ago, when my parents lived in Red Deer, a friend asked what central Alberta was like. I remarked the traffic jams on Sunday mornings were heavier than during the week. Of course, that was before I realized the closer one gets to the Alberta–U.S. border, the closer one gets to public religiosity. An example is the small town of Cardston, only a few kilometres from the American border. It has fewer than four thousand residents, but claims the first Church of Jesus Christ of Latter-Day Saints temple built outside the United States. The town was settled in 1887 by Mormon pioneers from Utah, who came in one of the last covered wagon expeditions. The temple was announced in 1912 and dedicated in 1923. For almost seventy years, it was the only Mormon temple in Canada, and to this day, after being renovated twice (and rededicated twice) it serves a growing community of LDS adherents in southern Alberta, British Columbia, and northern Montana. (There are five other temples in Canada, all located in much larger centres than Cardston: Edmonton, Regina, Toronto, Montreal, and Halifax.)

Equal attention is paid to other religions in the province, although a sort of polite Christian fundamentalism seems to be bred in our bones.

Social Credit, which held Alberta in its political sway from 1935 to 1971, arose out of a marriage of fundamentalist beliefs with economic theory. The Social Credit Party, long moribund, has been revived in the past few years, but it is no longer the "Christian" party William Aberhart meant it to be, but a party that reeks of discrimination and far-right attitudes.

Once Aberhart became premier of Alberta he discovered that Social Credit theory was easier to preach than to practise, writes

University of Alberta academic Bruce Guenther in his paper entitled "Populism, Politics and Christianity in Western Canada." Guenther says in his conclusion: "Christianity not only shaped the cultural ethos of central and eastern Canada, but also western Canada, albeit in fundamentally different ways. It underscores the fact that a commitment to Christianity is basic to an understanding of many leaders in western Canada. . . . A full exploration of the relationship between the 'west as protest' and the religious developments within the region would be a worthy project."

It is the curious demand that God and religion be publicly proclaimed that so differentiates Alberta from the rest of the country, which is more like Europe than the United States. In Europe, even in the staunchly Catholic areas, religion is a matter of personal choice, and the controversial issues that so plague our society are facts of life, especially abortion and birth control. It is not considered unusual or controversial that the presidents of France, Italy, or Spain, all Catholic countries, would head governments that approve of a woman's freedom of choice in matters of reproduction. Ireland, in that group, is still considered backward in its politicization of abortion.

In Canada, those who do not understand, appreciate, or accept the real separation of church and state continue, particularly in Alberta, to talk in shocked terms about how members, in good standing, of the Catholic Church – which forbids same-sex marriage and abortion (and birth control and, for that matter, fornication itself) – could approve of the Canadian government's liberal stance on sexual matters.

It is difficult to explain to someone not raised Roman Catholic, as I was, the concept of free will in matters of the soul. Not being a theologian, forgive me for any errors of Catholic theology I make in the following, but understand at least that one matter remains paramount, even under the strict rules of the Catholic Church: An act not only has to be a grievous sin, but I have to understand and agree that it is before I can be, as the fundamentalist Protestants are so fond of predicting – assigned to the farthest corner of the hottest hell.

I quote from the Baltimore Catechism, drilled into my brain so deeply I can still recite its questions and answers: "What three things are necessary to make a sin mortal? First, the thought, desire, word, action, or omission must be seriously wrong or considered seriously wrong; second, the sinner must be mindful of the serious wrong; third, the winner must fully consent to it."

So try and convince a few million Catholic women using birth control, who believe they are not sinning, that they are. I can point to many more millions of Catholics in North America who believe the Church's stance on birth control is born out of the Dark Ages and suits a patriarchy of old, celibate men, who have never birthed or raised children, nor ever had to make any of the reproductive decisions women face.

The convenient and workable separation of church and state in Canada, which allows our politicians to espouse whatever religion they choose without being called to account for any perceived or actual lapses in their public statement vis-à-vis that religion is not accepted by all Canadians, even though it protects all of us from the kind of discrimination "religious" governments can mete out to the unbeliever.

Bishop Henry announced that pro-choice Catholic politicians such as Joe Clark have a "weakness in their moral fibre," and, it was time, he said, for the Council of Canadian Bishops to "call some of these so-called Catholics to account." And that "account," according to Bishop Henry, was past due. "Now everyone in the church knows that it's difficult to mount a legal defence of life in a pluralistic democracy, and moral truth is going to be a hard sell sometimes. . . . But some of these politicians have either thrown in the towel, or given in to political expedience."

As if to add weight to his words – a weight that would be oppressive to any practising Catholic because of the threat – the bishop hinted if Clark died before him, he might not be around to bury him. It might seem just another minor threat to someone who isn't Catholic. Imagine, though, being denied a proper burial in your faith because the rabbi or imam or minister disagrees with your opinions. Because that's what it boils down to. I know. I went through this, long years ago, on the death of my first husband.

Clark's "error" was to separate his politics from his religion, a very Canadian decision. He supports a woman's right to choose in matters of birth control and abortion. My husband's "error" was, in fact, mine. Leslie George Elhatton did nothing but ask, as he was dying, to be reconciled with the Church of his and my childhood. As a baptized Catholic, he had that right. And also as a baptized Catholic, I had the responsibility to honour those wishes, and when he died, to arrange for a Roman Catholic funeral.

I took that obligation seriously, regardless of my lack of observance for so many years. Two days after his death, one day before his funeral, I was informed that I had offended the clerics and the church with Les Elhatton's obituary, written a month before he died and before his reconciliation. His obituary requested donations to his favourite charity, the Calgary Birth Control Association. I did not for a minute contemplate the furor my heartfelt obituary would cause. (More fool me. I would not wish the aftermath on any widow, regardless of her religion, her job, or her outspokenness.)

A more charitable group would have seen the inherent irony. After all, I had more on my mind than remembering a single line in a lengthy obituary I had not seen in all those long and painful weeks of watching my husband die.

I wrote his obituary while Les was dying, rather than wait and permit the funeral home to supply one to the newspaper that would not reflect the man himself. Once written, I had asked the advertising vice-president for the *Calgary Herald* to take it, to file it, and to wait. The details of his funeral were left blank. Writing it helped both Les and me. Les read it, and I loved the smile on his face that broke out. For me, it was a way of encapsulating my feelings and expressing them. There was nothing anyone could do but arrange for the inevitable. That obituary was part of those arrangements.

And when that night came and Les took his last breath in my arms, all of the final plans we had made together proved prescient. The decisions had been made and I was able to grieve.

But then his obituary was published and a single line, written a month before, was called into question. How dare I suggest donations to a group whose every effort was anathema to the Church? How dare I link Holy Mother Church with such godless work? That the linkage had never been made in my mind; that I had acted purely out of love, with absolutely no notion of making any kind of a political statement, made no difference.

The priest called and the bishop spoke. They hinted the Church, in whose faith this man had been baptized, and in which he had, in the final days of his life been reunited, would refuse his casket at the cathedral door.

They were not concerned with my grief. They were not concerned with my responsibility – also as a baptized Catholic – to make sure that my husband, because he had been given the last rites of our Church, receive a Roman Catholic funeral, despite his years of neglect of his faith. They worried, the bishop and the parish priest, only about their image.

They were profoundly unconcerned about my pain. They publicly repudiated me, in print, in my own newspaper. They judged, they threatened, and they gave up only when I gave the telephone to my sister and asked her to do whatever it was they wanted. Anything to satisfy the church so that the funeral would take place.

I was coerced in unctuous yet stern tones to change Les's obituary to something deemed less offensive. I was even held responsible for a predicted "demonstration" of the faithful over the coffin should it occur. It didn't, of course. There was no one at the funeral but our family and friends.

Subsequently, the parish priest denied he and the bishop had threatened me. Not to me, of course, not to the woman they had caused such pain, but to the late Pat O'Callaghan, then publisher of the *Calgary Herald* and coincidentally, a parish member. Father Stevenson wrote: "The original obituary was a cause of immediate public embarrassment to me and this parish, and it called for an immediate clarification . . . there was never an intention of cancelling the funeral service . . ."

This all happened in 1988, but the voices, the heartache, and the fear is as sharp now as it was that spring day in May. To this day, politicians who wear their religion on their sleeve and loudly proclaim their belief to anyone who will listen – just as George W. Bush does – make me very nervous.

The biggest challenge is yet to come. Too bad I won't be around to witness it: my own last rites. As a lapsed Catholic (bless me, Father, for I have sinned – I have no idea how long it's been since my last confession), the church will face a serious challenge when I pop off to see for myself if all this religious mumbo-jumbo makes any difference at all to eternity. (In keeping with another sturdy Catholic belief, I'll be making a deathbed reconciliation – just in case.)

Curiously enough, it was a Protestant minister and Mormon belief and not Catholic doctrine that planted in my mind the faint hope there would be an afterlife. Rev. Norman Vincent Peale was dismissed with obvious sarcasm by David Cloud in a 1994 article in a Baptist publication as: "one of the fathers and key promoters of the self-esteem gospel, the unholy mixture of modern psychology and the Bible which has almost taken over the Christian world." Worse, Peale was accused of attending schools which were "hotbeds of liberalism," according to Cloud, after questioning how "sound" was the faith of Peale's father, a Methodist preacher.

I'm going to presume more people know of Norman Vincent Peale than know who David Cloud is, and what his qualifications are for dismissing Peale's faith and beliefs as not true Christianity. Peale, who died in 1993, is best known for his book *The Power of Positive Thinking*. Peale believed in a God who takes care of all His children, not just those who are "worthy" of love, care, and redemption. Seems logical to me that God would be all these things, although we humans seem to usurp the name of God for whatever purposes we wish, from sports to amazing escapes from death. While it is comforting to believe God is on the side of the Miami Dolphins or the Calgary Stampeders, rather than the Green Bay Packers or the Toronto Argonauts, it is silly in the extreme. So, too, are the exhortations of godly intervention when one "miraculously" escapes destruction. The problem with such views of the Almighty is simple: If He's looking out for you or your side, why isn't he paying attention to everyone else? If we are all God's children, loved and cherished equally – indeed, if the Supreme Being is at all concerned with what is happening down here on earth – why war? Or famine? Why pain and suffering?

Fundamentalist Christians try to get around such conundrums by insisting bad luck is nothing more than a punishment from God, and there are religions that say we get more than one chance at life, albeit not necessarily as a human, before we are perfect enough to achieve nirvana.

No "true" believer seems to understand just how idiotic this kind of thinking is. We are the architects of our own destinies and the occasional victims of fate. We cannot know God's plan – or which team He bets on – and to credit or blame God for failure or success is ludicrous. As is, in some people's mind, the concept of heaven and hell.

Peale's view of eternity was of a perfect world on the other side of a curtain through which humanity cannot see, and which we cannot know, a heaven not unlike that promised by all faiths, minus the cherubs, saints, and in the case of a martyr for Islam, a slew of waiting virgins.

If you really want to ensure an eternal life, hope (or pray) for a Mormon relative or descendant. It is the belief of the Church of Jesus Christ of Latter-Day Saints that it is possible to ensure one's ancestors' return to God through salvation – even if they were not LDS members – through identifying who they are. Indeed, it is one of the duties of Mormons to research their families to enable as many to be saved as possible. It is this religious responsibility that has resulted in the LDS archives being one of the best sources for anyone researching genealogy.

As Alberta grows increasingly urban, welcoming more non-Christian immigrants into our cities and towns, the question of religion becomes less, not more, relevant. It may seem the opposite is happening, and for this you can credit (or blame) the increase of 29 per cent (Statistics Canada), in the number of Canadians identifying themselves as Pentecostals. If nothing else, they are vocal in their witnessing. Their whole is greater than their parts.

Canadian statistics still show the country about 46 per cent Catholic, 36 per cent Protestant, and a growing number of people – about 15 per cent – identifying themselves as having no religion at all.

The most obvious result of growing religious diversity – Sikh, Buddhist, Hindu, Muslim – is the need for public organizations, such as schools, and private concerns, such as workplaces, to adapt. Religious holidays, for example, are being questioned and such overtly Christian festivals as Christmas and Easter being the cause for holidays are being challenged, particularly in Canada's largest cities.

The questioning of public Nativity scenes in front of city halls, of traditional Christmas concerts, of religious hymns being taught to schoolchildren (Christmas carols in particular) is being hotly contested by those who see any change in tradition as bad. Nobody could count the number of complaints and the contempt and scorn levelled at officials who try to accommodate the multicultural and multireligious aspect of modern life.

Just mention changing the school Christmas concert to a Holiday Season concert or a Winter concert and wait for the opposition. The backlash against removing overt Christianity from Canada's public schools and public institutions has taken a page from the old book called persecution. The modern "persecution of the Christians" is one of the hottest anti-liberal topics in sympathetic newspapers, newsletters, and websites. Here's an example from the *National Review* book service, commenting on David Limbaugh's controversial but right-wing-pleasing 2003 book, *Persecution: How Liberals Are Waging War Against Christianity*. "Christians are increasingly being driven from public life . . . and even actively discriminated against for their beliefs."

The review continues: "In *Persecution* you'll enter the hotly contested battle for the soul of our public schools. Here are appalling – but true – stories of how anti-Christian social engineers not only prohibit school prayer and forbid students from wearing Christian symbols, like a simple cross, but even expunge the real story of Christianity in America from history textbooks. Worse still, in the name of 'diversity,' 'tolerance,' 'multiculturalism,' and 'sex education,' the social engineers actively inculcate hatred of Christianity as ignorant, repressive, and offensive. Not exactly the agenda of most parents whose tax dollars support the public schools."

There have been feeble attempts to "prove" that the above is happening right here in Canada, particularly in politics. One of the assumptions in the wake of the 2004 federal election was that the Conservatives lost the election because Canadians were suspicious of religion in public life. That was just plain wrong. Canadians may be suspicious of men and women who wear their religion on their sleeves, but mostly it just doesn't come up in conversation or in political decisions.

Fulminations against a "liberal agenda" are indicative of the hatred shown so-called liberals in the United States, but the forty-ninth parallel is no barrier to them. Yet, though this stuff seeps across the border and infects Canada, the status of religion in public schools, for example, is only rarely raised. When the issue of prayer in school was reopened a few years ago in Calgary, it resulted in a proposal from the school board to study and consider a "religious inclusion" program. Students would presumably learn about the world's religions without bias or prejudice.

Even there, the well-meaning trustees ran into protests when Wiccans found out they'd be excluded. They believed they were being discriminated against because they were pagan and thus not considered a "religion." Curiously, Wicca is most definitely a religion by any standard, celebrating what is called the Old Gods. It predates Christianity by a few millennia, as do its rituals, blessings, and beliefs.

The real reason behind the school board's attempt to have its cake and eat it too, is the overwhelming influence of Christianity in Alberta. What well-meaning public institutions fail to realize is that their attempt to take a middle-of-the-road stance is a non-starter. Regardless of what decisions are made by various school boards around the province, those supporting Christianity as the "state" religion in Alberta will never be satisfied until their bully tactics succeed.

But even in Alberta, even in the face of such a powerful special-interest group as Christianity, where the influence of evangelical Christianity far outweighs the number of adherents, most intelligent people recognize such arguments for what they are: the last desperate flailings of people who see their influence and their ability to mould public life in their own image rapidly waning in the face of a changing society.

12

Only "Real" Canadians Need Apply

All of us can remember some stunning example of our own ignorance. One of mine was not quite understanding the term "landed
immigrant." Nobody around me ever referred to the various newcomers as "landed immigrants." Nobody actually called them
immigrants. There were various scornful phrases employed for
identification, none of which are appropriate, let alone politically
or politely correct today.

Perhaps I could blame all those years in Edmonton, surrounded
by various "foreign" accents and, sadly, racist jokes, such as the one
about how the Ukrainian farmers would sew themselves into their
long winter underwear in October and leave themselves so encased
until spring seeding was finished. When they moved to town, they
saw no reason to change a lifelong habit. That was the reason, so the
explanation went, not to be anywhere near the Low Level bus
running from the east end into downtown on a Thursday late-
shopping night at Woodwards. Why anyone saw this bit of racism
as amusing still escapes me. I recall agreeing with all the inherent
biases of the era: DPs were dirty, stupid, and reeked of garlic;
bohunks (defined as anyone whose last name ended in "ski") would
sue their own mother; Indians were lazy drunkards living off welfare
and the sweat equity of others. Jews were beyond the pale. Everything

and everybody was U or non-U. As a child, I wasn't sure what that meant, either. (It's a particularly snippy British expression separating the favoured "upper" classes from everyone who wasn't.)

What did I know? Like other children of white-collar workers and professionals, I lived in a middle-class white ghetto where "foreign" was my Irish-born, war-bride mother. The children I went to school with all looked like me, shared a common religion and if not a common Canadian middle-class background, did not arrive at high school speaking their parents' broken English.

DPS? They were labourers with thick European accents. "Displaced persons" was the official designation for people uprooted by the Second World War and seeking a new life in Canada. They were to be avoided. Nobody ever explained why. It was just a given that "the other" was "not us," explanations unnecessary.

Luckily, none of this stuck beyond adolescence. I could see that my friends' parents who were Ukrainians, Hungarians (admired as freedom fighters after 1956), Poles, Russians, and all the other refugees from post-war Europe were no different than anyone else, notwithstanding the accents.

By the time I got to university, I was for all intents and purposes colour-blind. And in the first years of the 1960s, mores had changed and being exotic and different was desirable. So I applied at age sixteen to the University of Alberta as a "landed immigrant." I had no idea what one was, but I reasoned that my mother was raised in Ireland, I was born in England, and both of us came to Canada with the first wave of war brides patriated to their husbands' Canadian homes. That made me "landed" and an "immigrant." My Canadian father was dumbfounded to learn that his eldest child had no concept of who was really an immigrant to this country.

I was "born" Canadian, he explained, because he was Canadian and when he, Robert Ford, and my mother, Margaret Tunney, married in 1943, the law at that time made her a Canadian, also. Me, too, when I arrived in the middle of a bombing raid over London. (The real irony was that everyone but the Canadian government accepted my citizenship. When I first applied for a passport, I was shocked to be told I had to be able to "prove" I was Canadian, and thus had to apply for and keep a certificate of Canadian citizenship, the only member of my family to be so ordered. The expression on my father's face and the words he used to describe the government made the "landed immigrant" episode pale in comparison. I still resent having to produce the original of this certificate although I dutifully ship it off to Ottawa every five years to get a new passport.)

I offer this small story as an example of how endemic, how deeply rooted is the kind of racism that exists in "nice" countries like Canada. Racism of the more overt kind might actually be easier to handle because it's out there in public. Renaming Chinaman's Peak in the Rockies Ha Ling Peak may make us believe we are beyond such old-fashioned thinking, but we are fooling ourselves.

We no longer call the First Nations "Indians"; now they are aboriginals or the aforementioned collective. Has that changed our attitudes? Only by driving the bias underground and dressing it in smarmy and politically correct language. The only alienation Albertans acknowledge is that directed at Eastern bastards, of course. But there is more to alienation than the rest of Canada. We've done a fine job on some of our own, taking a lead from the prejudices imported here from Eastern Europe, Britain, France, and a host of other "white" countries.

One of the most glaring examples is the way we treated our own citizens of Japanese descent, and years later, in 1988, when the Canadian government issued a formal apology and offered financial redress for the treatment they received in the first years of the Second World War, the loudest voices were not of apology, but of outrage. How dare Prime Minister Brian Mulroney – or any Canadian prime minister – apologize to "them" in the face of implacable Japanese insistence there would be no formal apology offered to the Allied troops who were captured, imprisoned, and tortured by the Japanese when Hong Kong was overrun. The outrage was understandable, in light of fears that being captured by the Japanese was, indeed, a "fate worse than death." Those men who survived were the first veterans to be granted pensions in attempts to somehow acknowledge the vile treatment they received. The real surprise is that some actually survived the brutality of Japanese prisoner-of-war camps.

But the apology proffered by the Canadian government for the forcible disenfranchisement of Japanese-Canadians was not a quid pro quo. It wasn't offered to the Japanese government. It was offered to Canadians whose homes and businesses were expropriated – stolen, actually – and who were forced into internment camps and relocated from the West Coast to the interior. There is a comparison to be made between how Japanese-Canadians and Japanese-Americans were treated in the wake of the Pearl Harbor attack and how Muslims and other "foreign-looking" Canadians and Americans were treated by their respective governments after 9/11. There has been a similar hysteria about "suspicious-looking" men, which today is shorthand for anyone of Middle-Eastern or North-African Muslim heritage.

Like the Chinese, the Japanese were initially denied full Canadian citizenship, and when the First World War broke out, Japanese seeking to establish their loyalty to the country enlisted, only to be told they would have to serve in segregated units. It's a fact to keep in mind the next time we smug Canadians want to opine about the treatment of black Americans.

Unlike the situation of blacks in the United States, however, the Japanese were largely invisible to the majority population of the Prairie provinces because there were so few in the cities. Nonetheless, as the historical compilation, *People of Alberta*, says, "The arrival of Japanese settlers was viewed with suspicion and racism. A plan developed in 1908 to establish a sizeable Japanese farm community on irrigated land owned by the CPR east of Calgary did not come to fruition. The degree of public opposition the plan generated suggested that Albertans' underlying attitudes of prejudice differed little from the nativist sentiments that flourished in British Columbia. . . . In 1911, Alberta's Japanese population numbered only 244 individuals. By 1912, it had increased to only 493."

Those numbers remained stable until after the war in the Pacific began in December 1941 and federal legislation was enacted prohibiting Japanese-Canadians from living within 100 miles of the B.C. coast. Because of a labour shortage in the sugar-beet fields in southern Alberta, growers petitioned for some of the exiled B.C. Japanese-Canadians to be sent to work in the fields. They were promised much, including free housing and fair wages, but in fact were treated as little more than indentured labourers. And don't send too many was the attitude. As the late Ken Adachi wrote in his 1976 exposé, *The Enemy That Never Was*, "Although the labour shortage was critical, the Albertans did not desire an uncontrolled influx of Japanese, sensitized as they had been to the problems of colonies of 'unassimilable' people such as the Hutterites, already in their midst, and against whom they 'seethed with resentment,'" (according to a *Canadian Bar Review* case study). An arrangement worked out with the Alberta Social Credit government gave the province absolute control over the fate of the newcomers, preventing them from moving from farm to farm and forbidding them from settling in cities such as Calgary, Lethbridge, and Edmonton and the small towns of Picture Butte and Taber. "Indeed," writes Adachi, "most of the farmers looked upon the evacuees as a ready source of slave- or prisoner-of-war labour, ripe for exploitation which, under the terms of the agreement with the province, quickly became an accurate description."

There was only a single advantage for the Japanese – if families accepted relocation to Alberta, they would be able to stay together. Otherwise, women, children, and the elderly would be confined to crude camps in the B.C. interior, while the men and older boys were sent to work gangs.

Of the nearly 24,000 Japanese-Canadians affected, about 2,700 arrived in southern Alberta and were set to work in harsh physical conditions. Yet they persisted and made better lives for themselves through banding together as a community. Today, when an Albertan thinks about the Japanese in the province, he thinks of Lethbridge and the Japanese gardens, not about racism.

That doesn't mean racism and alienation is a thing of the past, just that we've found more pleasant memories on which to focus.

The price of forgetting, of not acknowledging the past truthfully, is not that the myth of an open, equal, accepting society is handed from generation to generation, but that it remains a myth. When Adachi was approached to write the history of the Japanese in Canada, in the wake of the Royal Commission on Bilingualism and Biculturalism, he embraced the task because, he writes: "Having been the victim since childhood of a particularly virulent strain of racism, I wished to reveal the demon in all its scaly ugliness and perhaps exorcise it."

Out of that vile episode of Canadian history came a tourist attraction: The Nikka Yuko traditional Japanese gardens in Lethbridge. Opened in 1967 as a Confederation centennial project, the name of the gardens means "friendship" in Japanese. They are, indeed, a beautiful legacy, but it is one born from ignorance and fear and is a lesson for the future. Adachi writes, obviously prior to the passing of the Charter of Rights and Freedoms: "What happened to the Japanese Canadians is an enduring monument to the fragility of democratic ideals in times of crisis in which, given the right circumstances, people so easily lose their perspectives on civil liberties."

That caution was written almost thirty years ago. It still applies, maybe even more so now the so-called war on terror has terrorized ordinary civilians into believing their next-door neighbour could be an embedded operative just waiting to be called into service.

It is far too easy for those of us living in "enlightened" times to forget how close we are to our roots of exclusion, bias, and fear of "the other." The Alberta Communal Property Act, for example, was abolished only in 1973. That Act, originally passed in 1947, restricted the Hutterite colonies of Alberta from freely buying land. They were forced to establish new colonies at least forty miles from existing ones. This legislation had replaced the 1942 Land Sales Prohibition Act, which prohibited the sale of any land to the Hutterites.

Who knows if it was the communal nature of Hutterite life, their pacifist stance, or the way the colonies kept to themselves that caused such a ruckus among farming communities?

The Hutterites (now numbering about twenty-five thousand, most of whom live in rural Alberta and Manitoba) are a splinter, strict Christian sect founded in 1528. They fled north to Canada from the United States in 1918, when they refused to observe military service.

They didn't get a much more friendly welcome north of the border and when Hutterites refused to serve in the Second World War, the resentment deepened. The colonies were seen as usurpers of farmland. Because all land is communally owned by the colony, and because colonies rarely failed to survive, the argument against the Hutterites was that they bought land and it never came back on the market. Farming communities lobbied for legislation to prevent Hutterites from amassing more and more acreage.

Unlike the Doukhobors in British Columbia, they didn't set fires and didn't march naked through communities to fight against discrimination. The Hutterites chose a more peaceful route, in keeping with their non-violent nature, but not with their tradition – the courts. Eventually, justice won out, and today the Hutterite colonies coexist peacefully with their rural neighbours. But discrimination still exists. While Hutterite families are a common sight at farmers' markets and in the stores and shops of Calgary, they are largely self-sufficient in their rural communities. They don't, as the expression goes, mix in. They buy little from local stores and don't participate in the life of the larger community. Some would argue this affects the social health and well-being of the entire community. They may not contribute, but they don't consume, either. Hutterites don't need the welfare of an outside community. It is an obvious source of resentment.

While Albertans persist in a belief that race, colour, and creed mean little and that we are all equal, the sad truth is that some of us are more equal than others. We participate in a mild form of racism toward minorities, but we reserve the real force of antipathy and alienation for ourselves and other Canadians.

It begins simply as a sense of isolation from decision-making. It escalates into discrimination against the so-called elites in Ottawa, and its bastard child, coddled and fed by Alberta neo-conservatives, is the discrimination against anyone who doesn't toe the "party" line. The only people really affected adversely by this attitude are any group of Albertans identified as have-nots. That takes in thousands of citizens who believe they have no voice in government, no leverage in the political process, and no way to change that.

They are dismissed as whiners, toadies to the left wing, and pawns in the political process. Yet they might only be rightfully asking for their share of the Alberta Advantage. Those men and women who have a right to participate in the good times as much as their richer neighbours find themselves systematically alienated. The complaints are ignored or characterized by the premier as "victims of the week," and they are seen as not quite U – not quite with the program; not "on side," as it were.

As far as the historical kind of alienation, we may not care for the hard-line separatists, but their intransigence and persistence in blaming the Ottawa bogeyman for perceived historical sins against Quebec and the West has served the cause well. In Quebec, it suits separatists to have a monster to blame. It suits them to talk about historical wrongs and how badly done by their "nation" has been under the yoke of English Canada.

On the other end of the country, the perceived grievances harboured by the West occasionally are fired up into an equally fervent expression of separatism. Only in Alberta's case, it isn't to form our own nation, but to join with the United States, to snuggle alphabetically – and geographically – between Alaska and Arizona.

The enduring myth of Albertans being born despising and distrusting Ottawa is a handy pot to keep on the simmer, ready to bring to a boil when needed. After all, a distant enemy deflects attention from any problems that may be the result of incompetence at home. Just ask the government of Quebec how convenient anti-Ottawa sentiment can be. Few Albertans would look upon their province as Quebec's twin, but the only real difference between Albertans and Quebeckers is that the latter have the guts to put their alienation to a vote.

Peter Lougheed defined the difference between Quebec and Alberta discontent as two sides of the same coin. Quebec, he said, wants to be master of its own destiny – *Maîtres chez nous* – while Albertans want to reduce their dependency upon Ottawa and the federal government. It's a subtle, but profound difference.

Alberta feels alienated through distance and being ignored; Quebec through culture and language. There are superficial, but interesting differences too: Quebeckers have partners; Albertans have spouses. In Alberta, a partner is the guy you went into business with. Albertans drink. So do Quebeckers, but they do so with considerably more responsibility than their Western cousins. Perhaps that may explain why Quebeckers watch the most television (drinking at home?) and Albertans, the least (drinking in bars?)

All things considered, Quebec sends fewer people to jail; Alberta sends more people to the polling booth. Alberta has the lowest rate of union membership; Quebec the second-best, after Newfoundland. Alberta has the highest standard of living of any province; Quebec shares the bottom with Newfoundland and New Brunswick. Both Alberta and Quebec have birthed political parties of dissent.

Indignation is fuelled by the history of economic favouritism toward Central Canadian interests, and comprises a list of political grievances headed by the notions that Parliament caters to Quebec and the majority votes of Ontario ignore Western interests. It can be something as simple and irrelevant as the Eastern media referring to former Ontario premier Mike Harris – on the day that he announced his resignation – as the Canadian politician who began the practical and political right-wing revolution in governance. Harris was lauded for his so-called Common Sense Revolution, which changed the face of provincial politics across the country. While Harris is said to have modelled his "revolution" on the examples set by U.S. Republicans, conventional wisdom believes he took more than a few pages of the playbook from Alberta premier Ralph Klein and his government, well into remodelling Alberta. What scorched-earth social policies were instituted in Ontario came from the example set in Alberta. Ralph Klein doesn't need a more inflated ego, but it would have been at least polite to have credited the Alberta premier with what he accomplished. That's not much of a reason to feel alienated, but it is an example of the irritation that Westerners live with daily.

Most historical grievances, from John A. Macdonald's national police that have become, as the RCMP, the most recognized police force in the world, to freight rates and the National Energy Program, have long been resolved. But it suits the West, as it suits Quebec, to keep that pot simmering. Ottawa helps keep the heat up by awarding government contracts to Quebec interests instead of to Western companies for what the West sees as purely political reasons.

Western alienation is a chimera, a mythical beast cobbled together out of things that go bump in the night and an overactive imagination. This is not to say it doesn't exist. But at its root it is not the desire to have a new country, as Quebec has worked toward for two generations, but the desire to have the old country pay attention. In this way, the West is much like the rebellious teenager who denies any relationship to his parents, but is afraid to cut all ties. The family metaphor is a favourite of Westerners who see Canada in those terms – dysfunctional, but nonetheless, family.

Safety, not lack of imagination, calls up such a prosaic metaphor. By invoking the comfortable thought of Canadian political and provincial dynamics being merely a family squabble, it avoids the real consequences of separation and alienation: get out, stay out, and don't bother to write. It avoids divorce, which only a few Westerners contemplate. It isn't Quebec-style separation the West wants, but a place at the head of the table. And at least half of Western alienation is resentment.

It is not a new construct. The roots are deep, buried in the rich central farmland, in the dry pastures of cattle country, in the rich reserves of oil and natural gas, but especially in the high-rise towers of Calgary, where the work ethic is strong, starts at 7 a.m., and seethes its way through the day, itching to be free of Ottawa's restrictions on the free market.

Today, three letters still make Albertan blood boil: NEP. The National Energy Program: Prime Minister Pierre Trudeau's 1980 decision to "Canadianize" the oil and gas industry and to set the prices for Alberta's resources inside Canada at half the world market price. It sucked about $6 billion out of Alberta and remains a metaphor for Ottawa's perfidy.

There's an aspect to Western alienation that has yet to be investigated – the idea that emotional and intellectual disconnect are a function of age, not just geography. The most prominent voices are those of older, disaffected neo-conservatives who have found tenured lodging in Alberta's (and specifically Calgary's) universities.

They promote a "firewall" around the province to stop the outflow of wealth, although there is no widespread public opposition to guarantees of regional equalization, where provinces share the wealth in somewhat equal measures. It's the "equal" part of equalization that grates on the sensibility of the more vocal critics. They believe, not without support, that he who pays the piper should call the tune: that if Alberta is to be dunned for what is seen as more than its fair share of the burden of supporting the have-not provinces, Alberta should have some say in where the money goes, and what it pays for.

Economist Robert Mansell, of the University of Calgary, asked this simple question in a media interview: "Why is it that we have to contribute so much and have so little say in how the money is spent?" He calculated that in the thirty-five years up to 1997, Albertans contributed more than two thousand dollars each to Ottawa while Ontarians paid more than two hundred dollars each – figures that are still skewed, even if the difference in population numbers is factored in. To add insult to injury, during that time the income of the average Albertan was 3 per cent higher than the national average, while in Ontario, the average was 16 per cent higher.

Thus far over the years, no acceptable answer has been forthcoming from any quarter.

Roger Gibbons, director of the Canada West Foundation, is one of the few critics to point out that equalization is not in dispute –

it's the use of Alberta money for federal programs that intervene in ways many people here find unacceptable that is in dispute. Loan guarantees to businesses is something that particularly rankles. Here in Alberta, as Ralph Klein likes to say, the government is out of the business of doing business. So much so it passed legislation to that end.

Critics of how equalization money is used whisper what in Canada is the unsayable: That maybe paying the Atlantic provinces not to adjust to reality is not the solution. It isn't that a single person – except for maybe a couple of cranks who believe paying any kind of taxes is an affront – objects to helping Newfoundland or the other Atlantic provinces whose traditional livelihood is threatened with extinction. After all, for many Albertans, they're helping family directly. Probably the second-largest number of islanders off the Rock live right here in Alberta. (The majority live in Toronto.)

Nobody ever suggests cutting off aid to the East Coast, at least until the region, the have-not of the Canadian economy, begins to realize the royalty profits from its offshore oil and gas reserves. The Atlantic Accord, reached in January 2005, fulfills a Liberal election promise of a 100 per cent return of royalties to Nova Scotia and Newfoundland and Labrador, and further guarantees continuation of federal transfer payments.

Six academics at the University of Calgary decided to address equalization payments and the use of Alberta's money elsewhere in the country, writing to the premier of Alberta suggesting it was time for a firewall around the province. It looked like a political document for more independence. It was really a call to decrease the amount of money Alberta contributes to the federal transfer system.

These academics, their degrees adding gravitas to what is essentially a mass bleat, are supported by a younger generation, in whose minds lurks no long-standing litany of complaints and abuse, merely self-interest. It is not a far stretch to link the voices of Western alienation with the demands of liberty from a centralized government, control of the marketplace, and a failure to commit to the social capital of the country.

Robert Putnam articulated this disconnect in a brilliant book on the corrosion of society, *Bowling Alone: The Collapse and Revival of American Community*. His opinions fit Alberta just as well. He posits late-born Generation Xers comprise a single less-tolerant cohort than their parents; a gathering of the disengaged and intolerant. He writes, "Communities whose residents bowl alone are the least tolerant places in America."

It is a question of community and who decides how it is formed. My generation believes community is local; Generation X sees it as electronic, without a physical reality.

As Alberta's population is among the youngest in the country, there are more disconnected-but-wired young people here than elsewhere. They make a heady combination – rootless young people who don't understand commitment to a greater good at the expense of their own desires; and an older generation determined to free Alberta from Ottawa's interference, their alienation born not from culture or environment, but from their own minds.

Out of this culture of alienation comes the disease of paranoia, and it is rampant in Alberta, as it is in the United States. We imported it on the wings of popular culture. While Canadians have never been as mistrustful of government as their American cousins, a similar paranoia about government and its actions lives and thrives in Alberta.

Ian Dowbiggin outlines exactly how and why paranoia has been accepted and has infiltrated our culture in his 1999 book, *Suspicious Minds: The Triumph of Paranoia in Everyday Life*. Most of the blame goes to electronics and the ubiquitous entertainment industry. For Dowbiggin, film producer Oliver Stone and his popular 1991 movie *JFK* captured the conspiracy motif. "Stone is just another in a long line of Hollywood moviemakers since the 1960s who not only indulge the public taste for conspiracy theories but appear to believe in them as well . . . (Stone) celebrates the paranoid imagination," writes Dowbiggin.

He cites programs such as *The X-Files* and *Millennium*. "In these programs the world increasingly takes on the appearance of a gigantic battle between right and wrong, good and evil, sin and innocence, light and darkness. Since the human psychological tendency is to take the side of persecuted righteousness in such struggles, it is little wonder viewers respond to such storylines. Paranoia thrives in the 'adversary culture' where estrangement, alienation, anger, fear and suspicion abound."

Since September 11, 2001, and the terrorist attacks on Washington and New York, that paranoia has been expanded and fuelled. Those horrific assaults on the fabric of North American life, on its citizens and innocents have served to reawaken some of the trust Americans had lost in their government, but they did nothing to alleviate the paranoia. They merely gave conspiracy theorists another target, and allowed what Dowbiggin calls "persecuted righteousness" to embody the U.S. government, instead of the individual being the one persecuted.

What this means to Alberta is simple: Suspicion and mistrust, especially of too much government and too many strangers, the thinking that characterizes the far right, extends northward from its headquarters in the wilds of Montana and Idaho to central Alberta, where Red Deer and its surrounding countryside are home to fundamentalist Christians (and the wacko contingent who believe that Bentley resident Jim Keegstra was unjustly persecuted for his Holocaust denials while he was teaching in an Eckville public school).

Canadians shouldn't pat themselves on the back for having no homegrown paranoid culture. We do. It's the notion that there is a mammoth conspiracy to sell out Canada and destroy it from within.

Anti-NAFTA lobbyists used this fear to great benefit during the free-trade debates, hinting that being too close to the United States, particularly doing business with them, instead of just being neighbours would inevitably result in Canada being sucked into America. Free trade would be just the first step in the takeover. As Dowbiggin writes, "To Canadian conspiracy theorists, the FTA was the first act in a carefully scripted scenario that would culminate in Quebec separation, the U.S. annexation of Canada, and the building of the

Grand Canal Project. This project has as its goal the damming of James Bay in order to make it a freshwater lake. Next this water will be diverted south through a complex system of dams so it can eventually flow into arid American regions hit hard by global warming and non-sustainable farming methods."

An offshoot of this thinking was that within days of the terrorist attacks on the World Trade Center and the Pentagon, the paranoid were predicting Canada would have to give up its sovereignty in order to protect itself against attack by allowing the Americans to provide defence. That was, of course, because commentators in the States had already begun to blame Canada for what they claimed were lax immigration and refugee policies, which allowed terrorists to freely pass over the longest undefended border in the world. Few pundits bothered to point out that whether or not Canada permitted "undesirables" into the country on humanitarian or refugee grounds had precious little to do with whether the United States border was porous. It is understandable, though, that a nation as confident in itself as the United States would seek to lay blame for perceived security breaches elsewhere. The unspoken truth is that if the terrorists were gaining access to the States through Canada, the hole in the fence must perforce exist on the American side, it being their responsibility to keep the undesirables out. A blunt truth would be that anyone leaving Canada is of little concern to Canadian authorities: a good riddance attitude.

Nonetheless, writes Dowbiggin: "A concept typical of paranoid popular culture is that government law enforcement agencies unwittingly aid the terrorist cause, underscoring the notion that, rather than being part of the solution, they are instead part of the problem."

A subset of that thinking is the less dangerous, but no less obtuse popular notion that the Canadian government is soft on criminals, and that whatever version of the Young Offenders Act is in place, it mollycoddles juvenile delinquents who would be, it is argued, better off in boot camp or jail until some sense is literally knocked into their heads. At least a century's worth of study of juvenile crime makes no difference to this kind of thinking, which holds that beating or lashing a youthful criminal will turn him or her into an upright young citizen. This, too, is part of paranoia.

Of course, as Dowbiggin points out, if they really are after you, it isn't paranoia. And in Alberta, sometimes it isn't paranoid.

Consider the fact that this province has had only four changes of political thought in its history. Back in 1975, David Bettison, John Kenward, and Larrie Taylor wrote in *Urban Affairs in Alberta*:

> This tendency to one party government and the relative ineffectiveness of left-wing ideologies reflects Albertans' stoic recognition of the value of individual rights, coupled to their consciousness that they have been the subject of thoroughly exploitive policies imposed upon them from elsewhere and especially from eastern Canadian companies. . . .
>
> Radical thought of the 1920s and 1930s in Alberta differed from left-wing thought in industrial Europe because Albertans themselves were title holders to agricultural land with obviously immense potential, or were owners of businesses in urban centres with equal potential. What was seen to be wrong was the world system outside Alberta. . . . Outside companies and political parties to whom their interests were tied had immorally crashed the economic system while still holding Albertans handcuffed to interest rates on borrowed money for Albertan exploitation. This in turn restricted Albertan capacities to take effective remedial action even inside their own province.

The surprise is not that Albertans talk about alienation, it is that after enduring more than a century of it, we're still here, still proud to be Canadians, and still wondering why we are so attached.

If Alberta were geographically located above Texas, rather than sparsely populated rural Montana, the situation might be different. Given the resonance between Texans and Albertans, the two powerful energy giants, both of which chafe against the East and their national governments and all of those regulations, might have banded together for the independent (and presumably landlocked) republic of Albertex, or Texberta, take your pick.

Permeating both cultures is the attitude of self-reliance and the raw dislike of weakness and dependence. (The cowboy attitude of taking care of the 'little woman' flourishes in both places. The cowboy culture is always surprised when those soft-voiced, dependent critters rise up and complain. It's no surprise, either, that charges of sexism, racism, or any other "ism" that flourishes in a dominant male culture is received with aggrieved sensibility, as if "we" weren't doing enough for "them.") The culture itself, regardless of gender, is one of lead, follow, or get out of the way.

University of Calgary historian and expert on military affairs David Bercuson, speculates on alienation as a product of attitude, rather than environment and culture. "Clearly some of the grievances that stimulate the growth of regional feeling . . . exist in the mind only. Attitude itself has created and sustained alienation and regionalism in the West," he wrote more than twenty years ago in the *Journal of Canadian Studies*.

Not much has changed, even though Alberta, its fortunes, and its people, are different today than they were a generation ago.

13

Drumheller and Dinosaurs of All Ages

I first visited Drumheller and its surrounding badlands, scored with hoodoos and canyons, more than forty years ago. I was more interested in the university agriculture student, who was riding across the hot, dry plain with me masquerading as a tall, lean cowboy, than in the topography or history of this small central Alberta town. I was a teenager, and he had taken me home to the farm to meet his parents and the horses.

I remember little of that hot, airless day in a summer's romance – except for a single breathtaking memory of a cloudless blue sky, dry grasses covering the ground to the southern horizon, and the vista down the Red Deer River Valley where the August sun lit up the variegated layers of the valley rocks, laid down over millions of years ago and subsequently polished bare by retreating glaciers.

By the time I returned thirty years later, Drumheller had become a magnet for paleontologists, geologists, and civilian dinosaur fans worldwide. The attraction of this small town was not only the 3.5 billion years of the Earth's life captured in the strata of the valley rocks, but what those rocks contained: dinosaur fossils, a treasure trove of calcified memories of the world's most famous extinct inhabitants.

Whatever killed the dinosaurs in the late Cretaceous period left them to sink into the tropical vegetation and be buried by river sediments and later covered with ice (more than a thousand metres deep at the thinnest point during the long, cold sleep of the ice age). When the glaciers melted and retreated, they left in their wake the Red Deer River Valley, its lakes, and the polished stone formations of the hoodoos.

(Pause for a moment in this millennial sweep of geological and paleontological history and consider the irony of the creationists' contention that man and dinosaur lived together in a world only six thousand years old. Anyone with even a basic knowledge of science would stifle a laugh at such nonsense. Nonetheless, one finds evolution still considered a "theory" and creationism or its euphemism, "intelligent design," taught as God's truth. And nowhere is this more evident, albeit pale by U.S. fundamentalist standards, than in the central farmlands of Alberta, within a couple of dinosaur lengths of Drumheller's fossils.)

Drumheller today is only marginally different from Drumheller of a century ago, when in the 1880s J.B. Tyrell stumbled across a dinosaur skull while prospecting for coal. The discovery of rich coalbeds around Drumheller spelled prosperity for the region. By the time the train connected Drumheller to Calgary in 1913, the first settler in the region, Sam Drumheller, was already exploiting the rich deposits. In time, there would be forty coal mines in the area and a thriving population dependent on what are still two of the three legs in the tripod of the Alberta economy – natural resources and agriculture. (The third, tourism, had to wait until Tyrell's dinosaur discovery, subsequently named Albertasaurus, proved to be the real economic future of the region.)

By 2005, Drumheller still had less than eight thousand people and after a brief foray into city status had reverted by vote to a town. It is possible to buy a house there for under $150,000 and a building lot for less than $45,000. In keeping with the evangelical Christian nature of the region, Drumheller has eleven churches, exactly the same number as hotels and motels.

Also in keeping with the tendency of small-town Alberta to employ a gimmick for visitors, just north of town on the forty-eight-kilometre loop of the so-named Dinosaur Trail, tourists find the world's largest dinosaur, a twenty-five-metre-high replica of a *Tyrannosaurus rex*, through whose "teeth" they can survey the expanse of the Alberta badlands.

But Drumheller's real tourist draw is the magnificent Royal Tyrell Museum of Paleontology, opened in 1985, which features the most extensive collection of dinosaurs in the world. It is a particular favourite with children, and with adults looking to keep their little darlings open-mouthed and curious for hours. Visitors can also watch technicians as they carefully separate fossils from the surrounding rock. That's not just for show, like panning for gold in Dawson City. It is the visible face of what goes on beyond the exhibits and walls of the Tyrell: the genuine science for which the museum is world-famous, and the research facility whose scientists are experts on dinosaur fossils and in demand worldwide.

The land surrounding Drumheller is an ideal place for philosophical thought – and a picnic, too. Unlike the Barney-the-Dinosaur made-up world of the creationists, the land reveals its real age and history mutely and softly. One must look for it in the layers of stone; adjust one's vision to appreciate the difference between the dusty brown rock and those faint squiggles that look like more of nature's handiwork left behind by the glaciers. Look closer and see fossils. Thousands of them, all that remains of those magnificent creatures who laid down to die on the wet grassy plain.

The philosophical question is, of course, Why in the face of proof to the contrary do creationists deny what they see with their eyes in favour of what they believe in their hearts?

To understand, one must first set a tare weight: Not all residents of rural Alberta are creationists. Not all are fundamentalist Christians or, as is the case in southern Alberta and the area around Cardston, members of the Church of Jesus Christ of Latter-Day Saints. Not all are even religious in terms of attending services. But for the purposes, let's assume the stereotype, then ask why does

Alberta seem to have more than its share of fundamentalist Christians, seemingly far outweighing the more mainstream Christians? Maybe the creationists/fundamentalists are just more vocal in their requests for prayer, discipline, and the Good Book in the schools serving their children; more intolerant of secular humanism; more, shall we say, "American" in their thinking. On the whole, they are against the gun registry; in favour of corporal punishment both in the home and in the school; dead-set against liberalism in any of its forms; suspicious of central government and programs that might usurp a parent's authority, such as daycare; patriotic and nationalistic in their expressions of citizenship and wary of "the other," the stranger, whether he be a dark suit from Ontario or a dark person from the even-more-distant East.

To understand, while you're lying on your back in the grass outside of Drumheller contemplating the nature of life, it is necessary to look south, down into the soul of Conservative America. It is even more necessary to appreciate that Albertans are Canadians with a healthy dose of American values.

There are a myriad of myths and hoaxes believed by Albertans, not just that men and dinosaurs were buddies only a few thousand years ago. Firstly, though, let's look at a fictional "map" of fundamentalism and its influence on Alberta. The map begins at the U.S.–Mexico border with a broad base excluding only California. It narrows as it sweeps northward, excluding states such as Washington and Oregon in the west and all of New England, New York, and Michigan. It crosses into Alberta from Montana and Idaho like a pyramid, with the tip extending as far north in Alberta as Red Deer.

Those Christian believers who live within the scope of that map have more in common with each other than with non-believers, agnostics, believers in other religions, or people of other nationalities, even if their next-door neighbour is one of those. When Americans came north into Alberta many stayed, and their influence in the cultural life of the province, along with their heavy influence on business attitudes, made southern Alberta almost a different country than the north of the province. A blogger named

Matthew Yglesias writes, not necessarily with tongue in cheek: "The real lines of cultural cleavage in North America do not track the international boundary very well. Quebec is obviously culturally distinct from the rest of Canada in a variety of ways. The American South isn't like the rest of the U.S.A. Meanwhile, the northern portions of the U.S. tend to resemble whichever bits of (English-speaking) Canada they happen to be adjacent to." He's slightly wrong in only one geographical area: when it comes to religious practices, the influence is more south to north in Alberta than the other way around.

In his 1995 study of Canadian social trends, *The Bibby Report*, University of Lethbridge sociology professor Reginald Bibby comments: "In Canada, we make much of our diversity. Yet, when it comes to what we want out of life, we have a great deal in common." Albertans share with other Canadians many needs and desires, the prime one being, to no one's surprise, happiness, the pursuit of which is guaranteed in the U.S. Constitution and nowhere mentioned in our own.

"There is nothing that Canadians say they value more than happiness," Bibby says. "The trick, of course, is how to find it . . . a close second 'want' is freedom. We seem to have the notion that happiness and freedom virtually go hand in hand. Most of us want the freedom to be able to do the things we want to do without having to be inhibited by people, lack of money, or lack of time."

We look for happiness through relationships: we want to be loved. We look for freedom through privacy, and, says Bibby, "We assume happiness and freedom will be realized as we experience success and the accompanying financial rewards that make for physical comfort."

It's over "freedom" – the quintessential American value – that Albertans (Westerners in general) start to look different from Eastern and Central Canadians. It is only in the West, in British Columbia in particular, where freedom is ranked "very important" by more than 90 per cent of respondents to Bibby's poll. (The national average is 87 per cent.) And it is only in the Prairies where family scores the highest (93 per cent) in importance.

Maybe a non-academic can draw the conclusion no scientist such as Reg Bibby would: The big difference in values across the country, the big difference between Alberta and the rest of Canada, is centred on this concatenation of freedom and family. It reflects the strength of the rural community here and shows, in a subtle way, how much the West shares with the United States, where the family is considered the first source of community and strength, and where religious observance matters. And in matters religious, Albertans do appear to be more like Americans, at least on the surface.

Nearly half the population of the U.S. consider themselves to be born-again Christians, an expression not in common usage in Canada. Rather than being identified as "born-again," similar Canadians are grouped, says Bibby, under the heading of "conservative Protestants," and are the only religious group in Canada to show an increase in attendance at weekly services. The phrase "conservative Protestants" embraces the evangelical Christian movement, including Baptist, Pentecostal, Mennonite, Salvation Army, Nazarene, and the Alliance Churches. The influence of the born-again Christian movement in the United States has affected Alberta in a more pronounced fashion than in other parts of Canada. The steady influx of Alberta's largest invisible minority – Americans – keeps religious movements in the public eye more than in the rest of the country, where religious observance is a more personal, less public act. It is not a stretch to suggest that when Texans, among the more religiously observant of Americans, move to Alberta to work for its oil and gas companies, they bring with them strong cultural influences. One of those is church observance and attendance.

As in the United States, religious observance – what you do, not just what you say – is a normal component of weekly life in Alberta's small towns, cities, and rural areas.

In the rest of Canada, the two most influential religions – Catholic and mainstream Protestant – seem in a curious way to "cancel" each other out. It makes for a secular country that works, despite a long history of discrimination against minority religions, particularly Catholicism in once-determinedly Orange Order Ontario. Certainly, it isn't that the rest of Canada is "less" religious than Alberta, but that there's a lot less public discourse about it. At a time when God is invoked on both sides of a war, when fundamentalist ideologues hold far too much power, to be able to live peacefully in a secular country is worth celebrating.

That doesn't mean that Canadians outside Alberta aren't involved with their religions. When Opinion Canada, a publication of the Centre for Research and Information on Canada, commissioned a poll on religious practices across Canada in 2004, results showed 61 per cent "believe that religious practice is an important factor in the moral and ethical lives of Canadians." That's an impressive number for a country regarded by some as amoral, immoral, godless, or secular humanist.

Unlike our neighbours to the south, Canadians are more willing to mind our own business about religion. We do not demand our leaders make a public show of attending Sunday – or Saturday – services to "prove" they believe in God. In much the same way, we don't wave the flag or pronounce our patriotism in public fashion by reciting an oath of allegiance daily in our schools and our lives. But for many in Alberta, this doesn't sit well. They take from our American friends, in the literal as well as the figurative sense, the idea that public demonstration of nationalism and patriotism are a good thing.

A significant number of Albertans, if public noise is any indication, want the Lord's Prayer back in all public schools and have demanded the national anthem be sung daily. Sadly, they have righteously defended these demands by trying to demonize those Albertans who do not approve of overt displays of nationalism and religion.

There is a reason public schools are called public and are different from private, religious, or, particularly in Alberta, charter schools. But we have been slow to achieve truly non-religious schools in Canada. While the "public" schools have been theoretically free of religion from the beginning, in fact, what they were free of was Roman Catholicism – "papism" to quote the bigotry brought from Protestant England.

Until the last ten or so years, until immigration started to make a huge difference to our urban schools, there was no real attempt made to appreciate, understand, or allow for a truly public system, such was the weight and the power of the majority Christian culture. So Jewish or Hindu or aboriginal children were the sometimes bewildered, sometimes oppressed captives of a system that insisted they attend a non-religious school, but did not insist the system actually be free of religion.

The belated move to de-Christianize the system across Canada has met with resistance and contempt, and not only in Alberta, from groups who presume a Judeo-Christian heritage means the public school system was therefore Christian. (The irony of Judeo-Christian meaning only the latter is not lost on those who choose to acknowledge it.) Howls of protest came when schools began calling the Christmas concert the "holiday concert," although it is passing curious that Christians minded. Presumably, for a true Christian it wouldn't matter what an event was called, what would matter is the observance of what one believes.

There are many who propose that children of other faiths whose parents choose to send them to public schools can be absented from the class while everyone else prays. Bad idea. This is simply an open invitation to separate kids into "us" and "them." Ask anyone educated in Alberta public schools prior to the 1960s how it felt to be "excused" from daily prayers, and the answer will likely be "singled out and different."

The danger of religious discrimination was highlighted by the attacks on New York and Washington on September 11, 2001. For far too many ordinary people, the attacks were carried out by Muslims, not by crazed terrorists with a warped and twisted view of God and religion in general and their souls in particular. It became risky for Muslim women to wear the hijab, their religious head scarf, on the streets of Canada and the United States.

Religious discrimination is never far from the historical memories of many Albertans. Between 1899 and as late as the early 1950s, when Dutch Calvinists brought their Christian Reformed Church to a welcoming Alberta, victims of religious persecution have sought refuge here. It was likely the promise of being able to buy land in uncrowded areas, rather than a reputation for freedom, that attracted more than 7,500 Doukhobors from Russia to Saskatchewan, Alberta, and British Columbia in 1899. Eventually, the Doukhobors concentrated their colonies in British Columbia. Both Alberta colonies, one at Cowley-Lundbreck, the other at Arrowood-Shouldice had disbanded by 1945.

When ten families of Mormons fled Utah for Alberta in 1887 after the Church of Jesus Christ of Latter-Day Saints abolished the practice of polygamy, they were initially viewed with suspicion. That soon vanished as members of the sect eschewed polygamy and quickly integrated themselves into mainstream Canadian life. By 1905 when Alberta was named a province, there were ten thousand Mormons in southern Alberta.

Acceptance was harder for those immigrants who lived communally, especially during the First World War, when the pacifist Hutterites and Mennonites, who had fled persecution in Europe, were viewed with deep suspicion, given their federal government exemption from military duty.

Today, the Hutterite colonies flourish in southern Alberta, and Mennonites are indistinguishable from any other Christian sect. The public fear has abated, and we have returned to our benign acceptance of other beliefs and religious practices. Even in the United States, for the furor about "clean" television, the reaction to the brief sight of Janet Jackson's nipple during the 2004 Super Bowl halftime show (referred to as a "wardrobe malfunction"), and the subsequent five-hundred-thousand-dollar fine levied against CBS, has not resulted in a public demand for legislated morality. Church and state are still separate, all the loud protestations from Christian moralists concerning the dangers of secular humanism notwithstanding.

That belief in the evils of secularism finds its loudest voice in Alberta in the question of so-called family values. Faith and family values are so intertwined for many in Alberta, some have forgotten that these are distinct matters – just ask anyone who opposes same-sex marriage on the ground of what the Bible says.

So-called family values are so entrenched here, they've been invoked by successive governments. Yet few of those governments have ever explained what they mean by invoking family values. It is assumed we, all the members of Alberta's families, will understand.

Former premier Don Getty made family values a holiday in February, after his own family was publicly embarrassed by the arrest of one of his sons on a drug-trafficking charge. Before that pronouncement, which made the third Monday in February a statutory holiday, and which one columnist called a "twenty-four-hour spasm of insincere good intentions," Getty had announced there was a rampant attack on the family. Nobody was quite sure what he meant by that, but he received enthusiastic support from all sorts of groups who saw, in the increasing diversity of this province and its people, a threat to a way of life.

Maybe the critics should have relied less on the easy answer and more on simple demographic fact. It is demographics and not a shift in values that has changed the traditional concepts of family and marriage. In the 1996 bestseller *Boom, Bust, & Echo*, David Foot and co-author Daniel Stoffman predicted: "At the turn of the millennium, don't be surprised if it appears that society has once again begun to neglect family values and to rediscover sex, drugs and new music." And that is what has happened. "Social observers will herald the arrival of yet another value shift, but the real reason will be the demographic shift," write Foot and Stoffman. Of course, blaming demographics is not nearly as morally satisfying as blaming immorality, loose values, character flaws, and poor upbringing.

In the same way, there's no magic or mystery to the increase in young mothers choosing to stay home with their preschool children. Again, it's demographics. The one-parent working, one-at-home model usually referred to as the traditional family has been the norm for years. "This demographic trend in favour of traditionalism will be operating in Canada until the echo generation (those born between 1980 and 1995) reaches marriageable age, starting around 2005."

When Premier Getty announced the first Alberta Family Day Act, in 1990, he talked about the erosion of family structure and its values and promised his government would stress traditional family values. Some groups chose to interpret this as a denunciation of families that did not fit the mould of one man, one woman, and their children. Gays and lesbians took it to mean a direct attack on their families. They were right to do so.

In all the debate about family values, nobody explains what is the traditional family, what are its values, and what is so great about them. In truth "traditional" doesn't mean traditional at all. It means a form of family that was fleetingly prevalent in the 1950s. I was raised in one: father, mother, one sister, one brother, grandparents, assorted uncles, aunts, and cousins.

In this model the husband is at work, the wife at home, the children seen but not heard. I'm not saying there is something intrinsically wrong with it, but let's not call it "traditional." I loved it. I remember how good it felt to come home from school each afternoon to find my mother there, the house warm and welcoming. I still believe that model to be the best for children. But I also know exactly how lucky I was to be raised in a family that was stable and secure. My father was not killed during the war, as other children's fathers were. My parents were not divorced, my mother not single. When we are young, all of us must live with the choices made for us by adults, and it would be foolish today to believe that the only option we have for raising happy children is the nuclear family model. The operative word here is choice – all families choose to be constructed. Should the nuclear family option be the only one?

I am a lucky member of the first generation to have choices – the war children, the vanguard of the Baby Boom.

The nuclear family endured through the 1950s, in its saccharine sweetness, in its single, magazine-cover-glossy dimension as the

Western world attempted to regain what had been lost forever. But a generation of women, many of whom had held "men's" jobs during the war, were not prepared to believe any longer in the notion of man as master, or that their gender rendered them incapable of doing certain jobs.

By the middle of the 1960s came the real '60s' revolution – feminism and the refusal of women to be treated as chattels any longer. Much ink and thought has been devoted to the sexual revolution and to flower power and the effect of the Vietnam War, but it was feminism that really changed things. For the better.

Those who have been most adversely affected by the call in Alberta for a return to "family values" (a code word for the nuclear family) were all the people who thought they had a family until they realized the government didn't think so. This includes single mothers and people in same-sex relationships.

The question of same-sex marriage is the big one in terms of the definition of families. The Alberta government has described marriage as being between a man and a woman. And a majority of Albertans oppose same-sex marriage, even as they don't want overt discrimination over same-sex benefits or relationships. It is the word *marriage* that gets in the way.

But it has come to pass, regardless of existing legislation or roadblocks, or any attempts by provinces to build a firewall or use the notwithstanding clause of the Constitution to prevent it. In the same way that the province's attempts to limit adoptions by gays or lesbians and deny benefits to the surviving spouse of same-sex relationships were toppled by court rulings, so too will any discriminatory legislation against same-sex marriage.

Few Albertans, regardless of their religious or political attachments, truly want to live in a society that boldly proclaims discrimination is a provincially mandated exercise. That Quebec invoked the notwithstanding clause is not permission for Alberta to do the same. (Quebec did it for language, not for sexuality. The difference, while obvious – sexual orientation not being a matter of choice – can't be overlooked.)

228 • CATHERINE FORD

Countries such as the Netherlands have eliminated the definition of marriage as a union between a man and a woman. All the
benefits and responsibilities accruing to married couples stay in
place, regardless of the gender of the couple. The sky did not fall.
Society did not collapse. The only difference now is that men and
women who lived on the sufferance and whim of the state are now
legally responsible for each other, for their property, for any children, and for their lives. It is coming soon to Canada.

Witness a 2001 Alberta Court of Queen's Bench ruling on
Alberta's estate law. The case was about a gay man who died intestate and whose estate went only to his estranged wife and children,
instead of being shared among his partner and his children, as would
be the case if his partner had been female. When Alberta Justice Del
Perras ruled the Intestate Succession Act contravened the Charter
of Rights and Freedoms, he set into motion the requirement for
Alberta to investigate and alter about fifty other pieces of provincial legislation defining couples as exclusively heterosexual. The
time is coming when any law pretending some couples are more
valid than others will have to be rewritten, and that likely includes
any law limiting marriage.

Yet the feeling still exists, despite court rulings to the contrary,
that granting equal rights to homosexuals is somehow giving them
"special rights." Such court rulings raise the hackles of an overly
concerned minority. I don't pretend to understand such fear;
nonetheless, it exists. Similarly, I don't accept the basis for the
concern, but there are far too many people who feel threatened by
it to dismiss it out of hand.

Delays in legislation are inevitable. But a charter ruling has
legitimacy over whatever bills are passed by any single government.
And forget the notwithstanding clause, frequently cited as an escape
for Alberta legislators. Any hint of using the clause has always been
rejected vocally by Alberta citizens. (The government mused years
ago about using the notwithstanding clause to limit the amount
of compensation paid to citizens who had been sterilized during
one of the province's darkest periods of discrimination, when the

eugenics law was arbitrarily used to sterilize the mentally retarded – presumed or actually mentally challenged. It has also suggested the notwithstanding clause could be used against homosexual rights and other so-called moral evils.)

The notwithstanding clause is a much-misunderstood and frequently maligned section of the Charter of Rights and Freedoms. Howard Leeson, a political scientist at the University of Regina, has studied the clause and published a paper entitled "Section 33, the Notwithstanding Clause: A Paper Tiger, in Choices." It is a balanced look at both sides. Leeson takes the facts of the clause, how it is used, what kind of power it exerts, and studies it. And he asks an important question: Is the notwithstanding clause the appropriate legislative tool to limit the power of courts? The simple answer: only for the moment, and only with limited success.

Better still, Leeson outlines the heart of the notwithstanding clause: "This attempt at compromise has drawn criticism from both sides of the debate about how best to protect rights. Supporters of the judicial approach are outraged that legislatures may still apply majoritarian standards to questions of fundamental rights, while supporters of parliamentary sovereignty consider any devolution of sovereignty to non-elected judges to be a violation of democratic principles."

The clause represents the ultimate compromise between the British model of investing all power in Parliament and the American model of giving ultimate power to the courts. In Canada, as is our wont, we try to balance the two. And therein lies the rancour and divisiveness between groups who are more than willing to adopt one system, but not both, and certainly not the one they distrust. As Leeson writes: "It is the quintessential Canadian compromise, a compromise that leaves no one happy but no one hurt." Therefore, it is safe to assume the notwithstanding clause provides the perfect kind of system of checks and balances.

Curiously enough, Canadians like to have it, but don't like its use. While the majority of Canadians aren't comfortable with the notion of gay marriage, they are cognizant of human rights. It is easy to assume within a very few years the opinion of the majority will swing in favour of same-sex marriage. It exists in all but legalities already. Such arrangements certainly haven't destroyed the traditional notion of family. I would argue that bringing homosexual relationships into public acceptance has strengthened the meaning and reality of family life, much to the betterment of all of us, by recognizing there is more than one family model.

Leeson concludes that Section 33 is a paper tiger. It could become, he argues, the equivalent of reservation and disallowance – the provision whereby Parliament can overturn provincial legislation – available in theory, but rarely if ever used in practice. Leeson sees the clause as a stopgap measure to enable more dialogue on the powers of the courts and the responsibilities of the legislatures. No current politician seems willing to open such a dialogue. That's too bad, because it was a former Alberta premier, Peter Lougheed, who lobbied for the notwithstanding clause, to prevent the federal government from launching another NEP.

Ironically, the clause that was intended to support Alberta's ownership of its resources and its right to set the price for goods, a clause used only once in its history, and that to discriminate against the English language in Quebec, remains focused in the minds of Albertans as a method to prevent common human rights being extended to all of Alberta's citizens. The same Alberta government that prides itself on its focus on the family, was the only Canadian government to refuse, for many years, to endorse the United Nations Convention on the Rights of the Child. There can be no greater ringing call for families than this convention which guarantees children the basics of life – love, shelter, food, and comfort.

They are curious things, values. So many of them are based on simple concepts – honour, forthrightness, honesty, forgiveness, love, and respect. Few of us would disagree with any of those words. But why do so many believe they own the only dictionary?

Former Conservative senator Ron Ghitter wrote over a decade ago, "There can be little doubt that the shape of the traditional family, with stable marriages and the wife staying at home with the children is changing throughout the industrialized world. There are of course, many reasons for this development including the reality that more women are entering the workforce and the greater social acceptability of divorce. There is really very little that government can do about this." But neo-conservatives continue to believe it is possible to pass laws to determine whose family is acceptable and who is not. Despite court cases that have ruled against discrimination based on gender, there is still massive resistance to the idea that two men or two women can be a family, just the same as any other.

It is fear that underpins some of the argument against families with same-sex parents and even same-sex marriage, while the bulk of the discrimination is based on Christian fundamentalist thinking. This perversion of true Christian ethics is maddening. Those who have the grace to be embarrassed by the dichotomy between Christian love and their own discrimination offer a "hate the sin; love the sinner" explanation. It is as mealy-mouthed as it sounds.

"What is fascinating is the continual insistence by the far right on a return to the good old days when families stayed together, when they were the strength in the communities – yet exactly when were those good old days?" asks Ron Ghitter. "They were the times of F.D.R. and Lyndon Johnson in the U.S., the days of the good society of medicaid, family allowances, pension plans, workers' compensation. The days in Canada of St. Laurent, Pearson and Diefenbaker, whose very policies are decried by those who perpetuate this hoax for political purposes."

Tangled up in the entire question of family values is, naturally, the status of women. Those who rail against non-traditional families, are in spirit akin to those who once refused to accept women as "persons" instead of chattels and those, later in the century, who believed family property was the sole property of the husband and father.

Property is no longer a question in divorce. But it was more than thirty years ago, when the then-new notion of feminism gave women a voice, particularly on the farms, where a woman could work as hard as a man, contribute just as much to the prosperity of the family, and receive no consideration in a divorce settlement.

In 1971, Iris Murdoch, an Alberta farm wife, launched a court challenge against her estranged husband. She disputed the automatic assumption of male ownership of family property and the devaluation of women's work in the family. An Alberta court refused her title to any of the property. In 1974, the Supreme Court of Canada upheld that decision, provoking farm wives to organize in protest and lobby for recognition of their labour. This opened the doors for the redefinition of family property and a re-evaluation of women's unpaid work in the family.

What Iris Murdoch fought for – the equal distribution of family assets toward which both husband and wife have contributed, even if the wife does not work outside the home – became standard in divorce through the Family Law Act of 1986. (And yes, it works both ways. It was also an Alberta woman who was ordered to pay her ex-husband maintenance when they divorced after he had quit his job and moved with her to the Maritimes so that she could further her television career.)

Murdoch fought for a stake in the land she had helped work. Not only because she had worked the land and kept a home and family, but because she, too, was rooted in the land.

Iris Murdoch never won her case, but other women have not faced the indignity of being told their labours as wife, mother, and worker were worth nothing.

Young Canadian women who dream of being prime minister or long to be a carpenter; who believe there are no barricades to their achievement; that anything is possible with hard work, talent, and intelligence, might take a moment to thank the Famous Five for their persistence.

Nellie McClung, Emily Murphy, Irene Parlby, Henrietta Muir Edwards, and Louise McKinney wouldn't take a man's no for an answer and wouldn't be deterred by the passage of years. These five Alberta women took on the task of convincing the federal government that women should be deemed "persons" as defined by the

British North America Act. They had to take their argument all the way to the Privy Council in England.

There is great irony in that these five women now grace the fifty-dollar bill. That spot had been reserved for the prime minister – R.B. Bennett – who refused to name one of the five to the Senate. And the loudest voices in objection to placing these women on our money came from Albertans who said the Famous Five were racist and thus didn't "deserve" such an honour.

It began, as so many revolutions, with a single insult. Emily Murphy, a writer and journalist was told she could not be named a Canadian senator because she wasn't a "qualified person." This, regardless of what she had contributed to her community as reformer and suffragette, as social activist and police magistrate. She was, in the eyes of the British North America Act, a nobody.

Five prime ministers from various political parties affirmed her non-status. But when Murphy discovered, under the Supreme Court of Canada Act, that any five citizens as a group could petition for a clarification of a constitutional point, she found four well-respected and like-minded women and when to work framing the question for the court.

The question was: "Does the word 'person' in Section 24 of the British North America Act, 1867, include female persons?" The Supreme Court said it did not. The pronouns, the nouns, the adjectives, and no doubt the intentions were masculine and thus men were the only qualified persons.

The women appealed to the judicial committee of the British Privy Council, at that time the highest court of appeal for Canada, and the rest is history. On October 18, 1929, after a twelve-year fight for recognition, the Privy Council ruled on behalf of women.

The Conservative government of the day, led by another Albertan, the dour Richard Bedford Bennett, denied any of the Famous Five the honour over which their battle had been launched. The senate appointment that should have gone to Emily Murphy went to another famous Albertan, Calgarian and cattle baron Patrick Burns. The excuse for denying Murphy the appointment was simple and expedient – she was a Protestant at a time when the prime minister needed to appoint a Catholic from Alberta.

Less than a year after the Privy Council decision, that "the word persons . . . includes members of both the male and female sex," the first woman senator was finally appointed: Cairine Wilson of Ottawa, a member of the Liberal establishment.

The disappointment of being so ignored must have been sharp for Murphy and her friends. But then, like today, appointments to the Senate are political. They are rarely made on the basis of merit, with few exceptions.

The five women then faded into historical obscurity, ignored by writers, male historians, and history aficionados alike. They were, after all, just ordinary women.

Seventy years after their triumph, a determined group of Calgary women raised enough money and enough consciousness to watch their heroes honoured in bronze. Seventy-one years later, on October 18, 2000, a second statue was erected on Parliament Hill. The Famous Five have joined the only other women honoured in statuary on the hill, Queen Victoria and Queen Elizabeth II.

No discussion of the myths and hoaxes of life in Alberta would be complete without considering the province's second most-expensive public program, after health care, education.

The scaremongers insist there is a crisis in public education. Supporters of the public system insist the only crisis is in the number of teachers, the size of the classrooms, and the amount of money all that costs. Neither side is completely right or totally wrong.

What is a crisis is the apparent inability of the education system to act with a view to changes in demographics. The system seems to be perpetually surprised by change, when most of it could be predicted and steps taken years earlier.

Instead of adjusting the public schools, we've now got charter schools. The charter-school movement has banked on the hoax of the crisis in public education. As Ghitter writes: "We are told that public education is a failure, that our schools are teaching left-wing values, that they are secular, without discipline or standards. The solution? Private and charter schools – oddly, not to strengthen public education but to weaken it further."

(When the charter schools opened for the 2001–02 school year, the Calgary Board of Education expected 1,000 students would leave the system during the year. A report the previous January said the drop in enrollment would persist for at least another three years with an estimated 6,000 drop in numbers from the 1999 enrollment of 100,000. And this in Canada's fastest-growing city.)

Ghitter says the arguments about the failure of public education find favour with Protestant fundamentalists who favour school vouchers, which they will apply toward the cost of educating their children at expensive private schools.

No objective study that has been undertaken in the U.S. or Canada shows a catastrophic decline in the quality of most public schools. In fact, if the neo-cons who bemoan the supposed inferiority of Canadian schools to Japanese and German schools were sincere, one would expect them to favour Japanese and German remedies – national funding of local schools, national standards, and little (if any) role by the parents in the selection of curricula – certainly not the decentralization of the system.

Charter schools, from the athletic to the religious, are touted as offering parents choice, and as being open to all – this is one of the conditions of their charter. But no geek is going to be comfortable in a school for athletes, or a Christian in a school for Muslims, or the academically gifted in a school for slow learners. Yet each of these Calgary schools is supposedly open to every child of every socio-economic level.

Those who, like the former senator, dare criticize charter schools, are frequently accused of being elitist themselves, willing to let the rich be the only families who can afford a private education. The argument is often made that vouchers and choice are far more democratic than obliging every child to attend public school and accept the values taught there. According to the charters issued by the Alberta government, such schools must admit every student that meets its criteria. In reality, charter schools are segregated by religion or race, even though such discrimination is prohibited.

When the Ontario Secondary School Teachers Federation studied Alberta's charter schools, its conclusion was that they are divisive, selecting students by class and ethnicity. "Schools run by parents are allowed to select students," writes Ghitter. "Students requiring special programs or more attention such as those learning English as a second language or the mentally challenged, are excluded. As well, because of the intense involvement required of parents in the running of charter schools, students from families where both parents work may be excluded."

The impetus for the charter schools movement, now more than ten years old and fully entrenched into Alberta's school system, was the myth of crumbling and ineffective public schools. Supporters could always find examples of how Alberta's public schools had "failed" children. Few people acknowledged that "problem" students – those who can't keep up, those who are angry and disruptive, have been present since the beginning of the public school system. Two generations ago, such students would have been held back until they caught up, expelled if they were disruptive until they could behave themselves, and often sent out to work. Then there was valuable and satisfying work for young people with less than a high-school education. No longer. Today, we must educate all children and that means through at least high school, if not university.

That's not the only change over the past fifty years. We've also seen the emergence of a child-centred attitude that places the responsibility for a child not learning or not behaving, squarely on the shoulders of the school system and the teachers. It isn't the parents who have failed, it must be the system. But the system wasn't given the resources to adapt. And, as a result Alberta's city school systems have closed inner-city schools in order to find the funds to build schools in the rapidly expanding suburbs. Nature abhors a vacuum and standing in line to take over the schools being closed are charter schools, backed by success, public money, and parental determination.

Alberta's public system hasn't quite deteriorated into a dumping ground for all the kids the charter schools don't want, but Senator Ghitter's words are prophetic, even as they become irrelevant: "We need the strongest public education system possible so that all our kids will have the advantages of learning and understanding the new technology. The public system must not become a depository for the poor, the disabled, the disadvantaged and the vulnerable. That is not what our nation is about, and we will pay dearly in the coming years if that is allowed to happen."

The fourth and final hoax, and perhaps the most emotional because is it the most specious, is the belief that human rights are special rights. In no other province has this dubious idea achieved such currency as in Alberta.

Even after more than a decade of court decisions that regardless of provincial legislation to the contrary, discrimination on the basis of race, creed, colour, gender, or sexual orientation will not be tolerated, the argument still rages that for some, human rights are special rights.

Those who have faced discrimination know the difference. "It is not difficult to understand if you have been there," says Ron Ghitter. "If you have been refused accommodation because you are black, Asian or aboriginal, even though you can pay the rent and will respect the premises, you have been there. Or if you are a woman who is paid less than the man beside you for the same work, you have been there. If you were beaten up on the street by a bunch of skinheads and forced to grovel in the dirt or run for your life because of your sexual orientation, you have been there."

In the parlance of communities targeted for special attention by authorities, from airport security guards to the police, being treated according to what colour or ethnic origin one is is called racial profiling. On the surface, Canadians say they are offended when, for example, a young, black man driving an expensive car is stopped and questioned by the police for no other reason than he's a young black man in an expensive car. In reality, protests against racial profiling are few, regardless of ethnicity. For example, police in both of Alberta's largest cities, Calgary and Edmonton, blithely refer to the growing problem of "Asian gangs" and youth gang violence with barely a whisper of objection from the public. Nor does the public seem at all interested in where law enforcement agencies get their information or on what evidence such characterizations are made.

The result of such profiling is measurable in terms of heightened fear. A 2001 report from the John Howard Society on gangs puts a portion of the blame for heightened fears on the media.

"The media reports to a wide audience and has a significant impact on public perception," says the society. Not much has changed in the past few years to alter what the report stated: "The Edmonton public has experienced heightened levels of fear, concern, and moral panic due to media accounts of gang-related youth violence. There is speculation that the media has sensationalized the gang problem, raising unfounded issues and concerns. The repercussions of this sensationalism have produced unease and fear in the public, less tolerance for youth crime and youth in general, increased reporting of any gang violence and vocal public demands for action."

There is almost nothing a macho and conservative media relishes more than a good, seedy story. Prostitutes, the homeless, gangs, and addicts provide continuing fodder for the print media and television, both of which feed on emotional pictures. It's much easier than the difficult and expensive investigative journalism necessary to look beyond the obvious.

Easily identifiable groups – prostitutes, gangs, the homeless, addicts – are prime targets for sweeping generalizations and the indignity of being seen as fodder for media obsessed with the easy story and graphic pictures. Worse, consumers of media scare stories begin to believe their cities are overrun with people they see as undesirables.

Human rights, equality before the law, have become only a dream for entire communities. Their rights are called "special rights." But is it special rights to honour employment equality, even if protection against discrimination based on who you want to go to bed with was not included in Alberta's original human rights legislation?

Perhaps no government had considered the question. Nonetheless, when the question arose, the province had only to amend the Alberta Individual Rights Protection Act to include all Albertans. It chose not to, even though by 1987, Ontario, Manitoba, and Yukon had set the standard for individual rights by including sexual orientation in provincial legislation.

The issue came to a head when Delwin Vriend was fired from his teaching position at King's College in Edmonton, and the college cited its morals clause as the reason.

Vriend is gay. The Christian post-secondary institution did not think his sexual orientation fit their singular viewpoint. Perhaps the college has a case in saying that teachers hired by religious institutions should practise whatever religion and be driven by whatever moral authority is held by the school. But Vriend did not hide his homosexuality, did not lie to the school, and believed he was as Christian as the next teacher. After twenty-eight months the school fired him.

Vriend took the matter to the provincial human rights commission, discovered that homosexuality wasn't included in the act, and went to court to plead his case. In 1994, the Alberta Court of Queen's Bench ruled that sexual orientation must be added to the act. The province appealed and the Alberta Court of Appeal overturned the lower court's decision in 1996. Eventually, in 1998, the Supreme Court of Canada unanimously decided against the Alberta appeals court and ruled that, effective immediately, the Alberta human rights legislation would be interpreted to include sexual orientation, regardless of whether the province changed the Act or not.

By that time Alberta was the only province not to have changed its human rights legislation to include homosexuals. In the aftermath of the Supreme Court decision Alberta still balked at changing its legislation, even though the court decision rendered such action moot. Instead, Alberta was urged to impose the Constitution's Section 33, which permits any province to opt out of a decision "notwithstanding" the courts.

The Klein government had promoted the idea that protecting homosexuals against discrimination could be equated with special rights. It was an idea with no logical basis, but was sufficiently emotional to be seized on as a mantra. Some people still believe ordinary rights can be translated as special rights if the group under discussion can be trashed with impunity.

But the issue of special rights still lingers. We may wish to think the hatred comes from fundamentalist groups who see only one form of family and one form of sexual union, but it was the premier himself who talked about special status for homosexuals. "The moment you include and give some people special status then you exclude other people," he said. Who are these "other people" who would be excluded? In Klein's words: "Severely, absolutely, totally normal people." The slight is obvious.

Senator Ghitter – who set up the Dignity Foundation to monitor human rights in Alberta – tried to set the record straight. "We are not talking about special rights. . . . We are talking in terms of treating people fairly, equally, and giving them opportunities no different than anyone else."

All these long years, even after a 1995 review made seventy-five recommendations for changes in human rights legislation, the government has steadfastly refused to do what many Albertans believe is the right thing – to offer the umbrella of protection to every person in this province. That's the true test of government – acting in the best manner for the most number of citizens. Alberta failed.

14

What Now?

On September 1, 1905, Alberta became a province and elected a *Liberal* – Alexander Rutherford – as its first premier. Even more surprising than this to Albertans with a finely developed sense of humour but little sense of history is that 1905 was the year oil was discovered. Not in Alberta, but near Windsor, Ontario.

Alberta didn't have to wait for 100 years to make everyone forget oil was first found elsewhere in Canada; it took less than fifty. And since oil and gas started flowing in earnest, it took another fifty for the province to make itself the undisputed financial star of the country, a province without deficit or debt.

At the beginning of the year-long celebration of its hundredth birthday in 2005, Alberta was on the cusp of change and looking for direction for the next hundred years.

It was obvious to some (including Tory insiders) that the man who had led the province out of debt would not be the man for the future. Premier Ralph Klein had talked often about the great future that awaited the province, about the changes his government would make to ensure better services for all Albertans (health care and post-secondary education for example), but most of it was just talk. Dithering. And we knew it. We had listened to promises of reform in the health system before and little had come of it. Until it became impossible to ignore the billions spilling out of the provincial treasury, Albertans dutifully obeyed the strict mantra: Pay the mortgage first.

Unfortunately, what was a crowd-pleasing analogy – that the province could be likened to a household in terms of debt and repayment – was just a way to encourage Albertans not to look too closely at the vision of the Ralph Klein Conservative government. In simple terms the question we were encouraged to ask was, Can we afford it?

In our own lives, we pose that question about stereos, cars, houses, or debt. The answer underlies all personal economics. But it also underlies the country's economy and the provincial economy. Can we afford a first-class medical system? Can we afford a premier educational system? Can we afford to care about the poor and the homeless or the less advantaged? A number of Albertans would counter with, Can we afford not to? But that's not the mantra that has inspired this province for a generation.

Fear of crippling debt (which would leave Alberta vulnerable to Eastern banking interests) combined with an unwillingness to be seen as "socialist" (code for giving away money to those who don't deserve it) means the idea of an overflowing treasury is regarded more with suspicion than glee.

Frankly, if a family looked on its good fortune with the same attitude the provincial government does, we'd still be the kind of people who paid cash for everything, fearing debt and equating it with immorality. Our economy would be stalled.

This point can't be stressed enough: the idea of debt as immoral is ingrained in this province and it comes, I believe, directly from the Eastern European wave of immigration, where an unpayable debt could mean a family's demise.

That debt is a means to an end – a mortgage paid back over time is a means to home ownership – is not a popular idea. The result of this thinking is that even as the province wallows in windfall resource profits, the same narrow, mean-spirited, sock-the-money-away idea permeates every level of conversation. It also means the vision of the future is tainted with fear: long-term funding is unavailable because of this. Public institutions, everything from universities to hospitals, can't plan for the future because the government won't take chances. It's not that the money is unavailable – it's there. But it's given out as one-time financing. No guarantees for next year, therefore, no incentive to do the kind of long-term planning so essential to a balanced economy.

In bold analogous terms, it means Dad's driving a Mercedes, Mom's wearing diamonds, and the kids have all the modern toys. Except the house has got dry rot underneath the expensive new carpet.

The family and the country are not fiscally synonymous, no matter how simple the analogies. Yet one of the Alberta premier's enduring banalities is his analogy of how a household spending more than it takes in is a recipe for disaster; an invitation to beggar one's children and grandchildren. If neo-conservatives want to patronize Canadians by talking about the national debt in terms of household budgets, then let them at least get the question right.

One family's decision not to buy a new car or renovate the bathroom or move to a more expensive neighbourhood doesn't make much of a dent in the community's standard of living. But scare the pants off most of Canada's families and the flow of money dries up, the economy grinds to a halt, and scared people start looking for someone to blame. Add a genuine fear of job loss, and the last thing people do is spend money. That's why when dealing with the nation's economy or the provincial economy, the question of affordability takes on a different meaning.

For Alberta, the real question is: Can we afford not to do it? Can a province blessed with prosperity afford not to support job creation for young people, for example? Can we afford harsh fiscal policies based on a model drawn up when the province was deep in debt and deficit? Does that model even apply in the good times, to which each Albertan has contributed?

Albertans and their government are all-too-willing to take all the credit. But, as the British magazine *The Economist* noted in 2000:

"Skeptics see Alberta's success as owing much to a strong national economy and especially to a surging oil price. Even so, it is not surprising that Alberta's politicians should be touting their model to the rest of Canada. More surprising, perhaps, is that over the past few years the Albertan agenda, rather than that of Quebec, has come to dominate Canada's national political debate."

If Alberta is to look to the future, the first step is answering the question, Who replaces Ralph Klein?

All through the 2004 provincial election Albertans knew, although there was the polite fiction Klein would serve out another term, that a leadership race was already on. It is one which pits the rural social conservatives against the urban social liberals. The future of the province depends on which side a new leader would represent. Choose the wrong leader, and the Progressive Conservatives would be in huge trouble by the time of the next election, sidelined by ideology. The premier, who was in earlier years considered a jolly fellow with a loveable penchant for the grape – just another man of the people so the myth goes – has turned into a bored-looking, sober caretaker of an equally bored and uninspired government. Worse is his meanness, the nasty edge that was softened by drink, but is now out there for everyone to see. Ralph Klein, the person, has always had a thin skin for criticism; Ralph Klein, the premier, was openly contemptuous of all, particularly the media, who questioned his government record.

The Conservatives have proven they are very good at the politics of mean. Very good at slashing and burning jobs, wages, programs, and expectations. In the beginning, Albertans yelped, but showed a prairie spirit of toughness and helped get the job done, if not always willingly.

In the aftermath, the province downloaded costs onto municipalities, removed itself from direct responsibility (or tried to) for the costs of health care and education, and furthered the insult by instituting brand-new taxes in the form of ever-increasing user fees. In Alberta, we don't call them taxes. We call it "user-pay" when the costs of public services such as transit, libraries, and recreational facilities are downloaded onto the user. The only class of voters this pinches are those living on fixed and limited incomes, the lower working class and the working poor, who, not surprisingly, have a lower record of voting.

But now it's payback time and unlike the provincial surplus, the government is poverty-stricken for a vision, a plan for the future. Nothing has been forthcoming.

It isn't as if the government didn't have the time to work on a template for growth and investment in good times. Yet that opportunity has been wasted. Squandered. We are offered little more than vague, non-specific promises something will be done, and that we will have a chance to voice our opinions, an opportunity for public consultation.

Well and good, but there must be something to discuss. And in case anybody in this province still believes in a government that soothes us by talking about trust, remember that we were consulted about rising rates for car insurance and a goodly number of us replied perhaps a public system would work best. That was quickly and quietly stomped on; never quite making it into the public record. Instead, vague limits were placed on charges and more study was urged. Many Albertans, me included, wondered what was the point of getting pennies back in rebates from our car insurance companies. (My cheque was twenty-two dollars; my husband's twenty-five dollars.) As for public insurance, it will never happen.

One unanswered question is, What now? What will Alberta look like after Ralph Klein? Outsiders look at the Conservative caucus and see a rural-urban split, a contest brewing between the social conservatives and the fiscal conservatives. While the former pride themselves on their tight-fisted attitude toward fiscal matters, it is the latter to whom a changing province will look. Most Albertans accept the notion of fiscal conservatism, but it is also true that the same majority looks at need and want and responds by believing it is up to all of us, the provincial government included, to make the Alberta Advantage available to every citizen, even those believed undeserving.

To make the Alberta Advantage province-wide means shoring up the social programs. That means spending money as an investment in people's well-being. In a province that holds with the vestiges of pioneer ethics – help yourself, help your neighbour, ask for nothing – the idea of government programs to help those who cannot (or will not) help themselves sits uneasily in the public square. Even in the face of riches beyond the scope of most other provinces' dreams, the idea doesn't sit well with social conservatives, who cling to an enduring belief that only those who have worked for it should share the wealth.

But it's tough to hold to such righteousness when there's an overflowing bank account.

The entire politics of Klein-era "reform" has been the politics of anger, alienation, and antipathy to a ruling so-called elite. If one looks closely at the supporters of the provincial Conservatives, one finds the real elite: they are well-to-do, middle-aged, middle class, and white. The party echoes their federal cohort, although there is no admitted connection between the Alberta Conservatives and the Conservative Party of Canada.

The argument can be made and accepted logically that today's Alberta is reflected in its politics – still mostly white and rural. Alberta's cities and their elite are only now following the lead of urban areas such as Toronto in assimilating the colours, credos, and cultures of the world. They are our real future and they live in cities. We cling to our rural heritage and the icon of the straw-chewing farmer, but the tripod of Alberta's economy – oil, agriculture, and tourism – will be resting on uneven ground before too many more decades pass.

What comes after oil? is a question now being asked with some urgency, although most of us will be past caring by the time the oil runs out. Agriculture is turning into a corporate business, and unless we start refurbishing and upgrading our tourist destinations such as Banff and Jasper, tourist dollars will start to go elsewhere. Already, B.C. is intent on siphoning off the ski-tourist business.

Underlying the changes needed for a prosperous future is the simple fact of immigration and the much-loathed concept of multiculturalism.

Am I accusing Conservatives of racism? No. As a group they are committed to the words *tolerance* and *acceptance*. But its political elite is still a party of like-minded people whose social conscience is based on Depression-era morality and whose political philosophy is a simplistic one in which the Bible is on a par with Adam Smith's *The Wealth of Nations*.

Those who must rely on the government for medical care, for education, for welfare, and those who support such government handouts, are regarded by the elite as somehow less democratically minded than those who believe in self-reliance as the first great commandment. They believe taxes are welfare for the government, and that Canadians should share only with those they deem worthy of help, not with young people in trouble with the law, single mothers on welfare, drug addicts, alcoholics – the list of the "undeserving" is long, complicated, and cold-hearted.

Alberta's future has to rest on something other than the nasty and brutish abandonment of people who don't quite come up to economical, political, or social snuff. But the politics of mean and nasty have been so popular in this province, they are hard to abandon. In the name of fiscal prudence, all the people we believed weren't quite pulling their own weight were culled. Welfare bums. Limited social assistance. Workfare. Institutional poverty. User pay. User fees. Make prisoners work in road gangs, obvious in bright orange coveralls. What could be stripped from the public purse in Alberta, has been. No matter that user fees hit the least able to pay the hardest; that ten-dollar-per-year charge for a library card means nothing to people with their own libraries, but is a barrier to impoverished Albertans. And such "extra billing" hits hard at immigrants who often come with nothing and need merely some initial help to become full participants in the province's success.

In as little as a single generation, or two at the most, multiculturalism won't be an ideal, it will be a reality. And the people to whom the word applies, from all over the world, will remember how they were treated as newcomers.

Curiously, it is the people of the prairies, many of them descendants of "newcomers" to the country, who should appreciate what being Canadian really means. We are, out here in the snow, inexorably connected to the land and the weather. Albertans, along with their neighbours in Saskatchewan, understand what it means to be residents of a northern, cold, winter country.

One of the best descriptions of being Canadian comes from a little-known but wonderful novel entitled *Hunting Down Home*, written by Canadian Jean McNeil, who now lives in England.

"This landscape and its seasons has to do with survival: with gritting your teeth and taking yourself through whatever you have to come through. Each winter is a death which has to be accepted and negotiated, knowing that resurrection is not a matter of virtue, but of time. I am a Canadian. I survive every winter, so I know I can survive anything."

The land and the country itself accepts our presence as long as we follow the rules – rebirth in the spring isn't a matter of virtue, writes McNeil, but of time.

To ignore the rules of survival, whether they be the philosophical ones set up by our society, or the far more serious ones set by nature, is to die. This is a land with little tolerance for mistakes.

Maybe it's the climate that's part of the stern nature of Albertans in general. As Margaret Sweatman wrote in her 2001 novel, *When Alice Lay Down With Peter*: "In this country we have two religions: Winter and Summer. Our doctrine of Winter is stern and dutiful, an Old Testament faith in the laws of Cold Night."

It is sternness and duty that underlies the success of the fiscal revisionists, who brought us lessons on how to manage money in a world where *elite* is a five-letter swear word for a university arts education, *liberal* a euphemism for spendthrift socialist, and *unemployed* an alternative term for good-for-nothing.

AGAINST THE GRAIN • 249

The curious thing about the born-again fiscal reformers is that in the short space of only a few years their revisionism – the deficit-debt-denial mantra – has become accepted wisdom across the country, leading other provinces to adopt Alberta's attitude. The former premier of Ontario Mike Harris tried. His so-called Common Sense Revolution was modelled on the Alberta example. But Harris blinked. His fiscal revolution fizzled and failed. His Conservative government was tossed out.

Conservatives in Alberta, on a winning streak for more than thirty years, want to avoid the same fate. To ensure that, they want a clone to succeed Klein. That would avoid the question of what a different personality will bring to the political mix.

Succession brings with it no guarantee of competence.

When Peter Lougheed, the man who made *Tory* a proud word in Alberta, retired, he was succeeded by Don Getty, for whom the word *hapless* has always seemed appropriate. Getty's real legacy was crippling debt and deficit caused by the combination of his government's overestimation of oil revenues in Alberta's budgets and a concomitant depression in the industry. When Albertans should have been tightening their belts, we were spendthrifts. And blind ones at that: we mostly ignored all the signs of disaster, preferring to believe that overspending and under-earning were nothing to worry about.

How different from the present. Now we are underspending and overearning, even though critics point to debt-free Alberta as a spendthrift province. It may look as if Alberta is tossing money around, but in reality Alberta's attitude to its good fortune is analogous to a homeowner paying off his mortgage and other debts and then putting all future money under the mattress, instead of using it to fix the roof, paint the siding, and resurface the sidewalk, all ignored while the focus was on paying off what was owed.

The true depth of the financial disaster came when Klein won the leadership and took over the premier's office. With the not-inconsiderable help of Rod Love, his chief of staff, often referred to as Ralph's Brain, and a cadre of other neo-cons, Klein took care of finances promptly. In a wave of purse-tightening, Klein chopped 5 per cent off the salaries of civil servants, including politicians, cut expenditures to the bare bones, and downloaded what couldn't be cut onto municipalities (which responded by passing the costs on to their citizens). The heartlessness of the cuts was downplayed in the face of hope of what they promised – prosperity, wealth, and lower taxes.

Mostly, what was promised by a reinvigorated Progressive Conservative Party was progress, growth, and power of a kind usually associated with Ontario or Quebec. It was a heady concept, that an "upstart" province could wield real influence and could challenge the powerful forces that inherited the elite Family Compact.

The debt-free future toward which Alberta has been working for more than ten years is here. Now what? What is the Alberta Advantage that will accrue to the next generations? The answer to those questions, posed in the waning years of the Ralph Klein Conservative government, is more political than practical. Right-wing Conservatives are mostly unwilling to invest in a government-decided future: that which will ensue if the current government invests each year's surplus into what they call social engineering, such as low-cost daycare, affordable housing, and greater assistance to the handicapped, among others. The social conservatives prefer to engineer the future through personal and corporate tax cuts, which, it is argued, would result in more charitable contributions, more money at the top to trickle down to the bottom.

The trouble is, such a theory has never worked, despite the late American president Ronald Reagan's belief, and can't be expected to work for the first upcoming generation, which curiously is among the least charitable in terms of giving. This is no surprise, nor should it be. Ten years ago, demographer David Foot, in his and Daniel Stoffman's bestselling book, *Boom, Bust & Echo*, predicted accurately what would happen to charitable giving when Generation X hit adulthood: "me first" would be the goal. Canada's Generation X, defined as those 2.6 million backend baby boomers born between

1960 and 1966, has had to fight since childhood for space with the older boomers who are taking up all the room, the jobs, the positions of seniority, and the attention of government programs. Generation X, writes Foot, has no choice but to look out for themselves in a crowded world. "Life experience," he says, "had led them to distrust any sort of large institution, whether in the public or private sector."

Such attitudes have had a dramatic effect on public policy and private charity. A study of philanthropy done by Indiana University showed only slightly more than half of Generation X households (53 per cent) contributed twenty-five dollars or more during 2000. (The twenty-five-dollar benchmark was used, report researchers, to avoid embarrassing the cohort with their stinginess.) By comparison, between 75 and 80 per cent of baby boomers and the pre–Second World War generation donate to charity. Is Generation X less interested in others? Not necessarily; they're just more interested in themselves. They'll get around to being philanthropic when they're satisfied with their own comfort.

By comparison, socially liberal conservatives, the red Tories, strike a balance between government engineering and private enterprise. Those "progressive" Conservatives believe the surplus should be used to ease the cost of post-secondary tuitions; to improve standards of health care; to provide for the future support of core programs and services (welfare, children's services, and the like), and maybe in the bargain, give a tax break to ordinary citizens.

As for the Liberal and New Democrat opposition in Alberta, nothing seems to make them happy, but criticism of government is, after all, their job. For their small number (seventeen Liberals and four New Democrats, excluding the single anomaly of one Alberta Alliance member, representing a party even more to the right than the rural Conservatives), they make a lot of noise and much of the time, a lot of sense. Yet they are overwhelmed by the sixty-one-seat Tory caucus and the Alberta news media who are categorically pro-Conservative, if not always pro-government. The opposition's major problem is not crowd-pleasing alternatives to a

Conservative platform, not lack of criticism of the Klein government, but the overwhelming optimism of Albertans coupled with
a kind of province-wide glee at being debt-free provincially, if
not personally.

This provincial optimism, which blankets most of the criticism
from those Albertans who are not in on the Advantage, is best
described by a comparison with our closest friends – Americans. In a
2003 essay in the *New York Times*, op-ed columnist David Brooks
described the growing gap in the United States between the wealthy
and the poor, and the surprising lack of conflict between them, thusly:
Americans "have always had a sense that great opportunities lie just
over the horizon, in the next valley, with the next job or the next big
thing. None of us is really poor; we're just pre-rich." In a boom-and-
bust resource-based culture, many Albertans believe the same. In
addition, it's tough for the voices of the needy and the working poor
to be heard above the din of self-congratulation coming from the
Alberta legislature that echoes through this province.

In 2004, the Fraser Institute praised Alberta's economic
freedom, which it defines as a measure of the extent to which "individuals control their own property without onerous taxation (and)
are able to enter into voluntary transactions without having their
freedom limited by government activities." Supporters of the dour,
right-wing think-tank applaud such attitudes, although "onerous"
when it comes to taxation is in the eye of the beholder (or property owner). There's not a single Canadian, let alone an Albertan,
who would ask to be taxed more, who would not welcome a break
in the annual tax bills we all face. But are our taxes really onerous?
Or are they the price of living in a country that understands the
concept of a common weal? There is no government case against
making as much money as possible, only the responsibility to pay the
taxes accruing. And certainly the concept of the government limiting so-called voluntary transactions (that means a free market in all
its meanings) is anathema.

The third of the Institute's economic freedom signposts, along
with low taxes and a laissez-faire government, is freedom to work,

the simple translation of the right to enter freely "into non-coercive agreements between potential employers and employees." It is this attitude that makes New Democrats weep and market capitalists grin. In almost half of the fifty United States, freedom to work is a reality under the 1947 Taft-Harley Act, which makes it illegal to demand union membership and mandatory dues as a condition of work, even in those companies with unions. In those states the average annual salary is US$5,000 less than in states with collective bargaining.

Right-to-work legislation would eliminate the few unions with which the Alberta government and companies must deal collectively. The very mention of being able to rid the province of unionized teachers, civil servants, nurses, et al., and replace union demands with individual wage negotiations (read that to mean salaries as low as possible) delights libertarians and any other group opposing unions and any government interference in the workplace, such as minimum-wage legislation.

It is a curiosity that the only union action in Alberta to meet overwhelming public approval was the Calgary laundry workers wildcat strike in 1995. On hearing the Calgary Regional Health Authority would be contracting out laundry services, 120 workers at Calgary General Hospital, members of the Canadian Union of Public Employees, walked off the job. The premier called them a "special interest group" and told them to whine and cry all they wanted, but he and his government wouldn't blink. Such bullying of a small group of workers faced with losing their jobs sparked public sympathy. Ralph blinked. But it was a small, even pyrrhic, victory. Three years later, in 1998, the General Hospital was demolished. Within ten years, all hospital support services had been successfully contracted out.

In the current flush of prosperity, it is unlikely that anyone in Alberta has the interest or time to worry about right-to-work issues. The demand for skilled labour, tradespeople, technicians, all the way up the social, economic, and class ladder to doctors, lawyers, and other professionals is such that Alberta makes room for willing workers and pays them well. The average weekly wage in Alberta is $726, exceeded only by Ontario with $740, even as the minimum wage in Alberta, the lowest in the country, is raised from $5.90 per hour to $7. (The average hourly wage is $18.55.)

At the same time as congratulating Alberta on its economic freedom, the Fraser Institute remarked that Alberta's provincial spending spree is damaging "Alberta's ability to maintain high levels of economic freedom and, ultimately, prosperity for its citizens."

It isn't any spending spree that threatens prosperity, it is the simple, cyclical nature of boom and bust: the vagaries of the market and the weather for agriculture, the effect on tourism of world panic over viruses such as SARS and avian 'flu, and the fragile nature of oil and gas revenues. To guard against another bust (a car bumper sticker says "Lord, give me another boom and I promise not to piss it away"), the Alberta government set up a $2.5-billion fund to sustain core programs and services in the future.

What makes this fund different from the Alberta Heritage Savings Trust Fund is questionable. The cynic would say that Peter Lougheed originated the Heritage Fund in 1976 as a "rainy-day" account for Alberta, and if it remained the only such fund Ralph Klein would get no credit for looking to the future. It is worth noting that from its inception until 1982, after the bottom fell out of the Alberta economy, all monies earned by the Heritage Fund were retained by it. Since then, all proceeds from Heritage Fund investments have been funnelled directly into general revenues, which is one reason it is difficult to assess the increase in value of the fund. Nonetheless, it is worth $12 billion today, although that number has been stagnant for a decade, and the billions can't be converted into cold cash, unless the government wants to sell a provincial park or two, ostensibly owned by the Heritage Fund.

On its centennial birthday, Alberta revels in a debt-free future promised by government in rather lyrical terms: "When we plan for tomorrow, it is to today's children, tomorrow's leaders, that we dedicate ourselves, as a government and as a province," stated the 2001 Alberta Throne Speech. In 2002, the government sponsored a "futures summit" with 250 delegates turning the opinions culled from four thousand Albertans into a statement of key priorities for the environment, economy, health care, and governance. In 2003, the government reported that many of the ideas had been incorporated into priorities for the future. It all made for interesting reading, as long as one didn't demand tangible proof. In 2005, we're still promising, planning, and prioritizing. The sentiment from the 2001 Throne Speech lingers but it is difficult to see, like the forest for the trees, what has actually been done. Why? Because so much is happening in Alberta that is not yet quantifiable. And despite our much-reputed aggressiveness and bravery, there is an air of hesitation over actually making change. Any change is likely to be accompanied by screeching and caterwauling, as any alteration to the status quo is greeted by those people who have been dispossessed or disturbed. Overlying it all is the thinking that whatever changes are made, we have to do it right. "What is happening here is a lot of adjustment," says a long-time Tory supporter. "Alberta is a 'bubble' society, all of a sudden pop! it's gone." Eliminating the debt mitigates that "pop" factor, he added.

Critics like me could point to the lack of imagination and interest shown by the provincial government in the centennial as an example of the letdown that follows unfulfilled expectations. With the single exception of a colourful, festive-looking numerical-with-confetti logo for 2005, the year has passed with little fanfare and even less interest shown by the government. With the single exception of renovations to the Jubilee auditoriums in Edmonton and Calgary, both built to celebrate fifty years of provincial status in 1955, government involvement in what is billed as a birthday party is decidedly low-key. Even the Royal tour through Saskatchewan and Alberta caused minimal public excitement. The biggest celebration, in fact, took place in Ottawa, where a two-week festival of Alberta artists at the National Arts Centre highlighted the talent of the province. The premier was noticeably absent for the entire event. One Tory supporter said she was "loath to give Klein an excuse to act like an uncultured boor," but perhaps the premier didn't attend for a good reason, such as an unwillingness to be badgered by the national press. Whatever, his absence was notable and noted. (Even here the Teflon Premier escaped much criticism. Shortly after the opening gala in Ottawa for what was billed as Alberta Scene, the premier was felled by a respiratory infection that kept him bedridden for a couple of weeks, causing Klein to miss an international health symposium and the annual Western premiers meeting. It also caused him to attempt yet again to quit smoking.)

In his 2001 book, *The Art of Innovation*, creative genius Tom Kelly warns that innovation and change take root slowly. "Not all futures happen at the same pace," he writes. Maybe that's the real barrier to predicting the future for a province in the unique position of having the time and money to innovate. By the time we sort out the chaos that has arisen from Alberta trying to address changes in health and wellness, education, the environment, and fiscal responsibility all at the same time, the future will be upon us. Albertans have every reason to be optimistic, it's the nature of who we are. We are just missing tangible proof that our optimism for every one of our fellow citizens, whether they currently benefit from the Alberta Advantage or not, is well placed.